Toward a
DEMOCRATIC
NEW ORDER

by

David Bryn-Jones

CHAIRMAN, DEPARTMENT OF
INTERNATIONAL RELATIONS
CARLETON COLLEGE

THE UNIVERSITY OF MINNESOTA PRESS
Minneapolis

Copyright 1945 by the
UNIVERSITY OF MINNESOTA

All rights reserved. No part of this book may be reproduced in any form without the written permission of the publisher. Permission is hereby granted to reviewers to quote brief passages in a review to be printed in a magazine or newspaper.

Printed at the Colwell Press, Inc., Minneapolis

Preface

This book has its origin in group discussions over a period of years. The discussions began in the years immediately following World War I, when it was the avowed purpose of most liberal teachers and statesmen to make the world safe for democracy. It seemed pertinent in those days to raise the question as to what democracy, for which the world had to be made safe, really is. It was found that a satisfactory answer was not as simple as had been supposed.

The discussion generally broadened into a discussion of other topics intimately related to, and all bearing upon, the vital question raised. To discover the meaning of democracy, the concepts of liberty, equality, and the rights of man had to be analyzed and as far as possible defined; analysis and definition inevitably led to problems of application.

The chapters that follow are the fruit of these discussions and of meditation upon them. It is of the nature of such discussions that no final answers are ever reached, and no absolute solutions are to be expected. They serve, however, to clarify thought, sometimes to reveal difficulties, and always, it may be hoped, to shape a philosophy of life that is helpful, though never final. It also helps in clarification of thought to try to crystallize the results of such discussions in the written word. That this should be attempted at this particular time is not strange, for our time imposes the obligation to attempt the task of rethinking democracy. Never was clarity more necessary, never was criticism more imperative, than in a world at one of the great crises of its fate.

Out of years of discussion one conviction emerges. The liberal tradition had in it elements of permanent worth—principles that are valid for ages beyond that which gave them historic expression. It also had, as all human systems have, definite limitations, which in time compromised its principles. These limitations made that tradition as interpreted in the nineteenth century inadequate for the new world of the twentieth century, the world that liberal principles had helped to create. It failed to meet the challenge of the industrialized and integrated world of today. The tragedy of our generation is the result. Men have found that they cannot live by the ancient faith as it was understood and expressed in the nineteenth century; they are seeking a new one. They have not always been wise in their quest, as the history of Europe in our time makes clear. When the old gods are discredited and pass into the twilight, new gods arise, and among them false gods. Unfortunately, these too find worshipers.

In such ages of transition, ages that are revolutionary, as ours is, a danger arises that may lead to disaster. In reaction against what is old there may be too great a readiness to destroy and cast out, too little appreciation of the vital elements that brought the old faith into existence, kept it alive so long, and gave to it the beneficent influence it once exercised. We are not rich enough spiritually to be able to dispense with those vital elements of permanent worth. We need them today, and tomorrow we shall need them more than ever. We may rediscover them in what men have meant, in their best moments, by democracy. The democratic faith needs to be freed from its nineteenth-century limitations and from the associated ideas that obscured its meaning, compromised its effectiveness, and came near to destroying it. It needs to be reinterpreted in terms that will make it a faith for the twentieth century, a faith by which man can live. This book is an exercise in reinterpretation.

"The defence of democracy, like other negative aims, is dead and barren," says E. H. Carr in *Conditions of Peace*. "The challenge of the revolution can only be met by re-defining and reinterpreting democracy in a new and revolutionary sense. The present crisis of democracy is the need for this re-definition." The chapters that follow are an attempt to meet the need for this redefinition of democracy. It is too much to hope that they will succeed, but it is not too much to hope that the attempt will contribute something of value to the achievement of that task. This is at once the justification and the explanation of this book.

Acknowledgments in a case of this kind can never be adequate. Students in my classes, both in England and in the United States, have contributed to it; how much it is not now possible to say. Indebtedness to other writers in the field is obvious in the pages that follow. I can express specific indebtedness only to my colleagues at Carleton College: Henry V. Cobb, Leal A. Headley, Robert W. MacEwen, and Reginald Lang. I am especially grateful to Ralph L. Henry, who has rendered invaluable assistance in preparing the manuscript for publication.

DAVID BRYN-JONES

Carleton College
June 1945

TO EDWINA

Table of Contents

INTRODUCTION 1

Part One. The Liberal Tradition

Chapter 1. THE IDEA OF DEMOCRACY 7
The Meaning of the Word, 8. Constitutions Do Not Make Democracy, 12. The Will and the Capacity to Govern, 18.

Chapter 2. DEMOCRACY AS A FORM OF GOVERNMENT 23
The Case for Democratic Government, 24. The Ordinary Man's Capacity to Govern, 27. Government by Experts, 30. Potential Weaknesses of the Democratic Form, 33. Emotion and Reason, 37.

Chapter 3. CONTRAST WITH DICTATORSHIP 41
Arguments for Dictatorship, 41. Leadership in a Democratic State, 43. The Question of Unity, 46. The Defects of Dictatorships, 49.

Chapter 4. THE WILL OF THE PEOPLE 54
The General Will, 54. Unity in Diversity, 59. The Rights and Duties of Minorities, 61.

Chapter 5. THE BACKGROUND OF THE DEMOCRATIC TRADITION 67
The Idea of Popular Sovereignty, 68. The Idea of Natural Law, 76.

Chapter 6. THE ETHICAL BASES OF DEMOCRATIC GOVERNMENT 82
The Idea of a Higher Law, 82. Democratic View of the State and the Individual, 87. Democratic View of Human Nature, 90. Human Welfare the Real Purpose of a Democratic State, 94.

Part Two. Basic Concepts of Democracy Re-Examined

Chapter 7. LIBERTY 98
The Negative Concept of Freedom, 99. Limits of Toleration, 105. Positive Freedom, 111.

TABLE OF CONTENTS

Chapter 8. EQUALITY 120

In the Thought of Greece and Rome, 121. Later Development of the Principle, 127. The Real Meaning of Equality, 130. Equality of Opportunity, 133. Achieving Essential Equality, 137.

Chapter 9. THE RIGHTS OF MAN 141

Revolutionary Implications of the Concept, 142. Burke's Doctrine of Rights, 145. Ideal Rights, 149. An Illustration: The Right to Work, 152. How Rights Win Recognition, 157.

Chapter 10. FRATERNITY 159

The Ideal of Brotherhood, 159. International Fraternity, 162.

Part Three. Reinterpretation and Application

Chapter 11. DEMOCRACY AND INDUSTRY 166

A Shift in Emphasis, 167. Industrial Autocracy? 171. The Increasing Power of Labor, 174. The Employers' Approach, 179. The Control of Capital Resources, 182. The Transfer of Effective Power, 185.

Chapter 12. SOCIAL DEMOCRACY 188

Industry and Political Power, 189. Inequalities of Opportunity, 193. Limitations of Freedom, 197. Inequality and Social Unity, 201.

Chapter 13. DEMOCRACY AND NATIONALITY 210

Nationalism in the Liberal Tradition, 211. The Meaning of Nationality, 214. A World of Variety, 219. The Principle of Self-Determination, 221. Suggested Remedies, 229.

Chapter 14. DEMOCRACY AND WORLD ORDER 233

The Totalitarian New Orders, 235. The Democratic Alternative, 237. The Leadership of the Great Powers, 242. International Economic Controls, 246. Political Principles of a World Order, 248. Conversion from War to Peace, 254.

Chapter 15. DEMOCRACY AND INTERNATIONAL RELATIONS 259

Rise and Decline of Imperialism, 259. Mutual Responsibility as an Alternative, 264. Empire and the War, 269. A General Principle, 272. A Mandate System? 274.

CONCLUSION 281

INDEX 283

Introduction

Long ago Socrates discovered that the simplest concepts are frequently the most difficult to define, largely because most people do not feel the need for definition. It was assumed in Athens, as it has been assumed ever since, that there are some ideals so obvious that they cannot be challenged, and do not need to be examined. This was particularly true in relation to those words that were on everyone's lips. Justice was talked about by the man in the street, who never stopped to ask what justice was. Meaning was taken for granted, and it was a part of Socrates' service to mankind to make it clear—at the cost of much unpopularity—that it could not be taken for granted. The unexamined life is not worth living, and the unexamined word is not worth using.

Democracy in the nineteenth century and the early years of the twentieth was in danger of falling into the category of unexamined words. The danger has passed; we know now that the meaning of democracy can no longer be taken for granted. The challenge of dire events has made that impossible, and such phrases as "democracy on trial," "the crisis of democracy," and "the survival of democracy" express a new and profound concern that is in marked contrast to the easy assumptions of an earlier period.

It may be said that at the end of the nineteenth century democracy was the accepted political ideal of the Western world. In many of the Western nations it had clearly not triumphed in actual practice, but this could be explained in terms of a time lag. Nation-states that did not have democratic constitutions were nevertheless on their way to democracy. They were politically backward, but in time changes would certainly come, and no one doubted that the changes would be in a democratic direction. A movement toward democratic government was progress; a movement away from it was reaction. In the realm of ideas, so it was assumed, democracy had triumphed. In time practice would catch up with ideas!

The last and best known frontal attack upon this general assumption in the nineteenth century was made by Sir Henry Maine in his book *Popular Government*, first published in 1885. The arguments of that book aimed at establishing three points: (1) "Popular Government has proved itself to be extremely fragile." (2) "It is, of all kinds of government, by far the most difficult." (3) "The perpetual change which . . . it appears to demand is not in harmony with the normal forces ruling human nature, and is apt therefore to lead to cruel disappointment or serious disaster."[1] Nevertheless, Maine admits that already in his day the basic tenets of democratic government were generally accepted. "Nine men out of ten look upon popular government as destined to last forever, or, if it changes its form, to change it in one single direction. The democratic principle has gone forth conquering and to conquer, and its gainsayers are few and feeble."

There was a chance, although a slight one, of avoiding the worst dangers of popular government. Human reason may discover "remedies for its infirmities," but whether people in modern times can be persuaded to adopt and apply these remedies is very dubious. The prejudices of the masses are strong, and the implication of Maine's argument seems to be that reason will be waging a rather unequal fight against them.

Ten years after the publication of Maine's book another writer, William Lecky, waged what may be called a rear-guard action in his *Democracy and Liberty*. Democracy, he concedes, has won its victories. It is destined to dominate the life of civilized communities, not permanently perhaps, but for a long time to come. Its triumph will almost certainly bring disaster. Lecky is less concerned than Maine with challenging the assumptions of the democratic faith, but he draws an ominous picture of its tendencies and results. In particular it menaced the institution of private property, and would in time destroy it; and with its destruction would pass the dominance in parliamentary England of the middle class, in whose political wisdom Lecky had such great faith.

"Lecky not only looked at the recent record of democracy, he also considered its future. He saw dark clouds gathering on the horizon; middle-class parliamentary democracy was threatened by the ultimate implications of universal suffrage, and by the abuse of wealth. It was his deep-seated fear that universal suffrage would ultimately lead to socialism."[2] Faced with these disastrous possibilities, Lecky has little to offer by way of constructive suggestions for avoiding them or even mitigating them. A minor reform of the House of Commons, increased power to the House of Lords, and a system of plural voting based on property and education—these measures, he thinks, might serve some purpose, but they would be frail defenses against the democratic tide. Lecky

[1] H. S. Maine, *Popular Government* (New York: Holt, 1886), p. x.
[2] B. E. Lippincott, *Victorian Critics of Democracy* (Minneapolis: University of Minnesota Press, 1938), pp. 229–30. See the whole essay for an excellent discussion of Lecky's argument.

INTRODUCTION 3

probably had little hope that the advocacy of such measures, even in his own day, would have much effect. The triumph of democracy seemed inevitable.

Maine and Lecky were survivors of a tradition that for a century had waged an unsuccessful battle against the advances of popular government. By the end of the nineteenth century it seemed that the battle was over. The struggle for democracy in practice would go on, but it was assumed that in the world of theory at least it had achieved an impregnable position. Democracy had triumphed; what remained for it was the task, which might indeed be long, of reaping the rewards of victory. In 1920 a distinguished American historian could write:

This universal significance [of the establishment of the United States] is that for the first time in the modern world, a new and potentially powerful nation was "dedicated to the proposition that all men are created equal," and founded upon the principle that the legitimacy of any government rests upon the will of the people instead of the will of God or of the State. And for a hundred years the example of the United States has been one of the strongest supports of this new faith which, however often forgotten or betrayed, *is now accepted by the better part of the world.*[3]

Even more familiar, and written in the same year, is Lord Bryce's judgment in *Modern Democracies:*

A not less significant change has been the universal acceptance of democracy as the normal and natural form of government. Seventy years ago, as those who are now old can well remember, the approaching rise of the masses to power was regarded by the educated classes of Europe as a menace to order and prosperity. Then the word Democracy awakened dislike or fear. Now it is a word of praise. Popular power is welcomed, extolled, worshipped. The few whom it repels or alarms rarely avow their sentiments. Men have almost ceased to study its phenomena because these now seem to have become part of the established order of things. The old question,—What is the best form of government? is almost obsolete because the centre of interest has been shifting. It is not the nature of democracy, nor even the variety of the shapes it wears, that are today in debate, but rather the purposes to which it may be turned, the social and economic changes it may be used to effect.[4]

It is true that Bryce goes on to utter a warning which in some

[3]Carl L. Becker, *The United States, An Experiment in Democracy* (New York: Harper, 1920), p. 53. The italics are mine.
[4]James Bryce, *Modern Democracies* (2 vols., New York: Macmillan, 1921), vol. 1, p. 4.

measure qualifies this judgment. He is not certain that democracy has necessarily come to stay or that it is possible to claim it as the natural, and therefore the inevitable, form of government. In words that today sound curiously optimistic in their assertions and almost prophetic in their recognition of possible change he writes:

> Nevertheless, although democracy has spread, and although no country that has tried it shows any signs of forsaking it, we are not yet entitled to hold with the men of 1789 that it is the natural and therefore in the long run the inevitable form of government. Much has happened since the rising sun of liberty dazzled the eyes of the States-General at Versailles. Popular government has not yet been proved to guarantee, always and everywhere, good government. If it be improbable, yet it is not unthinkable that as in many countries impatience with tangible evils substituted democracy for monarchy or oligarchy, a like impatience might some day reverse the process.[5]

It did not take long for the apprehension expressed in this closing sentence to materialize. Already, when these words were being written, there were in some countries signs pointing to approaching change. Within a year or two the reaction made its first dramatic gesture in the March on Rome, which was to end the democratic regime in Italy. Soon Fascism had not only brought the era of liberalism to an end in the land of Mazzini and Garibaldi, but had renounced the democratic faith and denied the ideas that are its essence. Mussolini became at once the expression and the vehement exponent of the widespread reaction against the liberal ideas and the liberal tradition.

The reaction spread rapidly. Before it culminated in the triumph of Hitler in Germany, one half the governments in Europe and many of the governments in Latin America had adopted systems of outright autocracy or had maintained democratic forms only as masks for what were essentially dictatorships. By 1933 it would have been difficult to find survivals of democracy east of a line drawn from the Baltic to the Adriatic, except in the case of what was still Masaryk's Czechoslovakia; while to the west, Spain had emerged for a brief and checkered experiment in democracy and Portugal occupied a dubious position that by no stretch of language could be called democratic. The triumphant democracy of Bryce's description was, it seemed, in retreat. It was now not merely unrealized in practice; in many countries it was challenged in idea as well as in fact. The challenge was not without effect.

[5] *Ibid.*, p. 42.

INTRODUCTION 5

Fascist movements under many different names developed considerable strength in Belgium, France, and Denmark, while even in Great Britain, the United States, and two Scandinavian countries, Norway and Sweden, they were not entirely negligible. In every Western country fascist methods and ideas were professed and propagated. The fascist faith was winning sympathizers even where it failed to recruit followers.

It became necessary, therefore, to dispel the illusion that democracy had won its battle, in the realm either of ideas or of practice. Once more it became necessary to defend it; and, clearly, to defend it effectively it was first necessary to understand it, to define it, and to try at least to formulate clear ideas as to its real nature. It is not surprising, then, that our day should be prolific in books on democracy; nor, in view of the changed temper of our age, is it surprising that the tenor of these books should be in marked contrast to those from which we have already quoted. It is a far cry from the tempered optimism of Bryce's book to this chapter heading in a recent book: "Democracy in Jeopardy—The Success of Democracy not Assured." And consistent with this chapter heading is the author's judgment, which few will question today:

Twenty-five years ago, although the era of debunking and disillusionment had already set in, the great mass of the American people, and the great majority of their leaders, were unwavering in their adherence to the traditional democracy. Even today the mind of America is not profoundly altered. But since 1918 we have descended into a deep trough of skepticism and discouragement. The post-war generation of American youth has grown to manhood in an era of economic depression and conflicting ideologies. The declared enemies of democracy have been winning all the notable victories, and Americans admire success. The modern world is pervaded by a spirit of infidelity and distrust. It is a good time, therefore, to revive and reaffirm our common creed.[6]

It may also be a good time to re-examine the basic principles of that creed.

[6]Ralph Barton Perry, *Shall Not Perish from the Earth* (New York: Vanguard, 1940), pp. 19–20.

Part One

THE LIBERAL TRADITION

CHAPTER 1. The Idea of Democracy

DEMOCRACY is a word that comes to us weighted with a load of associations which history has created. It takes us back to that Greek world where the idea of democracy was born and where its principles received their first practical application. It is true that judged by modern conceptions the application was partial and imperfect. Even in Athens at the pinnacle of its glory the social order was based on a slave population that outnumbered the free population, while the aliens and "strangers" were more numerous than the citizens. Still, the Athenians in the age of Pericles believed in democracy and when their fortunes were at their brightest they gloried in its achievements.

It is this pride in Athenian democracy and in its achievements that gives immortal splendor to the Funeral Oration of Pericles. It must be quoted here in part, not merely because it cannot be quoted too often, but also because the oration gives us a clue to the "something more" that is desired whenever the definition of democracy as a form of government is felt to be inadequate.

Our form of government does not enter into rivalry with the institutions of others. We do not copy our neighbors, but are an example to them. It is true that we are called a democracy, for the administration is in the hands of the many and not of the few. But while the law secures equal justice to all alike in their private disputes, the claim of excellence is also recognized; and when a citizen is in any way distinguished, he is preferred to the public service, not as a matter of privilege, but as the reward of merit. Neither is poverty a bar, but a man may benefit his country whatever be the obscurity of his condition. There is no exclusiveness in our public life, and in our private intercourse we are not suspicious of one another, nor angry with our neighbor if he does what he likes; we do not put on sour looks at him which, though harmless, are not pleasant.

And we have not forgotten to provide for our weary spirits many relaxations from toil; we have regular games and sacrifices throughout the year; at home the style of our life is refined; and the delight which we daily feel in all these things helps to banish sadness. . . . For we are lovers of the beautiful, yet simple in our tastes, and we cultivate the mind without loss of manliness. Wealth we employ, not for talk and ostentation, but when there is a real use for it. To avow poverty with us is no disgrace; the true disgrace is in doing nothing to avoid it. An Athenian citizen does not neglect the state because he takes care of his own household; and even those of us who are engaged in business have a very fair idea of politics.[1]

These passages make it clear that although Pericles suggests a definition of democracy as government by the many, as distinct from government by the few, he was not thinking primarily of this in speaking of Athenian democracy. He was thinking not of the constitution and the laws merely, but of a social order. He was thinking too of a culture and a spirit that he believed were inherent in that order. Athenian democracy for Pericles meant more than election by lot, rotation of offices, debates of the ecclesia, and all the other characteristics of Athenian government in his day. In this, Pericles is at one with those in every age for whom democracy is a faith.

THE MEANING OF THE WORD

There is some ambiguity in the use of the term *democracy*, and this is confusing. Sometimes the word is used loosely to signify the people in general, the masses as distinguished from certain classes, the many as distinct from the few. "The democracy," it is sometimes said, "is sound at heart," "it can be trusted in the long run," and so on. This usage is too broad to have meaning and may be dismissed without discussion.

But the term may also be used in two other senses, both of which are justified but which need to be distinguished. When we speak of *a* democracy, we are thinking primarily of a form of government with definite characteristics, which broadly speaking may be summed up in the phrase "government by the many." Its features in the modern world are the responsibility of the government to the people; the choice of representatives by election on the basis of a broad franchise; the freedom of the people to discuss issues of principle, policy, and administration; and opportunity

[1] Botsford and Sihler, eds., *Hellenic Civilization* (New York: Columbia University Press, 1915), pp. 241–42.

THE IDEA OF DEMOCRACY

for the people, when they have formed an opinion, to make that opinion effective. Some writers insist that the term must be used in this sense and in no other. Bryce says: "The word Democracy has been used ever since the time of Herodotus to denote that form of government in which the ruling power of a State is legally vested, not in any particular class or classes, but in the members of the community as a whole."[2] Sir Henry Maine is more emphatic. For him democracy "is simply and solely a form of government. It is the government of the State by the Many, as opposed, according to the old Greek analysis, to its government by the Few, and to its government by One. Democracy remains a mere form of government."[3]

These assertions do not carry conviction for the simple reason that it is no longer possible to restrict the use of the term to the political order. Democracy still means a social order, a way of life, which is not entirely a matter of politics. The important thing is to make and to keep the distinction clear. If men speak of democracy today without any qualifying article they may be thinking of government, but they will also be thinking of a stream of tendency in human history, an agelong aspiration for a better world. It is a spirit that on occasion has inspired men to fight with sublime and heroic passion. In many of those struggles they have sought political change but often they fought for something greater—social justice, opportunity, fraternity, or sometimes a dream to which they could give no name. In both senses of the word, democracy has been something for which men have been prepared to die. But it is as an ideal of human society, as a way of life, that democracy has the greater appeal in our world today. True democracy in this sense is not so easy to define, for ideals are never easy to define. Nevertheless, when men speak the word *democracy* today, they think not merely, perhaps not primarily, of a form of government, but of a condition of society, a culture, and a tradition. They mean by it a social order that secures, or at least promises, a definite measure of well-being to those who share in it. Pericles would not have objected to this use of the term.

Political democracy has a narrower connotation. A democratic government is the attempt to embody this ideal of democracy as an order of society and to further its realization through the instruments of a political order. The state may provide conditions

[2] *Modern Democracies*, vol. 1, p. 20.
[3] *Popular Government*, p. 59.

necessary for the pursuit of the ideal and perhaps, in time, for its achievement. Political democracy will never create the democratic society. It will always fall short of complete achievement. It can aim at social justice but never quite attain it. This, presumably, is what Rousseau was trying to express when he declared that "there never has existed, nor ever will exist, a true democracy." And "Democracy has not failed; it has been found difficult and not tried," is an expression of the same idea. Democratic government is a means to an end; it is this end that we have chiefly in mind when we speak of democracy without qualification.

Plato, we know, was far from sharing in the appreciation of democracy that finds such splendid expression in the Funeral Oration. As Maine reminded the readers of his day, Plato thought democracy a bad form of government. But Plato *was* thinking of a form of government, and thinking of it in only one of its aspects: the number that participated in it. For him democracy meant government by the many, government by the mass, which Plato thought must necessarily be ignorant, or at least untrained and incompetent in the art of government. The many would be indiscriminate in choice, haphazard in the assignment of tasks, as indeed Plato believed the Athenian people were in his day. What Plato would have thought of democratic government in a more modern form—what, for instance, he would have thought of representative government in a modern democracy—we do not know. But at least it may be affirmed that if democracy meant merely government by the many, few even of those who today profess the democratic faith would be wholehearted in its praise or enthusiastic in their devotion to it. This point is made effectively by Delisle Burns:

Democracy seems to mean the rule of the undistinguished and ignorant "demos"; and even if we declare that it does not mean mob-rule, many of its advocates seem to believe that democracy will be distinguished from other social forms by reference to the number of members of a group who control its policy. But if this is its meaning, no reasonable man could desire democracy. A mere counting of heads without regard to their contents might result in successful journalism, but would inevitably lead to political lunacy. A flock of sheep would then be the most complete democracy: and if the majority established tyranny it would then be democratic to acquiesce. But that is mere nonsense. Obviously democracy is to be known not merely by discovering how many in the group have political power.[4]

[4]Delisle Burns, *Political Ideals* (London: Oxford University Press, 1919), p. 277.

It may seem paradoxical to suggest, in view of Plato's unqualified condemnation of democracy, that a clue to the content of democracy as an ideal may be discovered in a critical study of the *Republic*, the classic of the extreme aristocratic tradition. The fundamental principle of Plato's *Republic* is surely that men must be given the functions and the tasks for which nature has fitted them. The guardians are to be chosen on the basis of *nature's endowments*. It is quality that matters *and nothing else*. Extraneous considerations of birth, wealth, status, have no place in a society in which, as far as the guardian class is concerned, both the family and private property are abolished. It would, of course, be absurd to suggest that this makes the teaching of the *Republic* democratic, or Plato a democrat. What is suggested rather is that the republic of Plato's construction is a society in which every man is given, or should be given, that place and that opportunity of serving the whole for which nature has fitted him. The individual is assigned his place simply on the basis of what he is. In constructing the republic on that basis, it is true that Plato departs from any accepted conception of democracy. This is because he assumes fundamental differences within human nature which the believer in democracy would of course repudiate. He assumes that men are separated by natural endowments and capacities into sharply defined classes. He falls back upon myth to justify this assumption. The gods have placed gold in some natures, silver in others, and base metal in still others. Plato knows the myth for what it is; nevertheless it expresses precisely his view of fundamental differences within humanity—a contradiction, as we shall see, of one of the basic assumptions of the democratic faith.

Still, in spite of himself, Plato does base his construction of the ideal society on what he believes are the essential human qualities, and assigns functions to people on the basis of their natural capacities and qualities. At least he would agree that a social order would be good according to its success in giving to men the place and position for which they are fitted by their natures and their aptitudes. The modern democrat would not agree with Plato in the application of this principle, but he might agree that the principle is not without value in suggesting the content and the nature of the ideal of democracy. We may even suggest the following as a tentative definition implied in the principle: Democracy is that order of society in which natural capacity is given its rightful place, in which it is given free play, in which each individual finds the place and task for which by nature he is fitted. Artificial restrictions, whether of birth or class, of wealth on the one hand or economic necessity on the other, are eliminated or reduced to a minimum. This, as we shall see, comes near to what is meant by equality in the democratic tradition. It may be compared with another definition that puts in other words the same essential idea: "Democracy is the ideal of a Society so organized that every man shall have equal opportunity to develop what is finest in him."[5]

In this sense certainly democracy is nowhere realized. Real democracy is an ideal that transcends the achievement of any existing society or state. Historically both opportunity and the capacity to seize and use it have been in the main the result of fortuitous circumstances rather than the consequences of differences of talent or of character. Ability and function have never been correlated. Social custom and organization and economic conditions have been and still are more effective in determining the individual's place and work than the distinctiveness of his talent or his aptitude in some particular direction. The lines of social demarcation or of social function have never been determined on rational grounds and they are not now. In spite of this, however, the ideal is not futile, unreal, or valueless. It provides a criterion and a goal, and gives both inspiration and direction to human endeavor and to social policy.

CONSTITUTIONS DO NOT MAKE DEMOCRACY

From all this it follows that constitutions and governments may be more or less democratic, while no government does or can achieve the full realization of the ideal. It follows also that the constitution of a state does not in itself determine the measure of its achievement of democracy. It is clear, for instance, that the provisions of a particular constitution may be honored in the breach rather than in the observance. Sometimes too the democratic implications of a constitution are denied in the actual policy or nature of the government that functions under it and is supposed to observe its provisions. On paper the Russian Constitution of 1936 was admirably democratic; nevertheless the Stalin regime evidenced not the slightest intention of abandoning the single-party system, under which democracy in the customary sense of the term is inconceivable. The constitution was an admir-

---

[5] Burns, *Political Ideals*, p. 276.

able document but a declaration of intent rather than a political fact.

This may be an extreme case, but even short of this the democratic structure of a government does not necessarily give the people actual control of their own destinies. Much depends on the spirit of the people—their ideals, their capacities, their enlightenment, or their lack of it. The Roman Republic is an illustration in antiquity of a system that was formally democratic but essentially oligarchic. In the days of the Republic the long struggle of the plebs for political recognition was over, and social recognition had also been achieved, but wealth was still a passport to influence and power. The Roman Republic, as Warde Fowler puts it, was "the perfection of Oligarchy."

The people are sovereign in legislation, and in the most important judicial cases; they decide on peace and war; they elect their magistrates yearly. They are sovereign whenever they are called on to act, and they must of necessity be called on frequently. "One might reasonably conclude," says Polybius, describing the position of the Demos at Rome, "that it has the greatest share of power, and that the constitution is of the most pronounced democratic type.

But this constitution, as it was actually worked in practice, was no more a democracy than the British constitution is a monarchy. It was not even what Polybius pronounced it to be, after surveying its several parts,—a constitution in which the elements of monarchy, aristocracy, and democracy were all to be found, acting and reacting on each other in a perfectly happy and harmonious combination. . . . As we see it in Livy's later books, and as we see it put to the test in the history of its fall, it was neither a democracy, nor a mixed constitution, nor a government of the best men in the State, but an *oligarchy*—the most compact and powerful oligarchy that the world has ever yet seen. As Athens realised the most perfect form of democracy of which the City-State was capable, so did Rome realise the most perfect form of oligarchy.[6]

The question as to the reason for this apparent paradox may be as significant for the political scientist as it is interesting for the historian. The answer, at least in part, seems to be that the Roman people had neither the capacity nor the will for self-government. With the means for effectively controlling their own destinies within their reach, they preferred to leave them in the hands of a minority. It is this minority that determined the personnel and constitution of the senate and effectively ruled Rome in the days

[6]W. Warde Fowler, *The City-State of the Greeks and Romans* (New York: Macmillan, 1921), pp. 219–20.

of the Republic. This was the case in spite of the checks and balances and the division of powers that Polybius imagined he had discovered, and in which he found the secret of Roman power; and the Roman people willed to have it so! It lies beyond the scope of our discussion to consider whether the Roman people were wise in willing that it should be so. Certainly something may be said for a system governed by a body of the character of the Roman senate. Nevertheless, the Roman Republic was an oligarchy that wore the aspect of democratic government and indeed held the instruments of democratic control, without, however, possessing the desire to use those instruments.

There may be many explanations for this political inertia. Warde Fowler mentions three, of which the last and probably the most important will serve to illustrate this point.

It is plain that they were not the men to govern themselves; government they could leave to their betters, who understood the traditions of the art. They were not fitted to guide, but they were always ready to obey; by their obedience they conquered the world, but left it to their leaders to make the best use of their conquests. . . . Democracy, then, in the Athenian sense of the word, could never have been realised at Rome. The people had neither wish nor ability to govern themselves, but they were perfectly content to elect their magistrates, and to express their opinion occasionally on projects of legislation, of which perhaps they only half understood the import.[7]

The essential clue to the situation is expressed in that passage. When the "wish and ability to govern" are absent, no form of government will constitute or achieve democracy. The spirit of the people, their history and traditions, their outlook on life, their various interests, and the relative values that they attach to them will largely determine the measure of their attainment of democracy in actual fact. There is at least an anticipation of this point in Aristotle, in his discussion of constitutions on the basis of number. Monarchy was government by one, aristocracy by the few, and democracy by the many; but he adopts this basis of classification only to find it unsatisfactory and to abandon it. Those who govern in an oligarchy are few, but this is an accidental rather than an essential feature of oligarchy. In a democracy the many rule, but again this is not the distinctive mark of democracy.

Aristotle is not concerned merely with forms of government.

---

[7] *Ibid.*, pp. 236–38. See also the whole of Chapter 8. For a brief account of the Roman constitution see W. A. Dunning, *A History of Political Theories, Ancient and Mediaeval* (New York: Macmillan, 1902), Chapter 4.

Governments cannot be classified, or states evaluated, on the basis of mere form. All normal states will aim in some measure at the true end, which is the good life, and may be classified according to the measure in which they manifest and express this aim and hold consistently to it. All true states also must display what we would call public spirit, and their relative possession or lack of this quality will determine their essential character. Aristotle would not say that forms of government are unimportant and that "what is best administered is best." He would almost certainly say that even more important than forms of government are the ends that a people seeks and the spirit it displays in seeking them.

We may say, therefore, that in any given state, if there is an undue adulation of wealth, if material success is recognized as the great end of endeavor, under *any* constitution the actual government will tend toward oligarchy. Again, if there is a subservient temper and an emphasis on birth among any particular people, no constitution will weld that people into a real democracy. Power will gravitate in the direction indicated by the trend set by the deepest desires and aspirations of the people. A broad franchise will not emancipate a servile race, nor will any device give government control to people who do not desire it.

The history of the German Republic may be cited as an illustration in modern times of this fact. The Weimar constitution, whatever else may be said of it, was an extremely democratic document. It made provision not only for election on the basis of universal adult suffrage without distinction of sex; it also included what were supposed to be the ultrademocratic devices of proportional representation and the referendum. It is no exaggeration to say that from the formal standpoint no constitution existing in 1921 —not even that of the United States—could excel it or exceed it in democratic character. The Weimar Republic in every respect *except in substance* was a pattern of democracy. That however did not make Germany really democratic, and "Weimar" never evoked enthusiasm, let alone devotion. In the course of time the very word was made a reproach. There may have been particular reasons for this; for example, one of the first tasks of the new regime was to accept a peace settlement that was indignantly resented. This, however, is far from being an adequate explanation of the fact that the republic did not make good. The truth seems to be that the Bismarckian tradition was still very much alive, and German character and sentiment had been imbued with its spirit. The military had suffered eclipse in their defeat in World War I, but the eclipse was only temporary. Germany still believed in the army, and the army certainly did not believe in the republic.

It is not difficult to understand why the Weimar Republic met the fate that befell it. Germany had been trained in the hard school of militant nationalism for nearly a century. In reaction to the privations and humiliations of the Napoleonic period there developed an intense and ardent desire for German unity. It found expression in economic policy under the leadership of Prussia and crystallized in the Zollverein. It also pervaded, and indeed in large measure inspired, the political liberalism that brought the Frankfort Assembly into existence. It is one of the tragedies of history that German liberalism failed to achieve German unity; that unity was secured under other auspices and by means undreamed of in German liberalism. Where the liberals of Germany failed Bismarck succeeded! And he succeeded by concentrating on military power and creating a strong and efficient German army. This army he used as the instrument of his own ascendancy, recognizing consistently that his position and power depended upon it; and this army enabled him to lead Germany to the successive victories that he believed necessary for the creation of united Germany. Throughout his career he was contemptuous of popular favor, distrusted democracy in any and every sense of that term, and believed in the sword as the ultimate arbiter in the fate of nations and governments.

That it was by such means and under such leadership that modern Germany began its career as a powerful and united state is obviously vitally important. The Bismarckian principles and methods had been vindicated by success, and the German Empire owed its existence to that fact. It was almost inevitable that the army and the bureaucracy which supplied the means for its maintenance should occupy a position of extraordinary authority and prestige in the German Empire. Liberalism had failed in Germany; autocratic bureaucracy combined with military might had succeeded. These were the potent historic facts that in great measure determined and colored the German tradition. Defeat in war did not destroy that tradition; indeed, as proof of its strength, the tradition made it possible to explain the defeat—or even to deny it—in terms that were harmonious with the essential implications of the tradition. Germany had not been defeated; it had been betrayed! Tradition triumphed even over fact!

Under these conditions a people bred in this tradition could not be expected to develop overnight either the capacity or the will to work a democratic system effectively. The Weimar system was from the outset a form of government which the German people had not wanted and which very probably they would not have chosen had not President Wilson, by implication, almost insisted upon its adoption. The democratic constitution was accepted reluctantly by the majority as a possible means of securing more favorable treatment for Germany at the hands of the victorious Allies. When it did not achieve even that result it fell into disrepute.

The history of the Weimar Republic then is the history of a democratic constitution adopted by a people that did not have the will and proved that it did not have the capacity to make it work. It was of course not inconceivable that the German people in 1919 might forswear the tradition of militant nationalism that had once proved so successful both in war and in peace but which now apparently had failed in a supreme test. If that had happened it would have been something of a miracle. It would have needed a transformation of character and of spirit sufficiently decisive to wipe out the results of a tradition developed and nurtured for decades and strengthened by the actual fruits that it had to show in its own favor. It did not happen.

Therefore, in spite of the constitution of Weimar the Germany of the twenties was not democratic. It displayed the forms of democracy but lacked the will to attempt the achievement of the reality. Social Democracy could make a great showing at the polls—although in time even here there were distinct signs of a reversal—but it could not appeal with sufficient power to establish itself securely. It never rested firmly in the people's esteem or in their affections. It therefore had to depend, not upon democratic approval, but largely upon such forces as it could recruit from quarters where it could expect neither approval nor loyalty. It was still dangerously apparent in the early years of the republic that the real arbiter in German politics was force. Even the Social Democrats had to call upon the army for support, welding its scattered fragments into an effective force but certainly without changing its mentality or its principles. Noske with his improvised army, suppressing revolutionary movements with ruthless ferocity—and not always drawing the line at revolutionary movements—was a disturbing augury, an omen of coming events. The republic was a frail edifice because it was never "broad based upon the people's will." The farce of the trial of the Kapp rebels is as significant as the brutal severity displayed in dealing with

Ruhr workers at the same period. The democratic republic really did not exist, except in form and on paper. The election of Hindenburg in 1925 was an indication of the realities of the situation. Germany had not forsworn its faith in its bureaucracy and in its military chiefs. The form of democracy existed; it was valued by many and it was useful for a while, but the form passed because there was not sufficient spirit to infuse it with life. There was no deep faith to sustain the liberal regime of Weimar, and democracy will never exist, nor will even its forms survive where it is merely tolerated, as it was in the early twenties in Germany. More than a constitution is needed to make a democracy.

THE WILL AND THE CAPACITY TO GOVERN

Democracy, then, is not necessarily created by any particular form of government, although some forms may render its achievement difficult or impossible. Its realization depends on the existence of at least two fundamental factors, the will to govern and the capacity for government.

The will to govern is the product of various conditions and factors, many of which may now be beyond our control. It is in part presumably the result of characteristics of temperament, of long established custom, of tradition, and of history. The relative importance of these various factors we can neither measure nor weigh. There is no doubt that Romans differed from Greeks in ways that cannot be entirely explained by different historical experiences or different physical environments. And certainly history and its effects in the creation of tradition cannot be canceled. The clock cannot be put back. Bismarck *did* leave his impress, both for good and for ill, on Germany and the Germans.

This does not mean, however, that even here the means of change are entirely nonexistent. The effects of long tradition can be modified, and the desire for self-government can be implanted and nurtured and may grow even in the most unpromising soil. A sense of responsibility and a desire to assume responsibilities may come with changes of character. It may be that these are essential human characteristics; perhaps they have long lain dormant, covered over by the pall of tradition and custom, but they are never really eradicated. This indeed, as we shall see, seems to be one of the assumptions of the democratic faith. The will to govern, or the desire for self-government, needs to be awakened, but the desire is natural and human and once awakened will grow by exercise. A sense of responsibility is the common possession of man, and it is probable that the readiness to assume responsibilities can be evoked more easily than is generally supposed. This is a point that must be discussed more carefully later.

It is possible to be much more positive with regard to the second condition of the achievement of democracy. The capacity for government *is* something that can be developed and enlarged. There is no specific method for producing critical ability or sound judgment in individuals, but the conditions of sound criticism and judgment are known and can be secured. It is universally recognized that judgment should be based on evidence and that criticism should be informed by knowledge. And to develop the capacity to know and to judge, it is hardly necessary to say, is the function of education. No illiterate and ignorant people will achieve much more than the semblance of democracy, whatever the form of their government or however broad their franchise. There is no possible means of weighing votes, only of counting them! Nevertheless it is clear that a wide franchise and the casting of votes will contribute to the well-being of the whole only in so far as they represent informed opinion. Education is, therefore, of crucial importance in providing the conditions of real democratic achievement.

Need it be added that what is meant by education here is not indoctrination but the antithesis of it? It is training in the use of the powers of the mind rather than the imposition upon the mind of rigid dogma. The democratic faith demands that the keys of knowledge be placed in the hands of the many, that the instruments of knowledge be made accessible to the people. If the essence of the democratic method is discussion, the people must be fitted for discussion, trained as far as possible to judge, to weigh conflicting arguments, and to appraise conflicting policies. Somehow, too, they must be given access to the accumulated wisdom of the ages that constitutes our cultural heritage.

Here too, let it be admitted, we are in the realm of ideals, for nowhere has "an informed and enlightened public opinion" been much more than an aspiration, and nowhere is education an entirely free opportunity open to all sorts and conditions of men. The "educational ladder," it has been said, needs to be abolished, to be replaced with the "broad highway." Nor must education be regarded as a process that ends with school or even with college. Adult education movements have been born of a realization that education in a democracy is a lifelong task. As democracy progresses education will become more and more clearly a part of its technique and a condition of its effective operation. Even if these be ideals, ideals count, and certainly this is integral to any sound conception of democracy.

Concerning the nature of democratic education little need be said here, for this would carry us into the realm of the educationalist and the psychologist rather than that of the political scientist. Aristotle's principle holds. Education must express the spirit of the constitution and be harmonious with it. Given the assumptions of democracy it follows that education in a democratic society will be imbued with a real sense of the importance of free inquiry. Having provided the young with the instruments of learning, education in a democracy must become a quest. What Lord Haldane said of the true university may be said of democratic education in general:

It cannot live and thrive under the domination either of the Government or the Church. Freedom and development are the breath of its nostrils, and it can recognise no authority except that which rests on the right of the Truth to command obedience. Religion, art, science —these are . . . but special and therefore restricted avenues towards that Truth—many-sided as it is, and never standing still. It was Lessing who declared that were God to offer him the Truth in one hand and the Search for Truth in the other, he would choose the Search. He meant that, just as the Truth never stands still, but is in its nature a process of evolution, so the mind of the seeker after it can never stand still. Only in the process of daily conquering them anew do we, in this region also, gain life and freedom. And it is in the devotion to this search after the Most High—a search which may assume an infinity of varied forms—that the dedicated life consists; the life dedicated to the noblest of quests, and not to be judged by apparent failure to reach some fixed and rigid goal, but rather by the quality of its striving.[8]

Education, however, is only one of a great variety of conditions upon which capacity to govern depends. Social conditions in general will help either to develop it or to retard its development. Society is a broader concept than the state—the former being a complex of relations by which human beings live in interdependence with one another, the latter being the implementation of the existing form of interdependence by means of governmental authority and organization. Having said that democratic society will not necessarily be created by a democratic form of government, although a government that is undemocratic may prove an

---

[8] R. B. Haldane, *Universities and National Life* (London: Murray, 1912), pp. 105–6.

insurmountable obstacle to the realization of social democracy, we must now add that where society is undemocratic, political democracy will have little chance of being much more than a form. Its influence and effect will be continually impeded and frequently nullified. Democracy in the social base would seem to be a prerequisite of democracy in the state, even though the state must function in the end as the safeguard of a democratic society. In the long run, therefore, it is not possible to keep the two concepts of democracy apart, except for purposes of analysis. Political and social democracy must grow together.

Public spirit, it will be admitted, is a primary condition of democratic government and is a basic element in what we mean by capacity to govern, and this is not and cannot be the creation merely of a system of education, however excellent that system may be. For the system must function within a particular social order and its effectiveness will be determined by the conditions of that order. If these conditions are inconsistent with a fundamental community of purpose, if they create a deep division of feeling and of interest, public spirit will not be guaranteed by superimposing upon them any system of education, nor will a wide franchise or any other device achieve the reality of political democracy. If "half the world knows not how the other half lives," it is evident that under any form of government democracy will be far from realization. There indeed will be, as Plato saw, not one state but two—"the city of the rich and the city of the poor"— or not two but many. Divisions of status, of rank, of material condition may go so deep that community feeling has little chance of growth. There will not be a real capacity to govern in a people deeply divided among themselves in feeling and interest. A discussion of democracy, therefore, cannot ignore those conditions within which human beings live and act, except at the cost of unreality and sterility.

Political democracy, then, may be discussed in abstraction, but it cannot be left in abstraction. To say that education must fit men for it is not the whole truth, for education itself is never a process occurring in a vacuum. It presupposes not only a particular kind of instruction but also a particular kind of environment and a particular set of conditions. Suppose that economic necessity does not permit men to avail themselves of the opportunities that are offered. Long hours of labor, inadequate means of subsistence, insecurity and the anxieties that go with it, housing conditions that provide neither comfort nor peace—these are conditions that may be inconsistent with the aims of the educational system and that may destroy the effectiveness and value of even the best system. This is becoming clear in most advanced countries. We know now, for instance, that there is no sense in trying to educate a child that is only half fed; so much is recognized in the practice of most modern states, which provide meals for undernourished and necessitous children.

The principle implied in this recognition requires a much broader application than is usually given to it. It should be a reminder that material conditions cannot be ignored in considering ideals. A man's environment, if not a part of his capacity, is of very considerable importance in determining that capacity. If we insist that man at his best must be a citizen, we must not forget that the citizen remains a man, with needs that must be satisfied before he can fulfill the functions and the duties of citizenship or prepare himself for them. Both his will and his capacity to govern will depend in great measure upon the milieu in which he lives and works. The consideration of democracy, therefore, takes us into the realm of politics but it will not leave us there. Political democracy may come first in the order of discussion; it does not necessarily come first in importance.

CHAPTER 2. Democracy as a Form of Government

GOVERNMENTS will never be completely democratic, as the argument thus far has made clear. Their democratic character will always be a matter of degree. Any particular government, as we have already seen, is an attempt, necessarily imperfect, to realize the ideal of democracy. But there are certain marks that will serve to characterize democratic government, and these distinguishing marks may serve as the basis for a broad definition of political democracy. Here indeed we may follow the general trend of nineteenth-century liberal thought.

A democratic government is one in which the sovereignty or controlling power is vested in the last resort in the entire aggregate of the community, every citizen not only having a voice in the exercise of that ultimate sovereignty, but being at least occasionally called on to take an actual part in the government by the personal discharge of some public function, local or general. This presupposes the existence of what may be called the primary freedoms: of thought, of writing and speech, and of assembly. It also implies free discussion as the normal method for creating the conditions that permit the formation of a real public opinion. Since the exercise of popular sovereignty must involve decisions, properly registered and made effective, it is essential that the evidence upon which decisions must be based shall be freely available and subject to the fullest scrutiny and criticism. Democratic government presupposes discussion as the means to effective decision.

In the modern state the characteristic, and indeed the necessary, means for giving expression to political democracy is representative government. Direct participation in the sovereign assembly, as conceived by Aristotle and as implied by Rousseau, is now out of the question. The government will therefore be democratic, other things being equal, only if the franchise is broad and comprehensive and in the last resort is extended to the people as a whole. Exclusion from the franchise on the basis of property, education, race, or sex is from this point of view a limitation of the democratic character of government.

It is the argument of those who believe in political democracy that these are basic conditions of good government, and that they are the elementary and essential marks of the political order that is compatible with the realization of democracy. We leave out of account for the time being the question raised by Montesquieu and discussed by John Stuart Mill, indeed by writers of the historical school in general, as to whether the phrase "the best form of government" should be used at all. Obviously the *best* form of government will not necessarily be applicable to peoples without reference to their actual conditions. We are concerned here with the question of objectives. Is the goal implied in our discussion of government the goal at which peoples should aim? Is the ideal of political democracy sound? The methods suitable for its achievement at different stages of cultural and economic development in the life of nations and peoples will still need to be determined. In short, we are not now concerned with the tempo of the march toward the goal, but with the validity of the goal itself.

THE CASE FOR DEMOCRATIC GOVERNMENT

If we keep this in mind there may be some purpose in asking the question: Is democracy the best form of government? The logical alternatives are either some form of dictatorship or government by experts, which in practice becomes some form of bureaucracy. The argument for political democracy is usually developed in opposition to the case for one or the other of these alternatives. It will be well to follow this course and to begin with the more general considerations.

It is urged that democratic government is the only form of government that develops the qualities usually connoted by the term *citizenship*. This is expressed or implied in the oft-quoted phrase "self-government is better than good government," a phrase that expresses a truth while seeming by implication to concede the point that democratic government may be lacking in efficiency, that it is to be preferred in spite of certain disadvantages and relative weaknesses. This we need not concede at the present stage of our argument. What is certain is that a sense of responsibility can be created only by making people responsible. To the argument that certain people or classes are unfit to govern, the democratic answer is simply that fitness can be developed only by actual practice. In the days when women's suffrage was one of the outstanding issues in politics, those who were opposed to the extension of the franchise argued that women were not interested in politics. It was not the only answer but a sufficient one to say that interest is developed generally by creating interests. Actual participation in politics and actual responsibility for policy are the necessary conditions of an intelligent and lively interest. The most efficient government conceivable, government by experts, may do many things, but it will be incapable of developing citizens in the only real meaning of that term. It is by the exercise of judgment that the capacity for judgment grows.

It is a legitimate extension of this argument to point out that only in democratic government can there be a just correlation of policy and consequences. The decisions of representative bodies may sometimes be mistaken, sometimes foolish, but at least they are their own. And the people who have chosen these representatives know that indirectly these errors of judgment are *their* own also. They are not bearing the consequences of decisions with which they have had nothing to do and for which they are neither to be blamed nor praised. Experiences that are the result of policy are in a specific sense *their* experience, and these are the experiences that are educative. Criticism is curative when it is self-criticism. Catastrophe is remedial only when the people who endure it are aware that they made it or helped to make it. In this sense too self-government contains within itself the remedies for its own weaknesses and shortcomings. The remedies may be slow in operation but at least they are not entirely absent, as they are in the alternatives to democratic government. People may be slow to learn, but that they can and do learn is one of the assumptions of democracy. Experience is often a hard teacher, but in the long run there is no substitute for it and there is no possibility of it where there is no sense of responsibility.

It is also relevant to consider the converse of this argument, the effect of government upon those who exercise its powers where participation in it is limited. Even the most expert bureaucracy will not be immune from the influences that its own special character creates. Bureaucracies do not retain their expertness; they tend to lose their efficiency by virtue of the very conditions under which they exist. It is not entirely without significance that the very word *bureaucracy* has come to be a term of reproach and that red tape is regarded as the besetting sin of government departments. The point made by John Stuart Mill in this connection is still relevant.

The disease which afflicts bureaucratic governments, and which they usually die of, is routine. They perish by the immutability of their maxims, and, still more, by the universal law that whatever becomes a routine loses its vital principle, and, having no longer a mind acting within it, goes on revolving mechanically, though the work it is intended to do remains undone. A bureaucracy always tends to become a pedantocracy.[1]

Not only is there a tendency to ossification, but the possession of power and freedom from criticism are as dangerous for bureaucracies as for dictators. The possession of power corrupts, and absolute power corrupts absolutely, as Lord Acton remarked long ago. No individual and no institution can be immune from the healthy blasts of criticism without at least the danger of that self-satisfaction and self-delusion which are the most potent causes of deterioration and of smug complacency. And it is only under democratic forms that effective criticism is not merely justifiable but expected.

The argument may be pushed one stage farther. Man is more than a citizen and his duties extend beyond what are usually meant by the duties of citizenship. There is a moral argument for democratic government, which is not to be too easily dismissed. One element in this ethical argument has already been stated above, for a sense of responsibility is fundamental to personality. But there are other qualities that are important. Intelligence, quickness of apprehension, mental agility—these are not qualities that any form of government can produce, but they can be discouraged or stimulated by political conditions. Where obedience and acceptance are the cardinal political virtues they will have little encouragement and less stimulus. Here, too, Mill expresses an objection to absolutism in any of its forms or modifications with point and force. Under a bureaucratic government,

The nation as a whole, and every individual composing it, are without any potential voice in their own destiny. They exercise no will in respect to their collective interests. All is decided for them by a will not their own, which it is legally a crime for them to disobey. What sort of human beings can be formed under such a regimen? What development can either their thinking or their active faculties attain under it? . . . A person must have a very unusual taste for intellectual exercise in and for itself who will put himself to the trouble of thought when it is to have no outward effect, or qualify himself for functions which he has no chance of being allowed to exercise. The only sufficient incitement to mental exertion, in any but a few minds in a generation, is the prospect of some practical use to be made of its results.[2]

But beyond these considerations are the other factors that go

---

[1] John Stuart Mill, *Representative Government* (New York: Holt, 1873), p. 127.
[2] *Ibid.*, pp. 56–59.

to the making of character and the enhancement of personality. Besides a sense of responsibility and intelligence but related to them there is the factor of obligation. "The duties of citizenship" involve qualities that are also valuable in fields other than that of actual participation in civic affairs. They are the individual's opportunity for realizing the significance and the demands of community life; they tend to take him out of the restricted area of personal and selfish interests. That there are other fields of activity which may provide this opportunity for, and stimulus to, altruism does not alter the fact that isolation and detachment from personal obligation in the realm of politics is a definite and serious loss. Where evils exist and where wrongs need to be righted it cannot fail to blunt moral sensitivities if people are left to feel either that the evils and wrongs are no concern of theirs or that they cannot do anything to remedy them. The fact that many or even the majority of people in political democracies do not feel these obligations or do not fulfill them does not alter the ever-present expectation that they should. Life can be narrow for individuals under any form of government, but this does not diminish the force of the argument that democratic government provides a valuable opportunity for expanding sympathies and broadening interests.

All this is another way of saying that democratic government is one of the conditions for redeeming the individual from the isolation of selfishness and creating in him a sense of the reality of the common life. It is in part at least what Aristotle had in mind when he spoke of the citizen, and the citizen only, as the complete human being.

THE ORDINARY MAN'S CAPACITY TO GOVERN

Perhaps the oldest and certainly the most persistent objection to political democracy as seen by some of its critics is the denial of the capacity of the ordinary man to understand, still less to participate in, the difficult task of government. In its classic form it appears in the Socratic argument that government is an art and that, like all the other arts, its practice demands careful and arduous training. Proficiency in the art of government is not a universal gift of nature, nor is the capacity for it. Some will be gifted, others will not, and even the gifted ones will need to have their gifts and aptitudes developed by a special regimen of intensive cultivation. Specific education is a prerequisite to the kind of efficiency and competence called for by the complex problems of politics.

It may be pointed out—although this has been done so often that it is hardly necessary to do it again—that Socrates was speaking particularly of direct and active participation in the work of administration and legislation, and in that connection the modern democrat would not quarrel with his main point. In any form of government experts will be needed, and special education and training will have to be provided for them. In all democracies this is recognized in practice to a greater or less degree, in the civil services and the technical and administrative bureaus that are a normal part of the governmental structures of modern states. Special provisions are made for the training and recruiting of their personnel. Here obviously the analogy of the arts holds, and the case against the appointment of administrative and other officials by the haphazard method of lot, even with the special conditions and safeguards that were present in Athens, may be freely granted.

Modern critics, however, deny to the majority the competence to participate in government even to the extent implied in the choice of representatives and the expression of judgment on broad matters of policy. Sir Henry Maine, in spite of the fact that he wrote in 1885, may be regarded as typical of criticism of this kind even yet, although his criticism is stated in intemperate terms that few would use today.[3] The argument briefly is that democratic government is the most difficult of all forms of government, that the issues raised in modern politics are complex and abstruse, that only the educated are competent to form reasonable judgments relating to them.

Since the multitude is clearly not competent, Maine's criticism proceeds, democratic methods of winning the people's acquiescence and support resolve themselves into mass appeals that are not appeals to reason at all, but that aim at arousing passions and emotions that know neither the direction nor the restraints of calm and considered judgment. In practice the masses do not form opinions; they merely follow the opinion of those few who manage in some way to arouse their interest and engage their uncritical admiration. Indeed the many do not know even their own interests. Jeremy Bentham, so Maine declares, "greatly overrated human nature. He overestimated its intelligence. He wrongly supposed that the truths which he saw, clearly cut and distinct, in the dry light of his intellect, could be seen by all other men or by many of them. He did not understand that they were visible

[3] *Popular Government*, Essay II.

only to the Few—to the intellectual aristocracy. His delusion was the greater from his inattention to facts which lay little beyond the sphere of his vision. Knowing little of history, and caring little for it, he neglected one easy method of assuring himself of the extreme falseness of the conceptions of their interest, which a multitude of men may entertain. 'The world,' said Machiavelli, 'is made up of the vulgar.' "[4] And this is no mere temporary phenomenon! It will remain true, if not forever at least for as long a time as can be foreseen or need be taken into account for practical purposes. Men are built that way and society will always be constituted so.

The greatest difficulty of democracy, says Maine, is human nature itself, and human nature apparently does not change. The multitude has no mind of its own and therefore no will that it can make effective. In relation to any save the very simplest political question it is certain that no general agreement is ever possible. And most political problems are not simple! Opinions in relation to them will coincide only when trained minds study them and find demonstrable solutions. Such phrases as the "will of the people" and *"vox populi, vox Dei"* may serve to decorate the rhetoric of the orator but they do not correspond to any reality. The people have no will, they are not capable of understanding the complexities of politics, and therefore they certainly are not capable of governing.

Concerning the view of human nature implied in Maine's statement something will be said when we come to a discussion of the ethical assumptions of democratic government. Here the argument can be met in simpler terms. The truth is that the knowledge that is of practical importance in politics is no exclusive preserve of the educated few, the intellectual aristocracy of which Maine speaks. The knowledge that is important here is that which is frequently gained in the actual experience of men and women in industry and in commerce, in workshops and in mines, in those walks of life that ordinary people tread in the daily round of normal activities. Such knowledge does not enable them to formulate legislation or to organize machinery for the effective administration of laws, but it is invaluable for a sound opinion as to the merits both of the laws and of the administration that puts them into effect.

This is the real argument for giving the people as a whole the opportunity of election, of criticism, and of judgment. It is no

[4] *Ibid.*, p. 86.

effective answer to say that the people are not qualified to do what, as a matter of fact, they are not called upon to do. And as Professor Bradley suggests, if "the objection be raised that, if they are not fit to hold office themselves, they cannot be fit to choose officials and judge their conduct, the answer is that in many cases it is not necessary to know how a thing is made in order to judge of it. The head of a household, who could not have built the house, is a better judge of the product than the builder, the man who eats a dinner than the cook who prepared it."[5]

In relation to industrial conditions, to take only one example, the workingman who lives under these conditions is the specialist, if firsthand knowledge of a particular set of facts constitutes specialism. At least he is in the best position to know the value of a vast range of social and industrial legislation for the simple reason that he has to bear its consequences. He knows where the shoe pinches. It is this knowledge that the many frequently have and the few, even though they are experts, frequently have not. And it is this knowledge that for criticism and appraisal is peculiarly important. Experience teaches, and its lessons are not the least important part of the equipment necessary for the practice of the art of government in the sense in which we have defined that term.

What you want in a body of electors is a rough, shrewd eye for men of character, honesty, and purpose. Very plain men know who wish them well, and the sort of thing which will bring them good. Electors have not got to govern the country; they have only to find a set of men who will see that the Government is just and active. . . . So far from being the least fit for political influence of all classes in the community, the best part of the working class forms the most fit of all others.[6]

Knowledge indeed is a condition of effective citizenship in a democratic order, but it is as foolish to make a fetish of the knowledge of the schools as it is to disparage it. There is no effective monopoly of the knowledge that counts in democratic government.

GOVERNMENT BY EXPERTS

Less important is the argument that democratic government suffers from the dominance of class interests. The argument of the Victorians is that since the workers are of necessity the ma-

---

[5] A. C. Bradley, "Aristotle's Conception of the State," as quoted in E. Abbott, ed., *Hellenica* (London: Longmans, Green, 1907), p. 217.
[6] John Morley, *Studies in Literature* (London: Macmillan, 1891), pp. 133–34.

jority in any modern community, there is a grave danger that majority rule will favor them at the expense of the privileged and minority classes.

In all countries there is a majority of poor, a minority who, in contradistinction, may be called rich. Between these two classes, on many questions, there is complete opposition of apparent interest. We will suppose the majority sufficiently intelligent to be aware that it is not for their advantage to weaken the security of property, and that it would be weakened by any act of arbitrary spoliation. But is there not a considerable danger lest they should throw upon the possessors of what is called realized property, and upon the larger incomes, an unfair share, or even the whole, of the burden of taxation, and having done so, add to the amount without scruple, expending the proceeds in modes supposed to conduce to the profit and advantage of the laboring class?[7]

Mill recognizes that this danger of the abuse of power is inherent in the possession of power, and he is not blind to the other side of the shield. The privileged classes are as likely to be affected by it as the many, for they may be as determined in their resistance to encroachments upon, or threats to, their privileges as the many are in their attacks upon those privileges.

What is overlooked, however, is that no government by experts can ever contain any assurance of safeguards against the perils of class interests. Experts are never merely experts; they are also men, and of necessity they will have interests as members of a class as well as interests as members of a community. There is no reason to suppose that they will certainly rise superior to the insidious urge of the interests of their class. The concept of the expert as such is as unreal as was that of the economic man. The possession of power will always create the danger of its abuse. The history of modern democracies gives little support to the assumption that the peril is increased under democratic forms. Indeed it may be argued that the majority by virtue of its numbers is less likely to fall victim to this danger. Class consciousness may very well be diluted in the vastness of numbers, especially if among those numbers there are disparities of interest. Certainly cohesion of purpose and policy becomes more difficult of achievement as numbers increase, and organization for effective political purposes is rendered much less probable. This is not to ignore the danger but rather to place it in its proper perspective and in its

[7] Mill, *Representative Government*, p. 133.

relative position of importance. The assumption that experts will be immune from this danger is unfounded.

There is even less to be said for the implicit assumption that government by experts will necessarily mean unity of aim and cohesion of purpose. The disagreements of experts frequently go deeper and result in more bitter controversies than do the disagreements of an average cross-section of the general public. Particularly is this true in relation to issues raised in the social sciences. The political sympathies of any group of expert economists in any situation may range them all the way from extreme right to extreme left on matters of general policy. "In regard to economic issues," it has been said, "the expert emphatically does not know, or rather, as the history of recent years has only too plainly shown, what he 'knows' is often diametrically opposed to what is 'known' by a rival expert."[8] Some economists may believe in free trade; others, equally competent, may advocate autarchy. The beliefs in both cases may be largely influenced by considerations that lie outside the field in which the particular individuals concerned are experts, although these considerations are vitally related to policies within those fields. There has never been any monopoly of expertness in any particular political party.

This leads to, and is partly explained by, the fact that political issues involve ends, in relation to which there can be no expertness in the ordinary sense of the term. Here presumably the saint is the expert, if the term has any meaning at all in this connection. Certainly in the realm of ultimate objectives and of moral values, the ordinary man has as much right to consideration as any expert. The point is made effectively by Professor Joad:

> An economic expert, for example, concerned only with the increase of efficiency, may conceive and plan a community of willing industrial slaves, owning no desires save such as are consonant with the speeding up of production with a view to the maximization of output; a hygienic expert, concerned only with health, may demand that men should be required to live on rice, rusks, and vegetables; a military expert, that they should be drilled daily and sleep with gas masks hanging to their bedposts in the interests of security.
>
> Or again, though the ends of the expert may not be other than those of the community, the means that he proposes to adopt in order to secure them may be other than those which the community wills. Most men, no doubt, desire a plenitude of goods, health and security. It does not, however, follow that they are prepared to turn them-

---

[8] C. E. M. Joad, *Guide to the Philosophy of Morals and Politics* (London: Gollancz, 1938), p. 793.

selves into robots, vegetarians, or soldiers; and it does not follow, because they may and do acknowledge other ends with whose realization machine-minding, vegetable-eating and drilling conflict. Thus measures proposed by an expert, although ancillary to ends which the community desires, may nevertheless be unacceptable because their adoption conflicts with other ends which the expert does not recognize.[9]

The fact is that the argument for government by experts depends for its plausibility upon the ambiguity with which the term *expert* is used. Expert in what and for what? Immediately the question is asked it becomes clear that every man has a right to be heard in relation to the ends which he thinks conducive to his own welfare. For specific and limited objectives the expert, as already stated, will still need to be consulted; but welfare in general is a matter of universal concern, in relation to which the values held by people in general are of vital importance. It is what the people wills that is, and ought to be, the final determinant in shaping policy.

POTENTIAL WEAKNESSES OF THE DEMOCRATIC FORM

This brings us to the most definite and specific considerations urged in criticism of democratic government. It is urged that democracy is an inefficient form of government, or at least that it has weaknesses in action that are so serious as to constitute a basic inferiority. We leave aside for the moment the question as to what the proper connotation of the term *efficiency* as here applied really is. The defects usually stressed may be summarized briefly.

It is said that democratic government is lacking in speed of decision. In normal times this will not matter; indeed it may be a positive advantage. The appeal to the representatives of the people, the discussion in Congress or Parliament, the canvassing of public opinion —all these and more are safeguards against hasty and ill-considered action and are also a part of the educative influences of democracy. It is better to decide important issues when they have been understood and when discussion and criticism have minimized the possibilities of error than it is to rush precipitately into actions that may have serious unforeseen consequences. This is generally admitted.

But it is when situations are critical and positive action is urgent that the slow deliberation of democratic processes reveals their inadequacies and dangers. In times of crisis swift decision is

[9] *Ibid.*, pp. 793–94.

all-important; it is then as disastrous to be too late as it is to be wrong. The tempo of modern life in politics, as elsewhere, has been speeded up so that crisis is no longer the occasional and rare condition, but is the characteristic feature of our time. The age is an age of crisis, and it is in such an age that the cumbersome methods of democratic government reveal their limitations. The point has been underlined by the events and experiences of the twenty years' armistice that separated the two world wars.

It is unnecessary, and it would be foolish, to dismiss the argument too casually. All too often during our time the justifiable verdict on vital decisions in the democracies has been "too little and too late." Discussion has continued frequently beyond the point where it served the purpose either of education or of prudence, when the nature of the decision to be taken was a foregone conclusion. Too often the result has been delay and obstruction rather than a clarification of issues. There is in a democracy always the possibility of the abuse of the opportunities it assures and guarantees. A jealous regard for the freedom to express minority views may be necessary for the preservation of the elementary liberties that are the marks of democracy. It is possible that a wide latitude of debate may be worth the price exacted in the form of delay. Nevertheless it seems clear that the determination of the point where discussion has served its useful purpose, when the moment for decision has come, will always be a difficult problem under democratic forms. The solution of this problem must await the development of public spirit and a sense of responsibility. And whenever it is asserted that these grow slowly, it may be answered that only under conditions of democracy do they have a good opportunity to grow at all.

Closely related to this is the argument that democratic government involves the probability of disclosures of purposes, plans, or policies that in the public interest should remain confidential. Publicity, desirable from the viewpoint of democracy and characteristic of democratic government, is frequently dangerous and may be exceedingly prejudicial to the interests of the state. There are occasions when it is necessary to make decisions that other governments should not know, partly because they might be misunderstood, and partly because they might arouse resentment. There are, so it is urged, times when state secrets need to be kept, and when keeping them does not necessarily imply any sinister motive. Under democratic government they are not likely to be kept. A chance remark, a journalistic coup, a question in Parliament, the unguarded argument of a hard-pressed minister in debate—any one of these possible contingencies may result in disclosures detrimental to a sound policy which if all the facts could be revealed would be capable of relatively simple justification.

It is in relation to matters of international policy that this point is stressed most frequently. Dictatorships are able to plan with a secrecy that obviously is impossible for a democracy. In times of crisis, therefore, they achieve initial advantages that may prejudice or even determine the course of events in the future. The history of our own time affords abundant illustrations that seem to support this contention. The advantage of surprise, which has been a characteristic element in the successes of the totalitarian states, has rarely lain with the democracies. The stories of Norway, Holland, Belgium, and Pearl Harbor, to mention only a few of the surprises, make the point obvious.

But it is not only in war that the force of the argument must be recognized. It may not be as important or quite as evident in diplomacy, but it may be serious nevertheless. Would it have been possible for any one of the democratic governments to maintain so close a guard upon its plans as it was for Italy from 1930 to 1935 in relation to its plans in Ethiopia? Would the policies of democratic countries have been interpreted with so much uncertainty and confusion by the rest of the world as was the policy of Japan in the Far East between 1930 and 1940? Secrecy was not the explanation of Munich, but surprise was one element responsible for the democratic debacle that occurred there. The Russo-German pact came, if not like a bolt from the blue, at least with sufficient suddenness to find the democratic governments unprepared for it. Under conditions of this kind must it not always be the case that the initiative will rest with the government whose policy is determined by one or a few, and which has therefore the advantages of secrecy and surprise?

The argument might be extended into the realm of economic and commercial life, even in normal times of peace. Here too policies of economic penetration may have initial successes by virtue of secret planning and operation. These initial successes may make it very difficult to recover lost markets or to counter the economic drives of nondemocratic states. This is illustrated sufficiently by the history of German penetration in the Balkan countries and in Latin America. Where discussion is free and where publication is uncensored, the governments concerned automatically renounce at least some of the advantages of silent marches into commercial areas where competition is keen.

It may not seem entirely convincing to say that this particular objection has force, not because of the inherent weakness of democratic government, but chiefly because of the absence of democracy in other countries and the existence of a spirit that is incompatible with democratic methods and manners. Governments must be judged, not in the light of the demands and conditions of a desirable and ideal future, but in the light of the grim practicalities of the existing world order. If today that world is governed in large measure and over wide areas by considerations of power politics and predominant force, democratic government must prove its capacity to meet the conditions that actually exist. All its merits will be of little avail if it does not demonstrate the ability to survive. It is pointed out by a contemporary writer that "Democracy and Christianity are ill adapted to brutality and deceit, the potent weapons of war."[10] But what if, as the critics suggest, it is not only ill adapted, but disastrously ill adapted? The real answer to this criticism must be left to a later chapter, which will deal with the ethical assumptions of democracy. Its nature is perhaps suggested by Ambrose Vernon in the article just quoted:

But this initial and essential weakness, of which we are both ashamed and proud, is also the source of our enduring might. For now we know the vast resources of a clear conscience. It has at once united our nation. It has cleared our decks of the shining brass of argument. It has nerved us for a sacrifice which God has permitted us, though failing glaringly in justice and humility, to bring not only for our country but for the kingdom of the spirit.[11]

It is a mistake to assume that secrecy, and the speed of decision consequent upon it, can be relied upon under the most repressive dictatorship. It has been said, with a considerable measure of truth, that secret diplomacy is the surest method of securing the widest publicity for decisions and agreements intended to be secret. In the history of modern times, since the formation of the Triple Alliance, most of the secret agreements of the autocracies, Czarist Russia included, were known in substance long before

[10] Ambrose White Vernon, "The Two Sources of Our Strength," *New York Times Magazine*, December 21, 1941.
[11] *Ibid.*

they were published. The most stringent censorship has not prevented leaks, and the news has frequently attracted more attention and has had a more sinister aspect because of the attempted secrecy.

Let it be admitted, however, that political democracy involves risks such as this criticism implies. That they are risks against which safeguards must be sought is not to be doubted. But there are also compensations. Initial disadvantages may be less important than the confidence begotten of the knowledge and the appreciation by the people of its government's purpose and the steps taken to achieve it. There is something to be said for the vast resources of a considered determination as well as of a clear conscience. It may be trite to declare that "thrice is he armed that hath his quarrel just," but it is certainly true that a rational appreciation of what makes the quarrel just will greatly enhance the capacity of a nation both for action and for resistance. To enter a conflict or to confront a situation with full knowledge may be the essential condition of the maintenance of morale, and today we are in less danger of depreciating the value of that than were our forefathers.

EMOTION AND REASON

There remains one final objection to democracy as a form of government that must now be considered. It is frequently asserted that democratic government is merely a façade for something entirely different, that it does *not* give the people the decisive power in government. It is, so runs the charge, frequently an advantage that people should be given the impression that they are a sovereign people; it feeds their egoism and actually makes them more amenable to direction and control by powerful and interested groups. It is suggested that what matters is not that the people should rule, but that they should think they rule. Modern democracies are devices for creating the illusion in the public mind that it is master in its own house, when really the house is run by the few—those few characterized, as a rule, either by their wealth or by their capacity for mass appeal. In either case the instrument of power is propaganda, exercised directly or indirectly by dominant groups; its tools are radio, press, platform, and all other such devices that modern science has multiplied and placed at the disposal of those who seek to rule. The conception of the voter as a rational being, deciding carefully between issues and setting forth to register a considered judgment at the polls, is a survival of the naïve sentimentalism of Victorian liberalism. Actually, emotions and passions are more potent and more operative than reason, catchwords and slogans more influential than principles and sound arguments.

The anti-democrat who contemplates certain aspects of the public meeting may well say of democracy, if it is government by public meeting, that it is government by mass suggestion; that its implication is that people govern best by getting themselves into a state of mind in which they would never dream of getting to solve their own comparatively simple problems. No one supposes that in ordinary life the responses of people under mass suggestion are of any serious value whatever. No one in his senses, if he had to solve an ordinary scientific or practical problem, would put himself under mass suggestion. The anti-democrat contemplating much that goes on at a general election may well ask—what are we to think of a form of government in which people deliberately make themselves drunk, or allow themselves to be made drunk, before they decide the most important questions of government?[12]

Dr. Lindsay does not accept the implications of the argument he here states, but at least he does not dismiss it as entirely without foundation.

This particular point of view has been reinforced by the general trend of studies in social psychology in our time, as well as by the various schools of propaganda analysis that have grown out of those studies. It has been assumed too readily that with people in general it is reason that decides; it is still more dangerous to assume that with masses of people judgments are always, or even generally, determined in the light of pure reason. Emotions and passions may be more dynamic than reason in particular situations—a fact that, unfortunately, the propagandist and the demagogue are not likely to overlook.

The first and obvious comment that suggests itself in this connection is that propaganda is not peculiar to democracy. In fact, it seems more prevalent and more necessary under other forms of government. The use of myth even by the philosopher king is one of the concessions that Plato is forced to make in order to satisfy the feelings of the people who are to be governed for their own good. In modern nondemocratic states the myths have been numerous and none of them as good as Plato's in the *Republic!* Certainly it is significant that it is in the totalitarian states that propaganda has been reduced—or should we say raised?—to a

[12] A. D. Lindsay, *The Essentials of Democracy* (New York: Oxford University Press, 1929), pp. 30–31.

fine art, and it is a modern dictator that has been most frank in his avowal of its importance and most proficient in its use. It seems to be a condition of survival in an autocratic state that dramatic surprises, emotional appeals, floods of oratory, and colorful pageantry should be pressed into the service of the government. When conditions become normal, enthusiasm flags and boredom threatens, and this the dictator apparently dares not risk.

This, let it be admitted, is not to deny the fact that propaganda does play a part in democratic processes of government. It is perhaps unfortunate that the term has come to have a quasi-technical meaning that generally carries with it a derogatory implication. Ambiguity in its use may, and frequently does, confuse issues of great importance. Every appeal that aims at influencing opinion, whether to change it or to confirm it, is propaganda. The real question relates not so much to techniques as to the end that is aimed at and the validity of the methods used to achieve it. That the ends aimed at in democratic countries by the propagandist are always good, or that his methods are always justifiable, it would be absurd to suggest. But it is possible to argue that propaganda in the least worthy interpretation of that term will probably be resorted to less frequently and less habitually under democratic forms of government than under any other. That at least is the testimony of history in our own time.

It is also important to notice that there is implied in this criticism of democratic processes a sharp distinction between emotion and reason, which is of doubtful validity. It is true that people are frequently swayed by emotion, but this emotion is not necessarily lacking in rational elements nor does it necessarily follow that the emotion will be directed to irrational ends. Leadership, which is as necessary under democratic forms of government as under any other, will never be based on purely intellectual or rational appeal. It is the *quality* of the emotional appeal and of the emotional response that matters. It is important that reason should not abdicate, but it is also necessary that the motive power and the dynamic urge of emotion should not be sacrificed.

It remains true, nevertheless, that the extreme rationalism of the nineteenth century has led to disillusionment, and faith in democracy has been prejudiced by the too facile optimism of its earlier advocates. Man is a rational being, but he is also a creature of strong and sometimes violent emotions and he may be powerfully moved by his desires and passions. It is the task of leadership in a democracy to recruit those passions and emotions for democratic ends—to instruct, inform, and enlighten them rather than ignore them or attempt to repress them. Here the psychologist's function must be recognized and his findings carefully considered and applied in the practical concerns of active politics. Severe intellectual analysis and criticism will always be necessary in the social sciences, but these in themselves will never impel men to the adventuresome enterprises and arduous sacrifices that alone can achieve real progress. Democratic appeal has lacked color and drama. Logical demonstration may convince; it does not necessarily inspire.

It is unfortunately true that the dictators of our day have been more apt to learn this lesson than have the leaders of the democratic peoples, and they have been adept in putting the lesson into practice. It is not their use of emotional appeal that is to be decried, but rather the ends for which the appeal has been used and the methods to which they have resorted in making it. The real onus of the charge against them is not that the appeals have been dramatic, but that they have frequently been dishonest, that truth has been distorted to serve their ends, that passion has been with them not the ally of reason but the most unworthy substitute for it. That human nature has proved, under certain conditions, responsive to such appeals is a fact of serious import. But what the democratic faith refuses to concede is that human nature is so constituted that the response to such appeals, made under such conditions, is likely to be general or permanent. Drama and passion will not, in the long run, serve as substitutes for fact and truth. Democracy involves the uncompromising declaration that, in the final court of appeal in human affairs, reason is the arbiter and its judgments must stand.

The conclusion, then, is that a too abstract rationalism among thinkers and leaders in democratic countries has proved dangerous to democratic processes. The cause of democracy has too often seemed open to the charge of a somewhat repellent and arid intellectualism. It has not been dramatized, and it has not always been suffused with sympathy and humanity. It has not been advocated always with passion, because passion has been distrusted by the intellectual liberal. Democracy must be revitalized. Nevertheless, it will remain true and will still need to be recognized that rational standards will always be necessary to save society and nations from the vagaries of emotion and the dynamic and possibly disastrous surges of passion. If in the last resort reason does not control, then there can be neither consistency nor meaning in history.

CHAPTER 3. Contrast with Dictatorship

A COMPARISON of dictatorship and democracy on certain points has been implied in the preceding chapter. It is now necessary to discuss more specifically the arguments for dictatorship, with which the history of our time has made us familiar. No attempt will be made to consider the particular and detailed features of those types of dictatorial government that have appeared during recent years. The peculiar and characteristic ideas of fascism and communism respectively lie beyond the scope of this inquiry. We are concerned with them only in so far as they have the common character of dictatorial government and are thus definite alternatives to democratic government. The philosophical oppositions involved will receive fuller treatment later. Here we are concerned with the contrasting views only in so far as they affect the question of political effectiveness.

ARGUMENTS FOR DICTATORSHIP

The essential point made most frequently by the advocates of the new dictatorship is that there is peculiar merit in the distinctive type and character of leadership as achieved in a totalitarian state. The will of the dictator is the source of authority, supreme and absolute, and this achieves not only speed of decision but also a kind of corporate unity that is impossible under democratic forms of government. It crystallizes the spirit of the people and brings into the common focus of one will the varied and disparate wills of individuals and groups. That this is achieved by a certain measure of coercion is not denied, nor is such coercion regarded as particularly regrettable. Mussolini was perfectly frank on this point as on many others:

Was there ever a government in history that was based exclusively on the consent of the people and renounced any and every use of force? A government so constituted there never was and there never will be. Consent is as changeable as the formations in the sands of the seashore. We cannot have it always. Nor can it ever be total. No government has ever existed that made all its subjects happy. Whatever solution you happen to give to any problem whatsoever, even though you share the Divine wisdom, you would inevitably create a class of malcontents. . . . How are you going to avoid that this discontent spread and constitute a danger for the solidarity of the State? You avoid it with force: by bringing a maximum force to bear; by employing this force inexorably whenever it is rendered necessary. Rob any government of force and leave it with only its immortal principles, and that government will be at the mercy of the first group that is organized and intent on overthrowing it. Now fascism throws these lifeless theories on the dump heap. When a group or a party is in power it has the obligation of fortifying itself and defending itself against all.[1]

In time, as people become habituated to the new order, say the advocates of dictatorship, the need for coercion may diminish; and in any case, as a new generation arises, educated in the technique and ideas of the system, these conditions will come to be recognized as necessary and beneficial. What now seems strange will then seem natural. It is only the survival of antiquated ideas, aftermath of the age of individualism, that postpones this desirable consummation even to the next generation. A state in which only a single party exists, or is permitted to exist, is in the natural order of things; the supreme advantage of such a condition lies in the fact that it supersedes the chaos and confusion both of party warfare and of class interest. It gives unity of purpose instead of the divided counsels and conflicting purposes of the traditional system of representative government.

Central to the whole argument for totalitarian dictatorship is the conception of "the Leader." He is not chosen; he emerges. There is none of the make-believe of election in his assumption of authority and power. It is foolish to suppose that authority can be conferred by masses of ignorant people registering votes in the conventional and haphazard democratic manner. The Leader achieves authority by virtue of a "right," which is mystical in character. He is marked out for leadership by fate or Providence, according to the predilections of the particular interpreter of this philosophy, but his claim to authority is established by the fact that he possesses the power to enforce it and to make it apparent to the people. Not to all of them, however, for there are some so blind that they will not see. They are the recalcitrant minority who make coercion necessary. In general, however, the Leader will be known by what he does; his claim will be proved by the fact that he does lead. He will be known when he appears! In this recognition of the Leader and of his authority there occurs a kind of miracle. The wills of the many are fused in his, and the purposes of all are focused in his so that they become "One Folk." The Leader then is the embodiment of the national spirit, and he

[1] As quoted in H. Finer, *Mussolini's Italy* (London: Gollancz, 1935), p. 223.

is also the incarnation of the genius of the race. This is Rousseau's general will inverted and standing on its head!

But—and it is at this point that the argument comes down to earth—this leadership does create a measure of unity and a kind of unity that representative government can never achieve. Its justification must be found in the triumphs that this unity makes possible, not only in the conflict of nations, although there certainly it will display its power, but also in the struggle against those elements of class interest, of group selfishness, and of monopolistic greed that are the inevitable accompaniments of political democracy. It has, therefore, the promise of glory on the field of battle, but it also has the promise of a society in which divisions have been transcended and antagonisms have been resolved into a partnership of common effort. It is at this point that modern dictatorships, whether fascist or communist, seem to converge, in a common opposition to capitalist plutocracy, presumed by both to be the necessary concomitant, even the common characteristic, of political democracy.

It is true that the idea of the Leader as outlined above finds no place in the communist scheme of thought. The dictatorship of the proletariat that must be achieved as a necessary stage on the way to the communist classless society, is certainly a different kind of dictatorship from that of Nazi or Fascist. It is based on principles that have little in common with those of race and leader. In the communist ideology, since party is always a function of class interest, there is logically no room for parties, only for *the* party, the party of the proletariat. The orthodox communist insists that a dual or multiple party system is incompatible with the stability and effectiveness of the state; that it results in divisions which paralyze authority and therefore in the long run make progress impossible. In the case of Russia, as in the case of Germany, it was argued that the leadership of one man created unity and resulted in a common consciousness that could never be realized under conditions of "pluto-democracy." The arguments of communist and fascist, different on so many other points, converged at least on this.

LEADERSHIP IN A DEMOCRATIC STATE

What has the democratic faith to offer by way of reply to this argument?

It is important in the first place to recognize that leadership is as necessary in political democracy as in any other form of government. It may also happen in a democracy that a leader's authority is as decisive and his power as great as that of any dictator. Indeed, the line that divides popular leadership from dictatorial power may not always be easy to draw, and the point where leadership ends and dictatorship begins may not always be clear in the public mind. That is why so often the charge of dictatorship is made in democratic countries against popular leaders, sometimes with justification, more often without.

The leader is distinguished from the dictator not by the measure of his power, but by the sources whence it is derived, the instruments and methods by which it is exercised, and the purposes to which it is directed. An American president or a British prime minister may actually have as much power as a German fuehrer, but that power will be derived from sources entirely different—from the expressed wishes of an electorate and the declared preferences of a majority of the people. And democratic leaders will retain that power only by continuing to maintain their hold upon the people's political preferences and by remaining the people's choice. They will not engage in "purges," nor will they attempt the wholesale suppression of parties and of opposition, to which a dictator periodically finds it necessary to resort. They will retain their leadership only so long as they prove able to lead, and the test of their ability to lead will be whether the ends they seek and achieve are those that are actually sought and desired by the people. Thus, and thus only, can they hope to maintain the confidence and retain the loyalty of their followers. They must serve as the executives of the popular will, not as external agents of coercion. They must win men, not break them!

Democratic government, indeed, from one point of view, is a device for securing proper and adequate leadership. Here too, in a sense, leadership "emerges," but not in the sense in which that term is used in the fascist argument. There is here no assumption of mystic choice and certainly no assumption that the sign and seal of that choice is the power of the leader to impose his will upon others. Democratic leadership emerges out of the conflicts that are the characteristic and necessary presuppositions of political democracy: the clash of interests, of political parties, of policies—at its best, the clash of ideas. In a sense democratic government is one of the methods that nations have tried, and are still trying, to secure government by the best. But in democratic theory "the best" does not and cannot mean a mystic elite; it is interpreted in a strictly pragmatic sense. "We are going to ask ourselves what is the philosophical justification of democracy. Perhaps in the end we shall discover that democracy is the latest invention, up to now, for discovering a true aristocracy; that the real need for good government is to find an aristocracy if we can. . . . Now we are trying an aristocracy by popular selection."[2]

The character of leadership in a democracy is determined by the methods and the conditions of its emergence. It consists of an ability to interpret the desires and aspirations of the people as a whole, to express their purposes in such a way that these purposes shall rise from the realm of dim apprehension into clear consciousness. This is not to provide "what the public wants"; it is rather to read the inner meaning of the real and deeper yearnings that constitute the soul of a people. It is true, of course, that there will be those who may achieve a passing but dangerous popularity by pandering to the whims of the moment or the passions of a day. There is no specific against the wiles and stratagems of the demagogue, and democratic government, let it be admitted, has suffered greatly from the practice of his arts. This, however, is recognized as the simulation, or even the caricature, of what is really meant by democratic leadership. The true leader in a democracy is concerned to interpret and give effect to the will of the people—a concept which later we must try to define—rather than to the demands even of a majority. In doing so he may add something to that will, clarifying it, strengthening it, perhaps even modifying it.

It has been pointed out that great political leaders of modern times have had the rare gift of interpreting to people their own unspoken desires and aspirations. They do not impose their ideas upon people but bring to clear consciousness ideas that lie unformulated and therefore dormant in the minds of great multitudes. These ideas become dynamic in the speech and perhaps still more in the life of the true leader. He is recognized when he voices the aspirations and purposes of the common man, who has been blindly groping for what now is made clear to him and therefore potent. Gladstone has been mentioned as an example of the leader who possessed this gift of giving expression to the common notions of common men; Lincoln is a still more striking example. It was not his remoteness from the people or his superiority to them that constituted his strength and explained his power. He had remarkable gifts of sympathy and of understanding that enabled him to identify himself with them. It may

[2] J. H. B. Masterman, *Parliament and the People* (London: Headley, 1909), p. 6.

be said that he was the common man at his best, and Lincoln himself would certainly not have caviled at that designation. He led his people because he was able to interpret and make clear to them their own deeper purposes. He became the voice of their unspoken desires and of their better selves. This is the essential character of democratic leadership at its best.

THE QUESTION OF UNITY

With leadership thus conceived, the kind of unity achieved or even desired in a democracy will be different from that of a dictator-state. We may anticipate so far as to say that it will never be the unity of uniformity. Nor will it be sought by means of coercion. It is true that in all government the possibility of coercion must be present and the use of it on occasion may be necessary. But the aim of democratic government will be to minimize its use and, as an ultimate objective, to eliminate it by making it unnecessary. Force will never be the basis of a democratic state. Indeed, it may be asserted that even a dictatorship, however much it may glorify force and magnify its importance, can never be founded entirely upon it. "The most thoroughgoing despotism in the world," as Nettleship points out, "never existed on a basis of mere force. If it be said that everybody would break the laws if he dared, the answer is that if that were true, everybody would dare; there would be no force sufficient to frighten him from it."[3]

The real distinction here is that democratic government must rest on the consent and approval and, in the last resort, on the confidence of the people in its purpose, its ability, and its integrity. It will minimize the resort to force and its dependence upon it. Dictatorship on the other hand assumes the necessity of a continuous display of force and depends, in the last resort, upon fear for its continued existence. The difference is a difference of emphasis, of degree, and of objective—a difference that is of vital importance.

We are sometimes told that the state rests on force. That is not true. It is, I think, true that the possession and use of organized force is the distinctive mark of the state. The state indeed insists on maintaining a monopoly of such force. But its main purpose in doing so is to ensure that individuals and other organizations do not, as the saying goes, take the law into their own hands. The use of the state's force is to deny the use of force to individuals and organizations in

[3] R. L. Nettleship, *Lectures on the Republic of Plato* (London: Macmillan, 1901), p. 58.

settling their disputes, or to insist that disputes should be settled by legal process. . . . So far then from the state's resting on force, the state's organized force rests on men's confidence in government and their belief in law.[4]

What then must one say concerning the unities achieved by dictatorships and democratic governments respectively? Here generalization may be dangerous, but there can be little doubt of the greater desirability of voluntary cooperation in common enterprises, *if it can be achieved*. That of course is the issue. Is such achievement possible? At least some conclusions may be stated positively.

If the unity of a state is enforced, that unity will probably be more apparent than real. Fear is a very unreliable cement for human relationships. Discussion, it may be confidently asserted, will not cease under a dictatorship; it may, however, be driven underground. Discontent will not change; it may disappear through repression, but only to become more embittered and more dangerous in consequence. Two things are significant in modern dictatorships: on the one hand, the prevalence of violence against the government on the part of the governed, and on the other, the necessity for resort to violence on the part of these governments against those who are disaffected and antagonistic to them. Insistence upon unity does not produce it; repression and threats of punishment produce merely the false appearance of unity. It is not an accident that a powerful secret police organization is given a central and vital place in the organization of modern dictator-states. This is a symptom of what lies behind the feverish protestations of common purpose and the insistence upon "monolithic unity."

It is clear too that this unity, even when it is something more than appearance produced by fear, is not likely to have the resisting and staying power of the democratic unity that seems so much less complete. Based as it must be upon uncritical acquiescence and blind faith in the dictator and his government, it will be ill prepared for the blows that adverse fortune may inflict upon it. It will feed upon success—a diet pleasing to the taste but unlikely to give iron to the blood. Nothing was more remarkable than the rapidity of the collapse of Germany in World War I once the tide of battle had turned. It may be that nothing was more natural. It was the obverse of the confidence in government and army that victories and prosperity had created in the Ger-

[4] Lindsay, *Essentials of Democracy*, p. 61.

many of Bismarck and of the Kaiser. A people trained to implicit confidence in a government in which it has little effective part is ill prepared to face the ardors and rigors of defeat when that confidence collapses. History may not have repeated itself exactly. Even in 1945, however, the collapse of Germany when it had once begun was catastrophic in its speed and in its completeness. There is at least a strong presumption that the unity that comes from a conscious and deliberate collaboration in a common purpose is much less likely to be destroyed in a common calamity. Indeed, it is in calamity that the inherent strength of this unity may be most clearly manifest and most fully developed.

It is not without significance that it is the experience of critical danger or the common endurance of almost overwhelming difficulty that welds men most surely into a united people. In the fires of great trials the purposes of men are fused into a common spirit. That, for instance, is why Valley Forge has its peculiar and dramatic significance in the American tradition. It would be an exaggeration to say that democratic unity feeds upon defeat or hardship, as totalitarian unity does on victory and success. What may be said with some confidence is that where the democratic system prevails, "the slings and arrows of outrageous fortune" are less likely to have fatal consequences and are more likely to be successfully resisted. And only with successful resistance can there come the ruggedness and courage which are the qualities that assure survival.

Some qualification of this argument may be suggested by the unity displayed so conspicuously in the resistance both of the Russian army and of the Russian people to the German attack. Courage and hardihood were displayed for over two years in the face of overwhelming odds and under the stress of tragic suffering. These qualities were not created by victories or sustained by dramatic successes; they were manifested in spite of serious reverses. Whatever else may be proved in the future, the cohesion and unity of the people of Russia, even under a dictatorship, have been demonstrated to a degree that has impressed the rest of the world. To attempt an explanation of this phenomenon lies beyond the scope of this inquiry. It is sufficient to recognize it and to admit that unity is not the specific and peculiar characteristic of democratic nations if by democratic in this connection we mean political democracies. The case of Russia may qualify our argument at this point without disproving it. It still remains true that ready and willing collaboration in conscious purpose is a safer bond and a stronger tie than common obedience to a superior power. The unity achieved will have more staying power.

Esprit de corps is a quality that grows in conscious cooperation, and conscious and voluntary cooperation are limited when decisions are dictated from above and when policy is determined in the secret conclaves of the dictator's chosen few. It may be freely admitted that often enough this sense of common destiny and of sharing in a common life is lamentably absent in democracies, as was certainly the case in France during the years before World War II. But this was largely due, not to any inherent defect in democratic government itself, but to the fact that internal dissension was sapping the spirit of democracy in France. Politically and socially France in the tragic decade before 1939 was a house divided. Nevertheless the unity that, by contrast, the victorious Germany of 1940 displayed in its hours of triumph had less enduring quality than the core of unity that even in the darkest days of calamity and defeat survived in the hearts of French people. The case of France may come to be seen as a striking example of what happens when political democracy disintegrates and decays and when what was once a faith becomes for many a mere form. It will also bear witness to the unconquerable steadfastness of that faith in the spirit of those who have once learned to appreciate it and to live by it. It is an observant and critical Frenchman who writes:

France succumbed, among many other reasons, because Daladier and his government, having sought the support of the conservative, Fascist, and defeatist elements in the country, could never explain to the people and the army their war aims in terms that the common soldier and the common worker could wholeheartedly approve. . . . In fact, Daladier and his supporters took the occasion of the war to fight democracy inside France with even more energy and consistency than they fought the Germans.[5]

On the other hand France survived because though the political forms of democracy collapsed, the democratic spirit refused to die. The unity discovered in defiant resistance was the unity of freemen who *willed* to be free.

THE DEFECTS OF DICTATORSHIPS

In a world where omnipotence and omniscience are not granted to mortals it is a serious liability to the dictator that he cannot

[5] Raoul de Roussy de Sales, *The Making of Tomorrow* (New York: Reynal and Hitchcock, 1942), pp. 117–18.

afford to make mistakes, at least not serious mistakes. Statesmen under any form of government may be expected sooner or later to make one or many. What happens under a democratic regime, generally, is that the statesman pays for his mistake, if it is serious enough, by resignation or by loss of office and popularity. There is no necessary or inevitable derangement of the machinery of government. Things go on under new leadership. But dictators do not resign; they fall!

Even when a government makes mistakes—or when it loses the confidence of its people, there is no disastrous convulsion as a result. A general election may be a nuisance, but it is not a catastrophe. The orderly procedure of political administration and of social life goes on without serious interruption. Democracy, as someone has said, is a device for changing governments without violence and with a minimum of fuss. The assurance of this possibility of peaceful change is important in reducing to a minimum the tensions and uncertainties of communal life in all its aspects. Elections may affect business, but their consequences are rarely of first importance; and in spite of much that members of the business world say, they know really that this is the case. Elections at worst are only distressing episodes. In general they may give a necessary release to social and political tensions; at best they may prove valuable means of political education. They are at least a valuable opportunity for emotional expression, which is not likely to be explosive or destructive.

It is one of the major disadvantages of dictatorship that it cannot be changed or ended except by revolution—unless, indeed, it is ended by death, a situation that creates acute problems of the succession. When a dictatorship falls it is apt to fall in a welter of blood and violence. It is not often that a dictator can withdraw as unobtrusively as did Primo de Rivera from Spain, and even there revolution and violence were postponed for only a short period; even there dictatorship brought down the monarchy in its train and left the country a ready prey to the bloody conflicts that were to follow. The dictator in his fall leaves no alternative government. If one is improvised, it will probably have all the defects of improvisation and will be unstable and insecure. The dictator "may be killed at any moment, and some day he must die. He is a tree without roots. There is always a touch of uncertainty in the air. No Dictatorship can be pronounced even a relative success before we can analyse the situation that it leaves behind. The Spanish experiment began and ended in a revolution, and the discredited Dictator bequeathed a heap of ruins. The system which boasts of its stability and continuity hangs on a slender thread."⁶

How critical the situation created may be is illustrated by considering the future of Germany as compared with the same problem in 1918. Then there was an opposition that constituted the possibility of an alternative government, and it was this possibility that proved a safeguard against anarchy and chaos when both government and army collapsed. When the war came to an end in Germany in May 1945 there was no opposition to constitute the nucleus of an alternative government. The danger of anarchy and chaos under these conditions was far greater. Under such circumstances it was impossible to improvise a German government capable of carrying on, of maintaining order, and of establishing even the minimum of administrative effectiveness. Adequate focuses of organization did not exist nor could they be brought rapidly into existence. It was necessary therefore to recruit the required forces and instrumentalities from sources outside Germany itself. That is one reason why the postwar occupation of Germany for some time is not a matter of choice for the United Nations but a necessity. When a dictatorship falls it falls completely, and in its fall tends to tear apart the social ties that hold the community and the nation together. From this point of view it is the fatal weakness of the dictator that he must make himself indispensable. Presidents may come and go, prime ministers may rise and fall, even in the midst of greatest crisis. These changes may involve advantage or disadvantage, gain or loss, but they do not threaten the bases of order or imperil the structure of society.

Even apart from the ever-present threat of revolution, there is, almost necessarily, the absence of that sense of security which the rule of law gives in a democracy. The fate of individuals and of groups will be at the mercy of one man or a few men. Even if these are well intentioned, it is impossible to rule out the arbitrariness to which irresponsible rule will always be subject.

The bulwark against the whims of an irresponsible ruler erected during centuries of struggle is removed. "His will is my law," says General Göring in speaking of his chief. It is a return to the primitive, before the conception of impersonal law was born. Those who share the views, and therefore enjoy the favour of the Leader, possess all the privileges that omnipotence can supply. Those who do not are

⁶G. P. Gooch, *Dictatorship in Theory and Practice* (London: Watts, 1935), pp. 35-36.

exposed naked to the blast. It is as useless to seek redress from the Courts as in the old Turkish Empire, where the testimony of a Moslem was preferred to that of a Christian. Dictators usually claim to have united the country over which they rule. In reality they introduce a fresh and deadly cause of division—the differential treatment of first-class and second-class citizens.[7]

It is perhaps hardly necessary, in view of the course of our argument thus far, to stress the fact that a dictatorial government is not only irresponsible but also unresponsive. It can hardly be aware of the tides of emotion and the fluctuations of opinion, which even the most rigid dictatorship cannot afford to ignore. Censorship and the limitation on freedom of expression not only prevent the people's knowing what is happening; they also prevent the government's knowing what the people are thinking. It is difficult for the government, therefore, to discern the danger signals of popular disaffection, and it cannot easily adjust its policies to the currents of popular feeling and favor, which it is dangerous for any government to regard too lightly. In a sense the dictatorship is a prisoner of its own repressive measures. It is ignorant in a realm where ignorance is dangerous and may bring about the government's own destruction.

The alternative, to which a dictatorship is almost necessarily forced, is a widespread and meticulous system of espionage. Modern dictatorships have developed such systems to a high degree of perfection, but no system of this kind can be more than a poor substitute for the normal channels of information that the radio, the press, and public assemblies provide for those in authority in a democracy. The arts of surreptitious agitation will be perfected too, as rigorous surveillance in a dictatorship makes them more and more necessary. Besides, the existence of a system of general espionage and the necessity for its activities is itself a condemnation of the regime that makes it necessary. The social relationships of life are poisoned at their roots when individuals are forced to regard one another with suspicion, as the potential bearers of dangerous evidence to the headquarters of the secret police. It is difficult to believe that any real confidence or unity can be achieved under such conditions. If morale is important as a condition of social vitality and national strength, as of course it is, then here surely are the conditions most likely to endanger and, in the long run, to destroy it.

[7]*Ibid.*, pp. 36–37.

There is one other destructive characteristic of modern dictatorship that bears upon all the foregoing considerations. These dictatorships of our own time are based upon party, and the states concerned are definitely and avowedly single-party states. Particularly this bears upon the argument that stresses the supposed efficiency of dictatorships. In the single-party state the supreme virtue tends to be, in fact generally is, party loyalty. The sound party man is not only preferred, other things being equal; he is preferred without much regard to other things being equal. The important offices naturally are allotted to men upon whose loyalty and subservience to the ruling group the government can implicitly rely. Under such conditions it is clear that the government will never be entirely a government of experts, or necessarily a government of the best available men. Indeed, there is a presumption that the proportion of yes-men in office will be greater than under other systems of government, that independent critical judgment and intellectual initiative will tend to be bars to positions of influence and authority, rather than a recommendation. Where a premium is placed upon subservience and party loyalty, it is hard to believe that the government can ever approximate to the ideal of government by the best.

It seems a reasonable conclusion, therefore, that whatever may have been the advantages of dictatorships in the past, these advantages do not obtain now or are outweighed by limitations and weaknesses. In the ancient world the dictator had a justification in the conditions of crisis in which he assumed authority and in the temporary character of the dictatorship, which came to an end when the emergency had passed.

The Roman dictator was a constitutional officer, legally appointed, to meet a special emergency, and for six months only. Repeatedly, if the emergency was successfully met, he resigned before the end of his term, and fell back into the ranks of the ordinary citizens. But the essence of the modern "dictatorship" is precisely the opposite. Like the ancient tyrant, he means his office to be permanent.[8]

History will decide the issues that are here discussed, but there is good ground for believing that its verdict will not disappoint those who believe that the future lies with democracy and that government of the people, by the people, for the people is not destined to perish from the earth.

[8] E. E. Kellet, *The Story of Dictatorship* (London: Nicholson and Watson, 1937), pp. 15–16.

CHAPTER 4. The Will of the People

It is necessary at this stage of our argument to consider more carefully the real nature of democratic government. If it means government by the *people,* it is important to ask what that term means. Decisions are made in practice in all democratic governments by majority vote, and representatives are chosen by the same device. It may be that this is a device necessary in order that rule may be possible at all, but clearly the majority is not quite the same thing as the people. The minority is a part, often a very important and influential part, of the people in any given state. Is it to be assumed that its function is merely to accept, to acquiesce, and to obey? If it is, then government may be as oppressive and tyrannical under a democracy as under any other form, for there is no assurance that a majority will not prove despotic.

THE GENERAL WILL

The escape from this dilemma, if not a complete solution of the problem, is perhaps suggested in a pregnant idea to which Rousseau gave currency. Much of what Rousseau wrote was inspired by and derived from the writings of the social contract theorists, Hobbes and Locke in particular, and in relation to the contract he did little but make a vague conception more nebulous than ever. In his development of this idea, however, he pushed into a new and more fruitful field. The problem that Rousseau confronted was difficult enough: "To find a form of association which may defend and protect with the whole force of the community the person and property of every associate, and by means of which each, coalescing with all, may nevertheless obey only himself, and remain as free as before. Such is the fundamental problem of which the social contract furnishes the solution."[1]

It may be freely admitted that Rousseau was not successful in solving the problem, but in attempting its solution he clarified thought regarding the question as to whether self-government is a possibility. He gave meaning to the concept of *a people,* making it clear, as indeed others had done earlier, that a people means something more than the aggregate of individuals within certain frontiers and in a particular territory, and that a community is

[1] J. J. Rousseau, *The Social Contract* (New York: Scribner, 1905), p. 109.

more than, and different from, a crowd. It was his peculiar merit that in his attempt to show what this difference is he opened up a new and interesting line of approach to the problems of corporate life and corporate action. This he did by his conception of the general will.

In any community there is developed a sense of common interest that transcends the various interests of its parts, whether individuals or groups. There is a distinctive interest of the group as such, the interest of the group as it seeks its own real good. This is true of all communities, and therefore true of the social community that constitutes the state. Any people is more than the sum of the individuals that compose it, and its interest is not identical with the interest of each individual or of each group within it. As Rousseau puts it, its will is not the will of each, nor is it the will of all; it is the will of the whole seeking the good of the whole.

It is not necessary to follow Rousseau's detailed exposition of this idea, nor is it necessary here to discuss the vexing question of the reality of the general will. As developed by the Hegelians, the idea was given a metaphysical interpretation that achieved a measure of apparent precision at the expense of robbing it of reality. All that is necessary for our purpose here is the recognition that democracy is government by public opinion and that public opinion is not completely identical with the opinion of the majority at any given time.

Public opinion in relation to any particular issue may be registered by a majority, but two things can be said of a majority decision: it is not exactly what it would have been had there been no opposition to it and no criticism of it by the minority; and the majority decision never fully and completely expresses public opinion. Nevertheless, decisions may be reached that do not represent the mere triumph of numbers or of power. They are reached by "the concurrence of a number of people in a single decision." In so far as public spirit is highly developed, this concurrence may involve the possibility of collective decision and action in which there is little, if any, suppression or disregard of divergent views.

Take . . . the instance of a family deciding to go somewhere for a holiday. Each member of the family, we may suppose, wishes to go; but their conceptions of a holiday are not quite identical. One wants boating, one wants mountaineering, one wants cycling, one wants sketching, one wants to "loafe and invite his soul." How are they to decide? Obviously there are many possibilities. They may go off separately at their own sweet will, each one arriving at a separate decision. The head of the family may determine the matter, and the views of the others may count for nothing. That would be the will of one. They may find some place that would be suitable for the fulfilment of all their wishes, and they may unanimously decide on that. This would be a case of the joint will of all. The views of the minority may be overruled by the majority. This also would be a joint will, but only of some . . . Or, on talking it over, they may come to the conclusion that the requirements of one member—who perhaps is ill— are more important than those of the others; and the others may agree to waive their claims. I think this last is the case that might be most truly characterized as a general will. It is not a mere compromise between different points of view, but rather a decision arrived at by abandoning the individual standpoint and surveying the situation as a whole.[2]

Without raising the metaphysical question of the reality of collective personality, it may be said that in any community there develops a common consciousness, that in such a community ends are pursued in common, and that the community develops a characteristic way of life. Whether or not this justifies the use of the term *general will* depends largely on our definition of that elusive term.[3]

The important point is that in practice as well as in common speech we recognize the existence of communities as something more than the sum of the individuals who compose them. Public opinion is something more than the amorphous mass of divergent views and aims of men and of groups. There is a common interest that may override the particular interests of parties. The public good is in the last resort the good of persons; but of persons not merely as individuals but as members of the body politic. There is at least the suggestion of a common life having a character of its own and purposes that are something more than the sum of

[2] J. S. Mackenzie, *Introduction to Social Philosophy* (London: Allen and Unwin, 1918), pp. 53–54. For a fuller discussion see the whole of Chapter 2.

[3] For a penetrating and critical discussion of the concept of the general will see E. F. Carritt, *Morals and Politics* (New York: Oxford University Press, 1935). His conclusion is stated thus: "In thus attempting to describe the responsibilities and obligations I find in respect of my country's laws, I have not felt that I should be assisted either by using the term general will, or by supposing a contract. It has been enough to recognize responsibilities and duties to my fellow men." This does not invalidate the argument of this chapter, for if there is a mutual recognition of "responsibilities and duties," the basic conditions of communal being are already present. It is not necessary to assume that this implies the existence of a *real personality* or of a *general will* in the idealist sense of these terms. See also Joad, *Philosophy of Morals and Politics*, pp. 508–10, 757–58.

the purposes held by individuals. When we speak of "the soul of a people" or the "spirit of a nation," we are doing something more than using convenient metaphors. There is in the case of any nation with a history a "national being" into which has entered the traditions of the past, a wisdom perhaps learned in the fires of critical experience, a sense of right and wrong that is part of its heritage. Into its being also go the aspirations of the present and the hopes of the future.

A people, like an individual, has character. It does not always act in character, for it is not always true to itself. Like an individual, it may rise above its normal self and also, perhaps still more often, fall below it. "That was not like him," we sometimes say of an individual when we hear of some action that is not in accord with our conception of his real character. So too we sometimes say, "That is just like him." We may on occasion speak of peoples in some such way. There is an American way of doing things, a British way, and other typical ways. In our common speech we say of a nation, "It isn't like it" when it acts in some particular manner—implying praise or blame as the case may be, but always implying a character that is inconsistent with the action of the moment. Are there not certain attitudes or policies that we declare unworthy of Shakespeare's England, of the land that bore Milton and Wordsworth? There are deeds also that we say are worthy of a people that Lincoln led and that Whitman inspired.

Here, indeed, we are using metaphor, but metaphor that is significant of a reality. The point surely is that in such judgments we acknowledge something different from the spirit of the moment, the action of the hour, or the decisions of a particular occasion. It is difficult perhaps to find a term that describes it. We might call it an "enduring personality," or the "national being." But whatever we call it, we are thinking of a complex of tradition, ideals, purposes, aspirations; and this complex is something more than the traditions and ideals of the mass of individuals. A nation is more than, and different from, the sum of its individuals at a given period. It is this, presumably, that Rousseau was trying to express in part in his distinction between the will of the whole and the will of all.

A true leader in a democracy knows that it is sometimes necessary to appeal "from Philip drunk to Philip sober" or from the present to the past or from the present to the future. He may choose to abide by the judgment of posterity, ignoring the adverse verdict of his time. He knows that on occasion the judgment of the many will be perverted by waves of passion, that a decisive or even an overwhelming majority may be a transient phenomenon that dissolves when sanity reasserts itself. The will of the majority is not necessarily the will of the people, and the real leader may appeal from the one to the other, calling upon the past or depending upon the future to justify his appeal.

The will of the people, then, is the will of the whole acting for the good of the whole—a will, it may be said, that is conceivable but never existent. What is clear, however, is that in a democracy public opinion is not identical with majority opinion except perhaps for brief periods. Majority rule therefore is an expedient, necessary of course but imperfect, for giving effect as far as possible to public opinion. The best that it can achieve is an approximation to a considered public judgment, and it will achieve that only if the necessary conditions are fulfilled. Even after the fullest discussion the minority may remain unconvinced, and the fact that it is a minority does not mean or prove that it is wrong. It is a harsh practical necessity that a decision be reached and that minority objections be overborne. Obviously this is not the achievement of the common mind that is the ideal of the democratic process and method, nor is the decision changed in character by speaking of it as the will of the people. It remains the will of the majority, which prevails because the necessity for action does not permit indefinite discussion and delay. The members of the minority may acquiesce in it, may cooperate even in giving effect to it, but not because they are convinced. They acquiesce because they recognize that compromise is a condition of getting things done in an imperfect world, that even a wrong decision may be better under certain circumstances than inaction, that resistance and disunity may have worse consequences than the policy of which they disapprove. Or in the last resort they acquiesce because they must.

Nevertheless it is important to recognize that a majority decision under democratic conditions is never quite what it seems. "Under democratic conditions" in this connection means after full and free discussion, where the evidence has been freely available and where debate has been as long and unfettered as circumstances permitted. The issue, we may presume, has not been unaffected by the discussion, and the decision reached is seldom likely to be what it would have been without discussion. The majority decision has been influenced; into its making probably have gone elements contributed by opposition and criticism. Even if the decision has not been directly affected, it is made with fuller knowledge. An individual action may, in form, be the same after the most careful deliberation as it would have been without any deliberation at all and yet the quality of the action has been affected. This too is true of the actions of deliberative assemblies.

Besides, the majority is not a fixed and concrete quantity; it may frequently be made in the course of discussion. The minority will make itself a majority if it can, and if it fails, it has not necessarily exerted itself in vain. The majority decision is not quite what it would have been had it never had the opportunity or the necessity to listen to what the minority has to say. Public opinion is sovereign in a democracy; but that opinion is the fusion of many and diverse elements. What proportion of influence is to be attributed to the opinion of the many and what to the opinion of the few, is always impossible to determine. A small minority highly respected and trusted may by its influence tip the balance in many a sharp contest which from the point of view of numbers would have been an unequal battle.

UNITY IN DIVERSITY

These considerations bring us naturally and squarely face to face with the issue of the place and function of minorities in a democratic regime. Clearly the existence of a minority is not merely desirable; it is a necessity if government is to be democratic. It is democratic to tolerate minority opinion; it is more democratic to value it. For if democracy is essentially government by discussion, it becomes a pertinent fact that it takes at least two to make a discussion; and if these two think exactly alike, there will be none. The decisive opinion in a democracy gains color and meaning from the diverse elements that have gone to the making of it.

Here specifically and definitely the democratic view diverges from the absolutist. Here particularly it becomes clear that what the authoritarian governments mean by unity is entirely different from what the democrat means by it. From the democratic standpoint the most deadly of all diseases in the body politic is uniformity. The democratic faith demands unity indeed, but unity of purpose, not of political or economic creed, unity of spirit, which can never be achieved by toeing the party line or being made to conform to it. It is unity in diversity that is sought and prized; it is the unity of the living organism, not of the dead assemblage of similar units, that democracy values and that democratic government seeks, in so far as it is true to its essential ideals. It is this kind of unity that is congenial to the cultural tradition which finds its origin in the spirit of ancient Greece.

The State does not consist simply of a number of men, but of men specifically different from one another;—these are Aristotle's words, and he at once illustrates his meaning by referring to the distinction between a State and an alliance. In the latter the mere addition of a quantity of men of the same sort is a direct good; but in the State, a community in the functions of good life, the unity to be attained must issue from diversity.[4]

There is a sense too, as Aristotle realized, in which the public opinion of a diversified community is more reliable, is likely even to be more just, than the opinion of one or of a few, even though the one be superior or the few select. The idiosyncrasies and peculiarities of individuals are merged in it; what may be regarded as eccentricities are canceled out. What results is a practical wisdom and a rough justice that is not to be expected from the select few.

. . . we find that the judgment of the mass on poetry and music is better than that of a single critic; for one man appreciates one excellence, and another another, whereas the taste of an individual is necessarily one-sided. And again, as a large quantity of water is less easily defiled than a small, so it is harder to corrupt a whole people than an individual; and "it is not easy for them all to be enraged or mistaken at once."[5]

The practical significance of this is made clear in the general recognition that is accorded explicitly or implicitly to the opposition in most modern democratic governments. In Great Britain the leader of the Opposition is now definitely recognized as an integral part of the government, and his services in that capacity are rewarded by remuneration equivalent to that of a minister in the government. The title "His Majesty's Opposition" is not merely a courtesy title. It expresses the fact that criticism and opposition are normal and necessary functions in a parliamentary regime. The decisions of Parliament, and of Congress in the United

[4] Abbott, *Hellenica*, pp. 187–88.
[5] *Ibid.*, pp. 216–17.

States, are not the decisions of the dominant party at a given time, although often enough they may give that impression. The fact is that these decisions emerge from the give and take of debate, and, while it may be argued that debates seldom change opinions, it is also true that even the issues submitted for debate and the terms in which they are presented would have been different but for the fact that it was always understood that these would be debated. Besides, even if there is rarely a change of opinion, there is always a greater or less modification of opinion. This process of modification is continuous and in the course of time may have far-reaching effect. This is perhaps one reason why the onetime opposition on achieving office frequently gives effect to the measures that it formerly opposed. Stealing the thunder of the opposition is not always what it seems!

Government by majority, therefore, is the rule in democracies. The justification for this is to be found simply in the realm of practical expediency. A majority decision does not necessarily register and express the will of the people—in spite of the fact that Rousseau seems to have believed that in really popular assemblies of the whole people it did. But at least there is some merit in a device "that provides for counting heads instead of breaking them." A majority of voices, as someone has said, makes nothing right or wise, but there is no alternative.

Perhaps an alternative is not fundamentally important. Safeguards may be found in the recognition of the reality of debate and insistence upon its freedom, in an attitude of intellectual consideration for opposing views, and in the growth of a spirit of real deliberation in the assemblies and parliaments of the nations.

THE RIGHTS AND DUTIES OF MINORITIES

It is not merely the question of majority decisions in representative assemblies that is important in this connection. A majority may be tyrannical and oppressive; it may be intolerant and may seek to penalize minority opinion by social ostracism, by marks of disfavor or abuse; it may demand repressive legislation; it may restrict or deny the freedom of unpopular individuals and parties. That safeguards are needed to prevent what may in effect become the despotism of the majority is clear.

What then is the real place of minorities under democratic conditions? It is customary to speak of the *rights* of minorities; it is more appropriate and relevant to our argument to speak of their duties. The performance of these duties will demand courage and may frequently involve sacrifice, but if the members of the minority realize that in displaying the one and enduring the other they are fulfilling a function vital to the successful operation of democratic processes, something is gained. The vigor, the persistence, and the courage of minorities may be the safeguards against the worst dangers of majority rule. Minorities must assert themselves—in the public interest!

But if the minority is to fulfill its function in a democratic community, there are dangers that it too must avoid and principles that it must recognize. The minority must take care not to be in the wrong. This of course sounds paradoxical. It involves a presumption that although numbers are not decisive, they do count; and where the majority is overwhelming, there must be something, perhaps a great deal, to be said for the opinion it holds. Therefore the member of a minority group must be rigorous in examining his convictions. A minority by virtue of its position must have a keener sense of responsibility, and, shall we say, of humility, than may be expected of the majority. This means two things: a member of a minority group must be prepared to examine and re-examine the evidence on which his conviction is based, and he must neglect no opportunity of discovering both the flaws in his own line of thought and the elements of strength in that of those to whom he is opposed.

The minority also must be rigorous in self-criticism. Thought is never free from the influence of emotion, and thought processes are never conducted in the pure light of reason. No human being can be entirely free from party and class associations. It is not to be expected that anyone, whether of the majority or of the minority, will be able to eliminate these factors; but the member of a minority must be unusually open-eyed in his awareness of them and realistic in his recognition of their influence. There is such a thing as a "minority temperament": the critical mind that is prone to disagreement, that is generally "agin the government" and is tempted to take pride in that fact! To be entirely disinterested and to seek only the common good is an ideal at which all may aim, but which none attain. It is too much to expect that any minority should be able to rule out all these influences; but upon a minority there devolves a responsibility, by virtue of the fact that it is a minority, for a greater measure of, and a more thoroughgoing, self-criticism both as to opinion and as to motive.

Having emphasized the peculiar obligations of a minority as a minority, we must as strongly emphasize that the primary duty of the minority is to advocate as forcefully and as convincingly as it can the opinions to which it has come. It is the duty of the minority to assert itself, using the methods and instrumentalities of democratic processes for that purpose. Here too it will be confronted by temptations and beset with dangers. Some of these are obvious enough to be dismissed with a bare mention. The danger of bitterness evoked in contests of opinion that become hard-fought and keen, the danger of persistent and fervent advocacy reacting upon a mind made up, to transform conviction into dogmatism—these are all too apparent in political contests, but they are not always avoided either by minority or by majority. But the fact that it is more difficult to maintain a minority opinion, and that a psychological reinforcement is instinctively sought from depth of emotion and from inflexibility of conviction, makes a minority rather more prone to these particular tendencies and more susceptible to their temptation.

More important are two dangers which, if yielded to, may destroy a minority. The danger of discouragement is the first of these. The pressure of mass opinion is not easy to bear or to resist. Closely allied to the possibility of discouragement, and perhaps the normal consequence of it, is the danger of a fatalistic acceptance of impotence in the face of the magnitude and power of the majority. "The fatalism of the minority" is a phrase with real meaning. If the majority does not want to hear—and very often it does not—what purpose is served by pressing unpopular views upon it? It is easier and certainly safer to be silent, refusing agreement indeed, but not attempting to change the current of opinion. It is probable, so the individual in the minority may argue, that he cannot do anything and, this being the case, it is best not to try. Where such fatalism triumphs, democracy has already lost a major battle in the agelong struggle for emancipation. The minority is a part, an essential part, of the democratic process and where it fails, democracy to that extent fails also.

In a nation with a keen moral sense and a capacity for strong emotions, opinion based on a love of what is deemed just or good will resist the multitude when bent on evil: and if there be a great variety of social conditions, of modes of life, of religious beliefs, these will prove centres of resistance to a dominant tendency, like rocks standing up in a river, at which he whom the current sweeps downwards may clutch. Instances might be cited even from countries where the majority has had every source of strength at its command—physical force, tradition, the all but universal persuasions and prejudices of the lower as well as of the higher classes—in which small minorities have triumphed, first by startling and then by leavening and convincing the majority. This they have done in virtue of that intensity of belief which is oftenest found in a small sect or group, not because it is small, but because if its belief were not intense it would not venture to hold out at all against the adverse mass. The energy of each individual in the minority makes it in the long run a match for a majority huger but less instinct with vitality. In a free country more especially, ten men who care are a match for a hundred who do not.[6]

What are the implications for the majority of this argument concerning minority rights and duties? Here we shall merely outline an argument that is stated differently and more fully later.

If it is demanded, as it must be, that minorities be open to conviction, that they be prepared to "consider all the evidence," that they avail themselves of all the relevant information, the majority must not deny access to that information or withhold the evidence. It is the duty of the majority to provide the opportunities for free inquiry and investigation, to make sure that discussion shall be unfettered. This is "the right to know" for which Milton made his eloquent plea. The recognition of this right is inconsistent with the maintenance of censorship as a general rule, and of censorship of opinion always. Some measure of censorship may be necessary in a democracy in normal times, and an extension of censorship may be necessary, and will almost certainly be made, in times of grave crisis and of war. But in a democracy censorship must always be suspect and must always be confined within the narrowest limits consistent with the public interest. It must never be utilized to withhold relevant facts from its people or to restrain them in the pursuit of the knowledge essential to the formation of sound judgment.

If the majority has a right to demand that the minority should not be influenced and its opinion determined by selfish considerations, that it should be actuated by concern for the common good, then it follows that the majority has a duty to prevent the injection of such considerations into the determination of public issues. It must not allow governments to penalize opinions or to bias judgment by a system of rewards and penalties. It must not

---

[6] James Bryce, *The American Commonwealth* (New York: Macmillan, 1907), pp. 261–62.

make opinion as such the basis for preferences or hold out the hope of office as a reward for "sound opinion." A great capacity for ready conformity is not a high qualification for the functions that are important in political democracy. The majority must not make the disinterestedness it demands in the minority more difficult by denying the importance of disinterestedness in its own practice.

If it is the duty of the genuine minority to assert itself, to proclaim its views, and to urge its convictions in a justifiable manner upon others, then the majority must again provide the conditions that will make this possible. The elementary political freedoms, without which democratic government is impossible, are implied in the demand. The right of free speech, freedom of assembly, freedom of the press and of publication—these are the simple watchwords of the democratic tradition.[7]

When minority and majority are mutually jealous of their rights and mutually scrupulous in the performance of their duties, the conditions exist for the creation and emergence of a real public opinion. It will not be the opinion of all, nor perhaps will it ever be the opinion of both majority and minority. Mass conversions are not characteristic of political processes and discussions! But at least this public opinion will be something other, and probably something better, than majority opinion. Both minority and majority will have made their contributions to it, and the contribution of each may be vitally important. It will still be short of perfect agreement, but at least it will represent some progress toward agreement. If the minority has been given fair opportunity to fulfill its function and has taken advantage of it, the conditions of reasonable cooperation and of mutual understanding have been secured. The minority may still pursue its vital function of advocacy and persuasion, striving to convert itself into a majority if it can, but if it fails there will be some recognition that it has failed in a fair and open encounter. The asperities of conflict may be softened, the possibility of cooperation in spite of differences will have been enhanced, and the realization of unity in diversity will have been furthered, even though it may not be completely achieved.

It is this public opinion that constitutes the essential core of what is called the will of the people. Sometimes uninformed and often distorted by prejudice, it is never as enlightened as it should

---

[7] For a much fuller discussion see David G. Ritchie, *Natural Rights* (London: George Allen, 1903), Chapters 7–9.

be, never free from elements of selfish interest; nevertheless it is the dynamic of democratic government. A sound public opinion, like democracy itself, is an ideal, not a recognized fact; but the slow movement of peoples toward it is an assurance that it is an ideal worthy of our pursuit and one that is not entirely without influence and recognition even in the imperfect achievements of democracy in the modern democratic state.

CHAPTER 5. The Background of the Democratic Tradition

BELIEF in democratic government rests ultimately upon certain principles. These are assumptions, but assumptions only in the sense that moral convictions always involve elements that defy demonstration and go beyond what is usually meant by proof. At different points in the argument of previous chapters these assumptions have been implicit; it is necessary to state them and to appraise them explicitly. Before doing so, however, it is desirable to establish another point of some importance, that these assumptions are integral elements in the tradition of Western civilization. The background of the democratic tradition is the culture that is a vital part of our heritage. Democratic principles are the logical development of germinal ideas that go back far beyond the modern democratic era. They are not merely the assumptions of democracy; they are, most if not all of them, assumptions that are implied in the main stream of Western thought. Democratic principles do not constitute a break with the past, but are foreshadowed in the political ideas and theories of that past.

This does not mean that governments were democratic in practice during the centuries when the tradition was in process of development. For long periods in Europe authoritarian government in some form or other was the general rule. There were long periods too when the dominant trend in political theory was concerned primarily with the justification of systems of absolute power and of autocratic authority. The doctrine of the divine right of kings has a long history, and at times it has found wide, if not general, acceptance. It gave way very slowly before the advancing tide of the democratic ideas that took their rise in the Renaissance and the Reformation. But absolutism, whether in practice or in theory, was never unchallenged. It was always on the defensive. Even in the church the doctrine of divine right never achieved a definite and unquestioned ascendancy. It had to coexist with ideas and doctrines that were really incompatible with it, that limited its application and always constituted an effective challenge to it. Again and again the challenge became assertive, and conflicts resulted in which the position of the doctrine of divine right became increasingly precarious and the growing strength of the opposing tendencies became more and more apparent. For long periods the issue of these conflicts was uncertain, but in retrospect it is clear that the final outcome was never really in doubt. The tempo of change might vary, but the general direction, in spite of temporary reactions, was on the whole consistent.

During the whole period from Plato to today, it is possible to trace the continuing influence of concepts which, while not distinctively democratic, yet serve to conserve and to convey to future ages the principles that are essential to the democratic faith. When democratic principles are definitely formulated, as, for instance, in the parliamentary struggle against the Stuart kings or in the revolutionary period in America and France, they seem less the statement of new ideas than a development or new application of ideas that are very old. Democracy as a political form, or even as a political doctrine, may be a modern phenomenon; it may be, as Dr. Gooch points out, that modern democracy is the child of the Reformation, not of the reformers, but it has a long lineage and a very ancient heritage. The ideas that came to fruition in it can be traced to their origin in ancient Greece and Rome; they persist in the teachings of the great churchmen, and become active once more in men like Aquinas, William of Occam, and Marsilius in the Middle Ages. Democratic thought may have come to birth at the time of the Renaissance, but the spirit that gave it birth and the ideas it embodies can be seen forming in the long ages that stretch back beyond the beginnings of the Christian era. It is a natural development of vital elements which were inherent in the tradition of Western civilization, which were never quite dormant, and which became conscious and active in the modern democratic era.

It is not possible to trace that development here. This has been done by others, particularly by the Carlyles in their comprehensive survey of political thought in the West.[1] But two ideas in the tradition are particularly significant.

THE IDEA OF POPULAR SOVEREIGNTY

THE idea of popular sovereignty was stated in ancient times, and, persisting through all the centuries of Roman history, was transmitted and given new expression in the thought of the great medieval thinkers. At times it was neglected or obscured, but it

---

[1] A. J. and R. W. Carlyle, *A History of Mediaeval Political Theory in the West* (4 vols., Edinburgh: Blackwood, 1903), vol. 1.

was never entirely repudiated. It was always an assumption, even when it was not a definite assertion, that the people had a share in government and were never merely a passive element in the state, that they were in some sense or other participants in sovereignty.[2]

The germs of the idea go back even farther. As we have already said, Plato can hardly be ranked as a believer in democracy in any either modern or ancient interpretation of that term, but even he recognizes that government is justified by its concern for the whole community and its scrupulous regard for the people's welfare. The best practical government—since the ideal is beyond realization—is government in accordance with the laws, and laws are never merely the creation of the ruler. They grow in the soil of the common life and are a reflection or an embodiment of such precepts and customs as are dictated by the experiences of the people.

Perhaps Plato's most interesting contribution to the subject is that striking defence of the democracy he so much distrusted which is put into the mouth of Protagoras. Zeus allotted the faculties for other arts, some to one man and some to another, so that for medicine we go to a specialist; but he assigned to all men their shares of justice and decency, which are the faculties for the political art, so that in government we consult all men; and those who have no share in these virtues have no place in human society.[3]

This is not a doctrine of popular sovereignty, of course, nor is it necessary to regard it as Plato's own doctrine, but it implies clearly a recognition of the truth of which that doctrine is in a sense a corollary—the truth that in government "We consult all men and those who have no share in these virtues have no place in human society." And if it is admitted that Protagoras here does not express Plato's own view, he was at least expressing a view that was current and had its advocates in Plato's day. What is merely implied by Plato is explicitly stated by Aristotle: "As to the form of government, the many though individually inferior to the few wise, are collectively superior. At least they are the best judges of when they are badly ruled and should therefore elect and dismiss their expert rulers."[4]

When we pass from Greece to Rome, the idea finds clear ex-

[2] See Alfred Cobban, *The Crisis of Civilization* (London: Jonathan Cape, 1941), p. 74.
[3] E. F. Carritt, *Morals and Politics*, pp. 20–21.
[4] *Ibid.*, p. 22.

pression and definite formulation, not merely in the speculations of philosophers, but in the basic concepts of Roman law. With what under the circumstances was a remarkable unanimity, the great Roman lawyers declare that the source of political authority is in the people. It is true that the authority was actually exercised by the emperor, but he could not exercise it if the right to do so had not in some way been conferred upon, or entrusted to, him. His power was not inherent in his person. "The will of the Emperor has the force of law, because by the passage of the *lex regia* the people transfers to him and vests in him all its own power and authority."[5] Authority is derived from the laws and laws are prior to government. They are the people's laws, not indeed in the sense that the people make them, but in the sense that laws originate in, and are framed for, the effective regulation and direction of the common life. It is truer to say that laws make governments than to say that governments make laws, obvious as the latter statement is. Authority is inherent in the people and is derived from them.

From the second century, then, to the sixth . . . the Roman law knows one, and only one, ultimate source of political power, and that is the authority of the people. . . . The theory of the ultimate authority of the people subsisted, and so came down till it touched the new Teutonic theory of law and political authority, a theory which again knew nothing of any legislative authority in the State apart from the whole body of the State.[6]

In this respect the Roman law makes formal and definite what had been stated in more general terms in the political thought of Rome before the Empire. Here the theory was somewhat closer to practice. The general assumption, in such writers as Cicero and Polybius, is that authority and power both spring from the people's will or consent. "The commonwealth, then, is the people's affair; and the people is not every group of men, associated in any manner, but is the coming together of a considerable number of men who are united by a common agreement about law and rights and by the desire to participate in mutual advantages."[7]

This idea was remarkably persistent, surviving in the changed conditions created by the Empire's decline and fall. It survived also in spite of the wide acceptance of a doctrine that seemed

---

[5] Ulpian in the Digest as quoted by George H. Sabine in *A History of Political Theory* (New York: Holt, 1938), p. 171.
[6] Carlyle, *Mediaeval Political Thought*, vol. 1, p. 70.
[7] Sabine, *Political Theory*, p. 166.

inimical to it—the doctrine of the divine origin of government and the divine right of the ruler. It was natural that the church fathers should lay great stress upon the virtue and even the necessity of obeying the ruler since he is, according to orthodox doctrine, ordained of God; but they also stress the fact that the true ruler must and will respect the laws. If he fails to do so, he becomes not ruler but tyrant, and the tyrant is a ruler who has destroyed the real basis of his own authority. The ruler is a minister of God only if he uses his authority well, which means in accordance with law, and this in turn means for the good of the people. If he doesn't respect the law, how can he expect others to do so? And although the churchman thought of law primarily as an expression of divine law, he also recognized it as at once the creation and the safeguard of the people's life.

It is this conception of popular sovereignty that limits the acceptance of absolutist doctrine, in spite of the fact that in practice the ruler's power is actually unlimited. Even when the logic of theological tenets tended powerfully in the contrary direction, the concept of popular sovereignty held its ground. The teaching of the lawyers prevails in the mind of the ecclesiastic even at the cost of inconsistency. Tradition here is too strong for logic, and the lawyers and their ideas therefore triumph over the implications of theology.

... in the conception of the Roman lawyers as to the source of authority in the State we probably have one foundation of the mediaeval and modern theory of democracy. ... It is at least well worth observing that, if the ancient civilization ended in a system of monarchical though legal absolutism, yet the theory of government which the jurists of the old world handed down to the new was a theory in which all authority in the State is conceived of as coming from the people.[8]

The doctrine was transmitted through the Roman influences that persisted in the ninth and tenth centuries. Here, however, another influence gave to the tradition a powerful reinforcement. The Teutonic tradition, which was native to the new order now arising on the ruins of ancient Rome, was not formulated or expressed in a philosophy (in due time it would take over its philosophy from the Roman heritage, which it was predisposed to adopt), but the Teutonic world had its usages and customs, and these implied a conception of popular sovereignty. In that world indeed the king was not and had never been the source of law,

[8]Carlyle, *Mediaeval Political Thought*, vol. 1, p. 79.

even in the sense in which the emperor had been in the Empire. The law was the people's law, and it was the king's peculiar function to defend, enforce, and apply it. Justice in a ruler might have many elements, but one of them was interpreting the laws wisely and faithfully administering them. Laws were not of his making, although he played his part when laws were made. The ruler was a participant in the process of making laws, rather than the source of the law. "To the ninth-century writers," says Dr. Carlyle, "the king had his part in making law, so far as law is made, but he has only one part out of many. Other voices have been heard besides his, the consent of others has to be given before anything can become the national law."[9]

In the Middle Ages, therefore, popular sovereignty was more than theory; it was, to a considerable degree, given practical recognition. It may be that the recognition was largely a matter of form, but here form is important. The promulgation of a law followed a procedure which was emphatic testimony to the vitality of a tradition and which was incompatible with any conception of absolutism. The sections of the law were read to assemblies of abbots, bishops, counts, and others, and those present gave their assent and pledged themselves to observance of the laws. Signatures were appended, giving the transaction the aspect of a compact, which in a formal and yet real sense it was.[10] There was implied, or at least foreshadowed, in all this the concept of representation. The advice and consent of the "wise men" did, somehow, signify and express the participation of the whole people in the making of the laws, and their pledge to observe them. Moreover the concept of election found clear recognition, although again this formal recognition was given only in the manner suitable to the conditions of the age.

The circumstances of the ninth century tended thus to favour the development of the conception that the ruler holds his place in virtue of the election of the nation, and of his fulfilment of the promises on which that election was based; and there were not wanting in the century circumstances which tended towards the further conclusion, that if the king failed to discharge the obligations which he had undertaken, he might not improperly be deposed.[11]

Here indeed what we really find is the persistence of usage and custom in a new environment with which the Teutonic peoples

---
[9] *Ibid.*, pp. 234–35.
[10] *Ibid.*, pp. 236 *et seq.*
[11] *Ibid.*, p. 250. For a full discussion see the whole of Chapter 20.

were not familiar. The thought forms of Rome had been adopted or were being adopted, and frequently these had to be strained in order to accommodate the political habits of peoples who were only beginning to be familiar with the thought of Rome. The Teutonic peoples were doing things in the ways to which they had been long accustomed. Laws had grown; from time immemorial kings had been made and kings had been deposed. Mutual promises had been given of old; they continued to be given. These were practices that implied ideas—ideas congenial, as we have seen, to the theories of the philosophers and lawyers of the Empire, certainly not uncongenial to the theory of popular sovereignty.

It was, however, not always easy to harmonize these customs and usages with some of the doctrines of the great churchmen. This was particularly true in relation to the doctrine of the divine appointment of the ruler. Here it was possible to retain and repeat the teaching of Augustine and Gregory the Great only to the extent of paying lip service to it while refusing to recognize its implications. Tradition proved stronger than the teaching of the Roman church at this point, even though that church was regarded as the repository and guardian of the culture of Rome. The immense respect of the Teutonic tribes for that culture and its guardian was not sufficient to break the hold upon their minds that centuries of practice had established. They appealed from the theologian to the philosopher and from the churchman to the lawyer. They *had* made laws, made governments too, and unmade them! This was the fact that determined the whole trend of medieval thought.

Furthermore, throughout the Middle Age even the partisans of Monarchy were wont to concede to the Community an active right of participation in the life of the State. . . . No matter what the form of government, the People was always the true Sovereign, and this was expressly stated by the maxim *"Populus maior principe."* Hence was generally drawn the inference that the Community still retained a legislative power over the Prince and a permanent control over the exercise of the rights of Rulership. But, in particular, the further inference was drawn that, if the Ruler neglected his duties, the People might sit in judgment upon him and depose him by right and doom.[12]

Closely connected with the idea of popular sovereignty and issuing from it, as we have seen, was the concept of representa-

[12]Otto Gierke, *Political Theories of the Middle Age* (New York: Cambridge University Press, 1927), pp. 44–45.

tion. Laws when promulgated had to receive assent, and in some way those who gave this assent were regarded as representative of the people. This comes into much clearer expression in the controversies of the fourteenth and fifteenth centuries and particularly in the doctrines of the Conciliar party. A philosophy was then formulated to justify and rationalize practice, and theory gave its support to custom. The new doctrine of sovereignty could not destroy the assumptions that a long history had created; it was harmonized with them. When "men developed the theory of a Popular Sovereignty, existing everywhere and always, the partizans of this doctrine did not once more call in question the newly acquired idea of Sovereignty, but transferred it to an Assembly which represents the people."[13] The democratic idea was already in being, in embryo perhaps, but still in being.

It was destined to come to birth in the struggles that marked the beginnings of the modern world. The Renaissance and the Reformation gave the idea a new significance and a new impetus. There was a period, indeed, during which the leaven of ancient and medieval doctrine as briefly described above seemed to lose its potency and its vitality. The Reformation in particular raised new issues and gave a new direction to political speculation. For a time the question of divine right was argued with a vehemence far greater than that displayed in the age when the church fathers gave it currency. With the rise of the nation-state the agelong controversy concerning the relative spheres and authority of church and state took on new aspects. The question of political obedience, always perplexing, came to have a practical urgency when Protestant kings ruled Catholic subjects and Catholic rulers were confronted with the problem of dealing with adherents of the new faith.

Nevertheless, although these conditions changed the aspect and direction of political controversy, they did not weaken the urge and the conviction that had found expression in the conception of popular sovereignty. Obscured by the smoke of battles that raged around other issues, the idea was destined later to reappear in more challenging and indeed in more explosive form. During the years when the doctrine of divine right was in the ascendancy, the democratic idea was striking its roots more and more deeply into the consciousness of men, at least in the Western world. The revolutionary struggles that were soon to come would wit-

[13] *Ibid.*, p. 93.

ness the reappearance of the conception, now as an "armed doctrine."

The temporary eclipse and suppression of the idea of popular sovereignty gave to it in its rebirth a dynamic energy and revolutionary character that it had not displayed in the ancient and medieval world. Confronted and obstructed by the doctrine of divine right, it began to display its violent possibilities. It was a sign of the times that tyrannicide became a popular subject of discussion among the controversialists of the age. Soon it ceased to be merely a subject of controversy. When it was sought to give practical application to the doctrine of divine right, as was done, for instance, by Stuart kings in England, it became clear that the doctrine of popular sovereignty had become something more than a doctrine. It was now a cause for which men were prepared to fight and to die. It had passed from the field of speculation into the field of action and from the arena of ideas into that of battle.

Henceforth the concept finds a new and more challenging interpretation. Government is now explicitly based on a contract to which clearly the people must be a party and by the terms of which governments must abide. As we have seen, the idea of a contract, whether as the basis of society or as the basis of government, is not new. But it is in the seventeenth and eighteenth centuries that the idea becomes basic in political thought, and it is in this period that the full implications of the doctrine become practically important. The doctrine now may be used to justify a revolution, as by Locke in England, or to prepare the way for revolution, as by Rousseau and others in France. It is not necessary to consider here the various forms it took in the systems of Hobbes, Locke, and Rousseau; nor is it necessary to consider the practical consequences that flowed from it in the English Revolution of 1688 or the later American and French revolutions. What is clear is that the idea is vitally present in the main stream of tendency in European thought and is interfused with the political ideas of the West. It is, shall we say, characteristic of the tradition of Western civilization that whether the people do rule or not, there is always the assumption that in some way or other they ought to do so. And this is another way of saying that although democracy is, in one sense, a modern phenomenon, its elements are imbedded in the matrix of Western culture.

THE IDEA OF NATURAL LAW

The other idea, which is closely related to that of popular sovereignty and even more deeply rooted and perhaps more significant, is that of natural law. It is a primary assumption of the cultural tradition of Western civilization that the universe is rational. Apart from this assumption the whole development of European thought has little meaning or coherence. From Plato, and indeed from before Plato, to our own time, it has been almost an axiom that there is a pattern and purpose in the scheme of things, and that both pattern and purpose conform to, and may be discerned by, reason. There is therefore a law that determines the nature and the relations of things. It is the final criterion of right and wrong, the standard of judgment for human action and human institutions.

This idea is clearly expressed in the Stoic philosophy and may be regarded as its basic principle. It is with the Stoics too that the idea is interpreted in a way which makes it vitally significant in relation to the development of political thought. Professor Sabine states it clearly:

Reason is a law for all men, not merely for the wise. There is a sense in which all men are equal, even after allowance has been made for the inevitable differences of rank, native endowment, and wealth. They ought all to have at least that minimum of rights without which human dignity is impossible, and justice requires that the law should recognize such rights and protect men in the enjoyment of them.[14]

It was through the Stoics that the idea entered definitely into the structure and substance of Roman law, and probably it was through the influence of Stoic teaching that it entered also into the main stream of Christian thought.

Since the universe was rational, it followed that inherent in it there was a law that was applicable to all mankind without distinction of race or creed, a law of reason that transcended the civil law and to which all other laws must conform or be judged invalid by virtue of their lack of conformity. Natural law was at once the source and the criterion of all positive law. "It was assumed that 'nature' sets certain norms which the positive law must live up to as best it can and that, as Cicero had believed, an 'unlawful' statute simply is not law. Throughout the whole of the Middle Ages and well down into modern times the existence and the validity of such a higher law were taken for granted."[15]

---
[14]Sabine, *Political Theory*, p. 153.
[15]*Ibid.*, p. 170.

It is not necessary to trace the development of this idea or its manifold consequences in the centuries that stretch from the period of the Roman Republic to the Renaissance. Cicero states the idea in terms which remained characteristic and which were unchallenged in the Roman Empire:

There is in fact a true law—namely, right reason—which is in accordance with nature, applies to all men, and is unchangeable and eternal. By its commands this law summons men to the performance of their duties; by its prohibitions it restrains them from doing wrong. Its commands and prohibitions always influence good men, but are without effect upon the bad. To invalidate this law by human legislation is never morally right, nor is it permissible even to restrict its operation, and to annul it wholly is impossible.[16]

The principles of this law are discernible by all who possess reason, and these principles are to be recognized and applied in every situation.

How congenial the idea was to the fathers of the early church is indicated by the readiness with which they adopted it. It is ready to the hand of the Apostle Paul. "For when Gentiles, which have not the law, do by nature the things of the law, these, not having the law, are the law unto themselves; in that they show the work of the law written in their hearts, their conscience bearing witness therewith . . ."[17]

Evidently the law written in men's hearts is the "natural law" of the philosophers and the lawyers of the empire. It was a very simple transition for the church fathers to identify this law of nature with the law of God, thus giving to the idea the added authority of religion at the expense perhaps of some confusion of thought. The important point is that in both church and empire a principle was recognized that constituted a limitation upon any conception of absolute power. The ruler was never a law unto himself, nor could he disregard the precepts of right reason except at the cost of sacrificing his real character and betraying the basis and principle of his authority.

The general acceptance of the idea in the Roman world is evidenced by the necessity the great churchmen felt to come to terms with it. Nowhere is this more apparent than in the attitude assumed toward those institutions that could hardly be justified by an appeal to natural law: slavery, private property, and coercive government. Here, indeed, were institutions that by their

[16] Translated from *De Republica*, III, 22, in *ibid.*, p. 164.
[17] Romans 2:14–15.

very existence challenged both the precept of the philosopher and the doctrine of the churchman. If these were not in accordance with natural law, was there any course open for the advocates of the new religion, save that of unsparing condemnation and unwavering opposition? That this course was not adopted we know; what is significant, however, is that no attempt was made to challenge the authority of natural law as a means of escape from the dilemma that the existence of the institutions created. They were the consequence of, and the remedy for, man's fallen nature. It was much the same way of escape as had already been discovered and followed by the Stoics, although the teaching of the philosophers was clothed in different language, naturally, from that of the church. The Stoics too had conceived of a state of nature, a golden age when man obeyed the law of his being. Here neither subjection nor coercion nor inequality existed. The golden age had passed away because avarice and greed had appeared, and man had betrayed his nature. Herein was found both the explanation and the justification of imperfect institutions. The churchman had little difficulty in accommodating his doctrine to this conception. The Garden of Eden could take the place of the golden age of the Stoic without affecting the general argument, and it did. Both these ways of escape left the authority and validity of natural law unaffected and unquestioned, in the mind of Stoic and churchman alike.

From this conception of natural law were drawn conclusions regarding human nature and human equality that foreshadow the characteristics of eighteenth-century radical and revolutionary ideas. It may seem a far cry from the teaching of the Roman lawyers and the church fathers to the American Declaration of Independence and the French Declaration of the Rights of Man and of the Citizen, and there may seem to be little in common between Cicero and Thomas Jefferson. And yet nowhere is the continuity of the Western tradition more obvious than in relation to the idea of the law of nature and the conviction that certain rights were inherent in it. Here at least there is no gulf fixed between ancient and modern, for whatever elements the great schoolmen and ecclesiastics may have questioned or modified in the tradition of Rome, the conception of natural law was not one of them. Like a golden thread this idea, more than any other, gives unity to the political philosophy of the Middle Ages.

The validity and reality of this law of nature was, we may

say, the axiom upon which was reared the impressive structure of medieval thought. Any human law that could be shown to be inconsistent with it was by that very fact rendered void, if not for the official whose function it was to administer it, at least for the individual who might therefore be justified in resisting it. The sovereign power, however wide its extent and however decisive its authority, was still in some definite sense limited by, and subject to, the law of nature. No government and no ruler could abrogate that law. They, as well as all men, were subject to it. Gierke's statement of this doctrine is emphatic and clear:

Rulers are instituted for the sake of Peoples, not Peoples for the sake of Rulers. Therefore the power of a Ruler is, not absolute, but limited by appointed bounds. His task is to further the common weal, peace and justice, the utmost freedom for all. In every breach of these duties and every transgression of the bounds that they set, legitimate Lordship degenerates into Tyranny. Therefore the doctrine of the unconditioned duty of obedience was wholly foreign to the Middle Age. The properly Medieval and never completely obsolete theory declared that every act of the Sovereign which broke the bounds drawn by Natural Law was formally null and void.[18]

There was a tendency in some quarters, as Gierke points out, to identify the law of nature with the moral law and to look upon the limitations on sovereign power as "no more than the claims which Righteousness makes upon a Sovereign Will." But the medieval mind was not inclined to regard "the claims which Righteousness makes" as less imperative or less stringent than those of reason or nature. Indeed, the great schoolmen might substitute divine law for natural law without diminishing by one iota the limitation this imposed upon the ruler's authority and power. As a matter of fact this concession was not granted in medieval thought. It retained its definite emphasis on the validity and reality of natural law, and it interpreted that law in the most realistic manner.

None the less, there still was life in the notion that a duty of the State which was deducible from Natural Law was a legal duty. Although there was no sharp severance of Natural Law from Morality, the limits drawn round the legitimate sphere of Supreme Power were not regarded as merely ethical precepts. They were regarded and elaborated as rules which controlled external action, and so were contrasted with purely ethical claims made upon internal freedom. No

---

[18]Gierke, *Political Theories of the Middle Age*, pp. 34, 84.

one doubted that the maxims of Divine and Natural Law bore the character of true rules of true Law, even when they were not to be enforced by compulsory processes. No one doubted that a true and genuine Law existed which preceded the State and stood outside and above the State. . . . No one doubted that the formally unconditional duty of obedience that is incumbent on subjects was materially limited by the Law of God and Nature.[19]

It is not the purpose of this argument to suggest that the persistence of an idea is proof, or that such persistence even establishes a presumption, of the validity of that idea. What is suggested rather is that the persistence of this idea of natural law indicates the incompatibility of the tradition of our civilization with the assertion of unlimited and absolute power, whether in government or state. Natural law was the fundamental bar for many centuries to any such assertion. Authority in the last resort must be based on reason and right, and where it conflicts with reason and right, it has forfeited its claim to recognition. This may not be a lawyer's principle; it is, rather, a human principle, for it is an assertion made by the moral consciousness of man. What the medievalist was saying in this connection was substantially what the Stoics had said earlier and what the "natural rights" philosophers said later: that power unrelated to, and independent of, moral principle has a claim neither to obedience nor to respect. Today we may choose other terms to make the same affirmation, but the fact remains that in making it we are affirming a principle that is continuous and fundamental in the traditions of Western civilization. The concept of state absolutism clearly contradicts that principle and is alien to that tradition.

In the eighteenth century the idea of natural law served other ends as well. The doctrine became the basis of claims to natural rights, the convenient weapons of men who were determined to challenge arbitrary power. Rights deduced from nature became at first the positive declarations of philosophers from Locke onward, and then they became the battle cries of those who made the challenge not in word but in action. Whether the doctrines of the natural rights philosophers or the watchwords of the revolutionists were valid is not here in question. Later that too may have to be considered. What is argued here is simply that the democratic tradition is consistent and continuous with the main line of development of the culture of the Western world. Its ideas were sown in the thought of ancient Athens, nurtured in the world

[19] *Ibid.*, pp. 85–86.

view of the Stoics, watered by many streams—Christian, Teutonic, and others—and came to fruition in the struggles of Puritan England, the fight for independence in freedom-loving America, and the revolution in France.

It is therefore a fair conclusion that the idea of natural law endured by virtue of the necessary function it fulfilled. That function is still a necessity. Natural law was a principle formulated to justify the conviction that the universe is rational, a conviction that, as Professor Brierly puts it, "is a necessary postulate both of thought and action."[20] It served this purpose effectively. But it did more; by its emphasis upon reason, it made impossible the enthronement of force as the decisive factor in human affairs and as the final arbiter in the destinies of men and of nations. It was the final and effective obstacle to the general acceptance of absolutism or, indeed, to the recognition of any nonmoral basis for authority and rule. In this sense it may be said that the idea of natural law preserved the conditions that were essential to the emergence and triumph of the democratic idea. It denied the claims of mere power to the obedience and allegiance of men, and this denial was to become the battle cry of the men who fought for freedom. This denial, whatever form it may take, still constitutes the fundamental opposition to dictatorship, totalitarianism, or any other doctrine of state absolutism. To any form of state-worship the tradition of our culture is as fundamentally opposed as is the principle of democracy itself.

Whether natural law is true law—the question that has provoked so much controversy—is of no great importance in this connection. That discussion passes into the realm of morals in any case, and to it we must now address ourselves.

[20] James L. Brierly, *The Law of Nations* (New York: Oxford University Press, 1928), p. 14.

CHAPTER 6. The Ethical Bases of Democratic Government

BELIEF in democratic government implies a faith. The ancient and medieval doctrine of natural law was an expression of one element, perhaps the basic element, in that faith. It was, as we have seen, something more than that, but fundamentally it would seem that the conception of a law of nature was an explicit repudiation of the idea that government rested or could rest entirely on force. It is this same repudiation also that is implied in, and gives permanent significance to, the idea of a social contract. Neither of these ideas would be accepted now in their eighteenth-century form, but the history of both bears witness to the repugnance inherent in the tradition of Western civilization to the idea that coercion is the essence of government or that the exercise of power is its primary function. It must have some justification other than that—a justification that is more satisfying to the human mind. Might may be necessary to make right effective, but might never makes right. This of course is a moral assertion, and it is a conviction upon which democracy depends. It is, therefore, necessary to analyze the elements that are involved in this principle.

THE IDEA OF A HIGHER LAW

The principle that might never makes right assumes that the state is a moral entity and that, like every other moral entity, it must find its justification in the end it serves. This end, to quote Aristotle's familiar phrase, is "the good life." It follows from this that there are mutual obligations between the state and its members and also between different states. The categories of right and wrong are applicable to the decisions and activities of states, and the criterion of judgment in relation to such decisions and actions can never be entirely that of expediency. From the strictly legal standpoint it may be true that "the King can do no wrong," but it has been a characteristic assertion of political thought in the West that there is another court of appeal, which is not bound by the precedents of positive law. There is an "ideal implanted in all men's minds of what human life ought to be made for every man in the growing progress of political Society,"[1] and state

[1] Masterman, *Parliament and the People*, p. 39.

action will be judged according to whether it frustrates or furthers the progressive realization of this ideal. Whatever the practice of nations may have been in the past or may be at present, democratic governments have never repudiated the idea that there are some things a state ought to do or ought not to do in its relations with other states. This statement does not overlook the definite tendency of Hegelian idealism in the direction of such repudiation. For Hegel there were no moral laws by which a state could be bound. But whatever influence Hegel may have had, it is clear that no democratic government would have ventured to announce its adherence to the position that Hegel implied.

It is a significant fact that even where there has been a disregard or a violation of obligation, even by a nondemocratic state, the offending state has found it necessary to attempt some justification. The aggressive action is not really aggressive! In recent times a moral justification, or at least a quasi-moral one, has been claimed even by those states that seem to come nearest to a repudiation of moral responsibility. The action of Japan in Manchuria was a "defensive" action, and the attack upon Poland was necessitated by the threatening preparations of the Poles, by the injustices inflicted upon Germans through the existence of the Corridor and the status of Danzig; and the actual precipitation of attack was due to "the intolerable crimes committed by Poland upon Germans." Even the Ethiopian campaign was "to carry civilization to one of the dark corners of the earth, freeing people from barbarous custom and ending slavery in backward Africa." Hypocrisy is the homage vice pays to virtue. In all this there is a tribute, unconscious perhaps, to the vitality of a tradition, which indeed is being honored in the breach rather than in the observance. Machiavelli may have been followed by states and governments, but very rarely have his followers acknowledged him as the responsible inspiration of their actions. In the policies of states generally there has been a certain deference to the conscience of mankind, even when that conscience was being flouted. It has been found expedient, in most instances, by even the most ruthless aggressors to offer at least a quasi-ethical justification or defense for their actions.

The democratic states have frequently been charged with hypocrisy, and the particular state in which the development of parliamentarianism has had the longest history has been peculiarly open to the charge. "Perfidious Albion" may be a term of reproach, as it was of course intended to be, but it is not difficult to understand the source of the charge or its apparent justification. No democratic government would care to present a policy for approval to its people unless it were possible to offer some ethical justification for it. Certainly no democratic government could carry its people into war unless it found some issues capable of moral interpretation and containing the possibility of idealistic appeal. Granted that on occasion the interpretation is specious and the idealistic appeal hypocritical, but the fact remains. Here at least is witness to the fact that in a democracy there is an assumption that its government ought not to embark upon a policy unless that policy is right. By *right* in this connection people may mean different things, but certainly in general they mean something more than expediency and self-interest. "My country, right or wrong," may be professed by some, but it is doubtful whether in a democratic country there can ever be a deliberate and conscious acceptance of that dictum. What may seem like hypocrisy is, at worst, merely the evidence of the strength of a tradition, which may be evaded but which is too strong to be really challenged or ignored. Frequently, even if it is hypocrisy, it is unconscious hypocrisy. At best it may be much more and much better than that.

This is not necessarily to overlook the important fact that group action is never likely to achieve the ethical consistency of individual action. There will generally be a lag between the ideals of a group as a whole and those of the best individuals in that group. And for this reason, as well as for others, a state will generally not conform, or be able to conform, to the highest moral standards recognized within its own community at any given time. In pursuit of an ideal an individual may be justified in taking risks that a government would not be justified in taking. For the individual the risk is his own, and the consequences, while never quite limited to him or even to his own immediate circle, are at least confined within narrow limits. A government, on the other hand, acts for all the people, including all sorts and conditions of men, and its actions are never, perhaps ought never to be, very far in advance of the judgment and the moral capacity of the average citizen. Action receives its quality largely by virtue of the motive that it expresses, and leadership that goes far beyond the general motivation of those whom it leads not only loses touch but also may fail of its purpose, because there is no sufficient moral conviction behind it and no sufficient faith to justify it.

This is not the assertion of a double ethical standard; it is rather the plain recognition of the fact that a distinction must be drawn between the realm of absolute values and that of expediency and compromise. It is a distinction that has always been recognized—for instance, in the teaching of the early church concerning slavery, private property, and coercive government. These were institutions that could never be completely harmonized with the Christian ideal of brotherhood and love. The church fathers taught, however, that they did have a relative justification in the conditions that prevailed in the early Roman Empire, and in the fact of man's frailty and imperfection. This was not a repudiation of the ideal; it was simply a recognition of the necessary limitations imposed upon its application under the political and social conditions that prevailed.

The fact of compromise is not inconsistent with the assertion of ultimate values. That compromise is dangerous is as obvious as that it is sometimes necessary, and it may often be truly charged that what is called compromise is in fact repudiation or betrayal. But this does not alter the undoubted truth that the compromises necessitated in political and social life may be consistent with a clear recognition of the validity of ideals and the imperatives of moral obligation. This, however, tends to carry us beyond the justifiable limits of our discussion.[2] The fact is that the democratic tradition has never been able to accommodate itself to the amoral or immoral conception of the state. It assumes, and has always assumed, that the state is the subject of rights and duties, that moral principle is relevant to it, and that in the last resort its security depends on its being founded in "the nature of things."

This principle obviously applies, as has been said, also to the relations of the state to its members. Political obligation must have in it a moral element and indeed must have a moral basis. A good law from the lawyer's point of view is not necessarily good in another and a higher sense. The fulfillment of a legal obligation is never the unquestionable duty of the citizen according to the democratic tradition. Obedience to the law will normally be a part of the moral obligation of the citizen, but he will not be a good citizen if he does not recognize an obligation that goes deeper than this and may even conflict with it. There may be occasions

[2] For a fuller discussion of this important point see Reinhold Niebuhr, *Moral Man and Immoral Society* (New York: Scribner, 1934), and other works by the same author.

when the "mortal god" has to be disobeyed; they will be rare, but the recognition that they do exist is vital to the survival of the democratic tradition. And this follows from a recognition that there is something basic to the state's existence that is also basic in the moral consciousness of man. There is a law that is beyond all law; there is an obligation that includes political obligation but that goes beyond it. It is in this sense that a law constitutionally passed and therefore to be faithfully administered may still be a bad law; and whenever the citizen realizes its badness, it is his duty as a moral being to try to change it. In the extreme case it may be his duty to defy it. In so defying it he may be rendering to the state the highest service of which he is capable. That is the supreme justification of the martyr in every age.

It is on the death of Socrates, rather than on his life, that the thought and imagination of the centuries have fastened. Indeed we may almost say that the greatest lesson of his life was his death. He taught thereby (and Plato has elicited the lesson for us in the *Apology* and the *Crito*) that for the sake of conscience a man may rise up against Caesar, but that, in all other matters, he must render unto Caesar the things that are Caesar's, even to the debt of his life. If he were promised acquittal, Plato makes him say, on condition of silence and of refraining from his mission, he could not obey. Greater than the command of the Athenian State was the command of the god; and greater than civic duty was his service. This is the temper of the martyr; nor is it a mistake to enrol Socrates in the ranks of the martyrs. He was faced, after all, by a conflict of duties: and by his death he sealed his witness to the choice he had made. On the one side stood his duty to the Athenian State which throughout his life, and even in his death, he loyally acknowledged. On the other side stood his duty to the god, to testify at all times and to all men—old as well as young, foreigners as well as citizens, but above all to the men of his own blood and his own State—the gospel of Knowledge. He made his choice and he abode the consequence.[3]

In the name of an imperative higher than the law of the state, Socrates defied that law. The apparent paradox of the loyal son of Athens refusing obedience to its behest is resolved only with the recognition of the moral basis for the state's authority. It was his unflinching loyalty to conscience that made Socrates both the good citizen that he was and the martyr that he chose to be. The state has a right to demand everything of its subjects, but it does not follow that all its demands are right; and from this fact de-

[3] Ernest Barker, *Plato and His Predecessors* (London: Methuen, 1908), p. 96.

velops the conflict of duties in relation to which the democratic tradition is clear. Man may serve the state by dying for it; he may serve the state by living for it; he cannot serve the state by doing what he knows to be wrong or by refraining from the duty to which "the gods have called him." There is one supreme good, to which both men and nations must in some sense be subject, for that good is the ultimate end of both. "I could not love thee, dear, so much, lov'd I not honour more," is the statement of a truth that is profoundly significant here, for loyalty to the state must be rooted in a loyalty to those principles in which, in the last resort, both governments and peoples must find justification for all their willing and doing.[4]

DEMOCRATIC VIEW OF THE STATE AND THE INDIVIDUAL

It follows from our discussion that the democratic faith involves a belief in man as an end in himself. He does not exist merely as an instrument for the achievement of the purposes of any other organization or institution. The development of his personality and the achievement of his destiny as a moral being are issues having ultimate significance. Society and the state may both be expressions of his nature and both are necessities for the realization of his being, but in neither can he ever be so merged that his own responsibility ceases and his will is no longer his own. It is perhaps not strictly true to say that the state was made for man, for this would imply a conscious and definite act such as the theory of the social contract presupposes. But it is an assumption characteristic of the main trend of Western thought that the state exists for the realization of human purposes, and in the last resort for the perfecting of man. Whatever the origin of the state or the stages through which it has passed, the why of its being is to be found in the realm of human values. The individual is an end in himself.

It is this emphasis upon the ultimate reality and value of the individual that makes necessary the recognition of the possible conflict of duties in which he may find himself involved. Here too is the explanation and the justification for the view that where such conflict arises, it is the claim of the moral law, not of the state's command, that must be recognized. For in the democratic tradition man is a responsible being charged with the task of seeking and finding his own good. Therefore he cannot divest

[4] For a clear discussion of the problems here raised see L. T. Hobhouse, *The Metaphysical Theory of the State* (London: Allen and Unwin, 1918), pp. 88-95.

himself of responsibility by accepting unthinkingly and without question the decree of an external authority, even though that authority is the august authority of the state. A good imposed upon a moral being is a contradiction in terms.

This belief has been the nerve of resistance to the exercise of arbitrary power in the countries of the Western world. It has been expressed in the doctrine of rights, to which we shall have to return, but its essential character does not depend on any particular mode of expression. It insists that every man has a life of his own to live, that he must choose his own way, that in the final reckoning the choice he makes is a matter of infinite moment to him. Like a golden thread running through the tangles of political thought in the West there is this insistence upon the imperishable worth of the individual.

Moreover, a fugitive glance at Medieval Doctrine suffices to perceive how throughout it all runs the thought of the absolute and imperishable value of the Individual: That every individual by virtue of his eternal destination is at the core somewhat holy and indestructible even in relation to the Highest Power: that every man is to be regarded by the Community, never as a mere instrument, but also as an end:—all this is not merely suggested, but is more or less clearly expressed.[5]

There is no necessary opposition between man and the state, nor does the democratic tradition assume this opposition. It insists rather upon mutuality both of need and of purpose. But we live in an imperfect world, and it may often happen that the state, which should further the good of man, may be responsible for measures that retard and frustrate the achievement of that good. Absolutist rule in Stuart England and arbitrary rule in the Colonies later had just these consequences, at least so the Puritans and the Colonists respectively believed and declared. It is at this point that conflicts arise which have to be resolved, perhaps through violence. And it is in such circumstances generally, if not always, that the belief in the dignity and worth of man as man becomes dynamic and perhaps revolutionary. In the eighteenth century this was generally asserted in a positive declaration of rights, the "Rights of Man." In the last resort men refused to bow to an authority which their reason and conscience repudiated.

It is this assumption of man's worth that is most definitely challenged by the antidemocratic forces of our time. Here the

---

[5] Gierke, *Political Theories of the Middle Age*, pp. 31-32.

assertion of the principle is confronted by flat denial. Man exists for the state, not the state for man. According to Mussolini,

> The keystone of the Fascist doctrine is the conception of the State, of its essence, its purposes, its ends. For Fascism the State is an absolute, before which individuals and groups are relative. . . . A State which is based upon millions of individuals, who recognize it, feel it, are ready to serve it, is not the tyrannical State of the mediaeval lords. It has nothing in common with the absolutistic States before and after 1789. The individual in the Fascist State is not annulled but rather multiplied, just as in a regiment a soldier is not diminished but multiplied by the number of his comrades. The Fascist State organises the Nation, but then leaves sufficient margins to the individuals; it has limited the useless and noxious liberties and has conserved the essential ones. The judge of such things cannot be the individual but only the State.[6]

It is hardly necessary to add that in this case *l'état, c'est moi.*

It is true, so the argument continues, that liberalism, even in its insistence upon the individual, may have had a necessary function to perform in history. It was born and nurtured in the necessity for opposing and breaking the absolutisms that prevailed in other ages and in past time, but it "exhausted its historical function as soon as the State was transformed in its own conscience and popular will. Liberalism denied the State in the interest of the particular individual; Fascism reaffirms the State as the true reality of the individual."[7] The individual therefore must be absorbed in the state. "Each citizen must be completely at the disposal of the State. Nothing for the individual; everything for Italy!"[8] The new leviathan is no longer a mortal god whose commands must be obeyed for the sake of a security that can be found in no other way. It swallows its people whole, assuring them that in the process they will find happiness and realization! They will learn to live submerged and like it!

Where difference goes as deep as this between the fascist theory and the democratic faith, there is no room for compromise, nor much for argument. In fact, neither the assertion of democracy nor that of fascism admits of proof or refutation. They must be stated as opposing articles of faith and left in their stark and grim opposition.

[6] As quoted in Finer, *Mussolini's Italy,* pp. 204–5.
[7] *Ibid.,* p. 198.
[8] H. W. Schneider, *The Making of the Fascist State* (New York: Oxford University Press, 1928), p. 104.

DEMOCRATIC VIEW OF HUMAN NATURE

Belief in democratic government also involves certain assumptions concerning human nature. One is that human nature is to be trusted. This may be stated in different ways. The traditional way is the assertion that man is essentially a rational being. This, of course, does not mean that he always behaves rationally. Man is also a creature of emotion, of sentiment, and of passion, and often he may be swayed far from the path of reason. If this is true of the individual, it is perhaps more obviously true of groups and of masses of men.

The democratic faith does not involve a denial of this fact. It asserts, rather, that there is a kind of dead center to which the human mind tends ever to return, however far it may swing from it. To change the figure, human reason does not keep on a straight course; contrary winds of passion may drive it far and frequently from its true course, but reason can be trusted sooner or later to find that course again, and in the long run also to find port. The popular expression of this assertion is the familiar and oft-quoted saying, "You may fool all the people some of the time; you can even fool some of the people all the time; but you can't fool all the people all the time." A people "finds itself" in the sober moment of reflection, and if this sober moment comes all too infrequently, it is nevertheless sure to come sooner or later. A people makes mistakes, but experience of their consequences teaches it to beware of repeating them too often. In this sense at least we find human nature dependable.

It was one of the weaknesses of nineteenth-century liberalism, as typified by John Stuart Mill for example, to overstress the certitude of this return to the right course, and conversely to underestimate the power of the irrational forces inherent in human nature. The aftermath of this tendency and its penalties have been all too apparent in the twentieth century. It has given the expert propagandist, with his flair for drama and his exploitation of emotion and passion, a long lead over those who were still so impressed by the rationalism inherent in the liberal creed that they disdained to recognize the potency of emotional appeal. This in spite of the warnings of the political psychologists! Democracy will never depend on ritual, myth, drama, and demonstrations, but the democracies are learning now that it may be disastrous to try to dispense with them altogether. Propaganda is an art that may be directed to base uses, but it may also be used for worthy ends. It may be honest or dishonest, and in either case it may be potent; whether for good or for ill depends on the purposes it seeks to achieve and the method to which it resorts for their achievement.

Mussolini had no diffidence in avowing *his* method. "We have created our myth. The myth is a faith, it is passion. It is not necessary that it shall be a reality. It is a reality by the fact that it is a goad, a hope, a faith, that it is courage. Our myth is the Nation, our myth is the greatness of the Nation! And to this myth, to this grandeur, that we wish to translate into a complete reality, we subordinate all the rest."[9]

This quotation makes clear the point at which democratic propaganda must always diverge from fascist. It too may use myth, but only on condition that the myth in some true sense expresses reality and is recognized for what it is: a device to make vivid what is obscure although true. This divergence is necessitated not merely by the fact that the democratic faith involves a principle of morality that does not permit the end always to justify the means; it involves also the conviction that sooner or later the myth *will* be known for what it is, and if it is found to be empty or, what is worse, divorced from or misrepresenting reality, it will be condemned in a denunciation that will involve and discredit those who perpetrated it. If experience shows that it does not work, it may explode with disastrous consequences for those who used it. There is no sure foundation for stable and effective government except in reality, because although men may be fooled they do not stay that way! Reason reasserts itself as the lessons of experience are learned. Seeming triumphs may be achieved against it, in spite of it, or at its expense, but such triumphs are not lasting. There comes inevitably a day of reckoning.

This too is an affirmation of faith, for which no proof can be given or even attempted, save perhaps that which is to be found in the appeal to history; but it is an affirmation that is integral to democracy in any sense of that term. And, therefore, whatever methods of appeal the democratic propagandist may use, in the last resort they must involve or imply an appeal to reason, or else they will betray democratic principle. He may strive to arouse emotion, but only to reinforce reason, not to displace it or overcome it. The ordinary man must be trusted in the long run to discriminate between true and false, to decide between conflicting

[9] At Naples, October 24, 1922, as quoted in Finer, *Mussolini's Italy*, p. 218.

arguments, to know the difference between good and evil, though he cannot be expected to be able to explain that difference.

No one will suggest that man's ultimate choice or dependence on reason is easy to affirm or to accept. But it is less difficult than is the complementary affirmation, which may be put roughly by saying that belief in democratic government is based on the assumption that a man's better self is his real self. He is capable of appreciating the common good and of choosing it, and, being what he is, he *will* in the long run choose it. This is not true of every man, or of any man under all circumstances. It is true generally of man in society—true enough at least so that a community may be trusted to know its own good and pursue it in spite of the selfishness of individuals and of the varied and conflicting interests represented in any community. The creation of public spirit is a real possibility. The community too will make mistakes, will err in judgment, will perhaps be corrupted by selfish and sinister interests. When this happens it will pay the penalties that in a rational universe will inevitably be imposed upon it. It will learn, sometimes only to forget what it has learned; then it must learn all over again, perhaps by bitter experience. There is no dogma of inevitable or unbroken progress involved in this faith. There is only the conviction that man is made for the good, and that sooner or later he will come to the realization of that truth. He will remain unsatisfied until he does, and his dissatisfaction will be both the evidence of his real destiny and the spur to renewed effort and achievement. He will not be content always to live in the cave of illusion. Democracy accepts this difficult truth as a working faith. It asserts that human nature is to be trusted.

Closely connected with this, and perhaps implied in it, is the assumption that man by his very nature desires to make his own decisions. He is at once capable of choice and wills to do his own choosing. He is not only a responsible being, but he feels his responsibility at least to the extent of desiring consciously to assume it. Put in another way, this means that the democratic faith assumes that man prefers liberty—however this may be interpreted—to unquestioning obedience to authority. In the long run he will not be content to do merely what he is told or to remain in a condition where obedience is the beginning and the end of duty. There are, and there always have been, men of slavish temperament; but fundamentally man is not a slave, nor, in spite of Aristotle's opinion to the contrary, is there a human being who is naturally fitted for slavery. Man will obey orders, but he will not continue to obey orders to which reason is never asked to give consent. Unquestioning obedience may be demanded of him under certain circumstances and in certain conditions, but he will never entirely renounce his capacity or his right to question. He needs to know the circumstances and to accept the conditions. "Theirs not to reason why" may be true of men on occasion, but only for a specific purpose to which their reason and will have assented; never is it true of men as men.

A government therefore that demands unquestioning submission and that is based on subjection is not grounded in the reason of things and will not endure. It is contrary to human nature. It is true that nineteenth-century liberalism made this assertion too sanguinely. It assumed that oppression called into being the forces that would destroy it, and it appealed, not in vain, to history in support of its belief. The assumption may have been true under the conditions that prevailed at the time; what the liberal did not foresee and therefore did not sufficiently appreciate was the tremendous increase in power that modern science has placed in the hands of repressive and ruthless governments. A single airplane may overcome and destroy a multitude who have merely guns and barricades. Revolt is still possible, but it needs now a preparation comparable to that which is necessary for scientific warfare. The age of the barricades is not likely to return. A revolt may have succeeded in Spain, but the conditions that enabled it to succeed are not likely to be paralleled again anywhere. Even in Spain it was not the revolt that succeeded really; the issue was decided by the relative strength and determination of the powers that intervened in the conflict. Under twentieth-century conditions "the long run" in which oppression must come to an end and arbitrary power be overthrown may be a very long one.

But this does not invalidate the democratic assumption. It still must continue to insist that man must at least *feel* free in his quest for the good as he conceives it, if he is to display the essential human qualities. He will not be content under any other conditions. How he is to attain the good and what its nature when attained, are questions to be discussed later. Here it is sufficient to assert that man desires to conceive that good for himself rather than to have it determined for him by another, and he desires to pursue that good in his own way rather than in the way dictated by another, even though that other be a government or a dictator. And this is so in spite of the fact that the tendency to shirk responsibility is also a part of his nature.

The democratic faith need not imply a too optimistic or rosy view of human nature, although overoptimism is a danger to which it may be susceptible. It can be realistic, however, at this point as at others. There are for most men decided attractions in the prospect of a condition in which problems are solved *for* the individual, not *by* him; in which he is relieved of the stress and strain of mental and moral conflict; in which duty is clear because it is prescribed. The believer in democracy admits all this, but he asserts that the attraction will be recognized as a temptation to be resisted, or if it is not, its attractiveness will pall, and man will know that his good cannot be found in the acquiescence this condition implies. No abundance of bread and circuses will reconcile man to the kind of self-abrogation and self-abdication that unquestioning obedience demands. Man cannot forever renounce the demand for liberty. It is the characteristic democratic assertion that this demand is human.

HUMAN WELFARE THE REAL PURPOSE OF A DEMOCRATIC STATE

Finally, it is the assumption of democracy that the state exists to enhance and to further human welfare. In its tradition there is never a concession to the totalitarian assertion that the state is essentially power or exists for the achievement of power. It is true that there have been marked divergences of view in the democratic tradition as to how human welfare is to be conceived. The long controversy between hedonist and idealist, for example, makes that sufficiently clear. But whatever difference may have existed among liberal thinkers, there has always been a general consensus that the well-being of men and women was at once the aim of the state and the justification for its existence. Aristotle's "good life" for which the state continued to exist was general enough to permit of wide divergences of interpretation, but these divergences never led to a repudiation of the concept on the part of those who professed a belief in the democratic principle. Generally in the long history of Western civilization when a state was praised, it was for the actual good conferred by it upon its citizens and the benefits they derived from their citizenship. Pericles, for example, was proud of Athens for what Athens had done for the Athenians, ennobling their lives and providing stimulus for worthy interests and appreciations. The modern poet exclaims, "Here and here did England help me." Between Pericles and Browning lies the tradition that unites them by its consistency. It rejects the idea that the public welfare is necessarily achieved in the might and power of the state. The state must be able to demonstrate its beneficence in terms of personal good. Even Hobbes, in whom we would expect to find least evidence of the influence of the tradition, has to recognize it. The leviathan which he creates must in the last resort be justified by the fact that it does provide for the welfare of the people, a welfare that Hobbes identifies with the security of persons. It is his contention that the state does guarantee to people this fundamental blessing.

The state therefore in the democratic tradition must be judged by its fruits. It is never regarded as omnipotent, never as justified merely by the fact of its existence or its power. "The State exists for individuals; individuals do not exist for the State. Liberty has meaning only for the individual, and the welfare of the State has neither meaning nor value except in terms of the welfare of the individuals who compose the State. The State, in short, is not an end in itself, it is a means to the well-being of men and women."[10]

This then is the criterion of judgment in relation to policy: Does it make people better or happier? Does it add to the sum of human welfare interpreted in terms of personal good? The state must find some better answer than that this or that particular measure increases its own strength and enhances its own power; for, granted the democratic assumption, it is relevant to ask, strength for what and power to achieve what end? And if it is asserted by totalitarian advocates that power is an end in itself, the believer in democracy will always refuse to accept the assertion and will deny its validity. He will reply as Bertrand Russell does:

And a good community does not spring from the glory of the State, but from the unfettered development of individuals: from happiness in daily life, from congenial work giving opportunity for whatever constructiveness each man or woman may possess, from free personal relations embodying love and taking away the roots of envy in thwarted capacity from affection, and above all from the joy of life and its expression in the spontaneous creations of art and science. It is these things that make an age or a nation worthy of existence, and these things are not to be secured by bowing down before the State. It is the individual in whom all that is good must be realized, and the free growth of the individual must be the supreme end of a political system which is to re-fashion the world.[11]

It does not satisfy the democrat therefore when he is told that economic measures sponsored by the state are necessary to

[10] Joad, *Philosophy of Morals and Politics*, p. 736.
[11] *Proposed Roads to Freedom* (New York: Holt, 1919), p. 138.

strengthen the state. He must be shown either that the measures improve the conditions and the quality of life for the people, or that the particular element of strength that is sought can contribute to their well-being. It is not sufficient justification of the exercise of power to say that it will enlarge the bounds of that power and increase the range of its authority. Again the question arises, to what end? The whole idea of autarchy seems to be out of harmony with the democratic concept, for it substitutes state power for human well-being as the purpose of economic activity and as the acid test of economic policy. Democracy therefore presupposes a welfare economy rather than a power economy as the right and normal economic system.

The totalitarian may declare that in the last resort the well-being of the individual is meaningless apart from the well-being of the state, that people will be powerful and will rejoice in their power only in proportion as they feel the reality of the power inherent in the state to which they belong. The victories of the state will be theirs and its capacity to assert itself will somehow communicate itself to them, giving them a sense of mastery and a feeling of significance. This too, so it is argued, is a justifiable source of satisfaction and a species of well-being that is to be preferred to the satisfactions of material comfort. There are higher goods than those of economic well-being—pride of race, prestige gained in successful endurance and in victorious conflict. The smug complacencies of the well-fed pale into insignificance before the glittering prizes won by those who dare the hazard of living dangerously. The individual, then, is indeed merged in the state, his good made identical with its good and therefore with its power. He finds glory in the glory of his country, a vicarious achievement in the victories of its armies. This is what the individual exists for, and it is by this alone that his life can be redeemed from insignificance. Only as an instrument of the state's power can he be said to have any significance at all.

"All individuals or groups are relative, only to be conceived of in relation to the State," according to Mussolini. Here, indeed, is the reversal of the democratic assertion, its antithesis. It is really a distortion of a sound principle, the principle that the individual finds self-realization in seeking the common good. But in the democratic faith the common good can never become the good of the individual except in and through a definite act of will on his part. It is his prerogative, as it is his moral responsibility, to decide for himself. "Our wills are ours to make them thine." But the totalitarian argument means that the state's demands must be accepted because they are the state's demands, that the individual renounces his capacity for judgment in favor of the state, that he recognizes no criterion of judgment save the state's fiat. What is achieved is not self-realization but self-abnegation, for the implication is clear. What the state ordains must be *assumed* to serve the common good; its decrees must be accepted as the criteria of good and evil and the final tests of value. At this point the argument between totalitarianism and democracy breaks off, for there is no common ground upon which the battle can be fought.

Here democracy can only abide by its principle and continue to maintain its faith. Government must be for the people. This does not mean that there will always be an obvious connection between state action and the immediate advantage of the people, nor does it mean that the advantage will necessarily be conceived in terms of material good. Policy even in a democratic state may also sacrifice a present interest for a future good; it may aim at an intangible benefit at the expense of economic sacrifice. It may for instance choose to aim at a balanced economy in preference to a more profitable policy that it believes would result in deepened social cleavages. Frequently its policies will inflict what may seem like unnecessary burdens or unjust restrictions upon certain sections of its population. Welfare must never be interpreted narrowly. Nevertheless, it is the welfare of the whole, and of that whole as made up of persons, that must be the paramount consideration and the ultimate aim of the democratic state. It may be difficult to define what is meant by the welfare of the people. But at least it is something other than increase of power for the state or expansion of the bounds of its territory. It must mean the enhancement of personality for its members, the increase of their happiness, and the furtherance of their ultimate interests as moral beings.

When all qualifications are made, then, it still remains a basic assumption of democracy that the state is a means to an end, and that the end is the people's good. Whatever else the state may be or fail to be, it must find its justification in what it does for the people.

Part Two
BASIC CONCEPTS OF DEMOCRACY RE-EXAMINED

CHAPTER 7. Liberty

IN THE practices of modern democracy there have been strange and varied inconsistencies; in its fundamental assertions, however, there has been a remarkable consistency. In any group of men professing the liberal faith, there would be substantial agreement as to its primary characteristics. These are expressed in the watchwords made familiar and dynamic by the French Revolution: liberty, equality, fraternity. Until recent years it would have been difficult to find any government or any recognized political leader in the Western world who did not at least pay lip service to these ideals. The repudiation of liberty by Mussolini in the early twenties shocked the world, not only because of the vehemence with which liberty was denounced, but also because it challenged an almost universal assumption—that liberty, as an ideal at least, had passed beyond the realm of argument. If man has any rights at all, then freedom, it was assumed, must be one of them. What the nature of liberty might be and how it might be most effectively realized were matters of discussion or even dispute, but it was unquestionable that liberty is a good, that it is an end to be pursued, that governments exist for many purposes but primary among them is the safeguarding and development of freedom.

The same cannot be said quite so positively of equality and fraternity. Equality was regarded as a more debatable issue even as an ideal, and certainly more difficult to realize. Assertion of its validity as an ideal was hedged around with reservations. Frequently it was argued that there is an essential incompatibility between equality and liberty. Still there was a consensus of opinion that in some interpretation of it, perhaps only as "equality before the law," it is inherent in the democratic faith. Fraternity, on the other hand, was unquestioned as an ideal but rarely regarded as a principle of practical significance in the realm of politics. It was vague, indefinable, difficult to translate into terms of political obligation, and therefore frequently stated but rarely stressed.

But in the case of all three ideals definition was not easy, and except by philosophers the task was only too frequently evaded. "Everybody knew what freedom was!" It was easier to inscribe the watchwords on banners than it was to explain them. It was tempting to appeal to them when controversy became heated or when vital issues were in debate. What was not so simple was to respond to the challenge of those who asked for something more than words, who asked that the principles these words expressed should be stated clearly and their practical significance explained. As a matter of fact, these words have often inspired heroic devotion on the one hand and have been used as a cloak for gravest injustice on the other. In the name of liberty, for instance, men have endured the greatest sacrifices, and in its name also, men have perpetrated the greatest wrongs. The fact that these words have been potent does not obscure the fact that their meaning has been elusive. Men have sometimes pursued the ends they signify without asking themselves or others what they were or what they meant. Their objectives generally were immediate and practical and clear; understanding could wait.

Nevertheless, definition must be attempted, or if not definition at least a measure of understanding. A faith will not achieve its full dynamic effect if its rational foundation is never appreciated and if its essential principles are never analyzed. If democracy is to survive, those who subscribe to it must be prepared to give a reason for the faith that is in them. In the last resort this must mean a readiness to explain and to defend the basic concepts of their faith.

THE NEGATIVE CONCEPT OF FREEDOM

What is liberty? Like all those concepts that seem at once simple and ultimate, the word comes to us colored by its long history. Generally interpretation has swung between two poles as emphasis has shifted from the negative to the positive concept of freedom. From the negative point of view freedom has always meant the absence of restraint. Man is conceived as a being exercising choice, making decisions, and proceeding to put these decisions into effect. Whether this choice is ever real is the core of the agelong controversy concerning free will and determinism. This question we need not discuss here. Granted the assumption of essential human freedom, we may assume that man has desires, is conscious of preferences, and exercises choice; the curtailment of freedom occurs when the effect of this choice is frustrated, when limits are imposed so that his decisions cannot be put into effect. This is restraint.

Restraint in itself, however, is not necessarily a limitation of liberty. It all depends upon the nature of the restraint. If desire is completely unregulated and passion holds sway without check or hindrance, the result is not freedom but license. There are justifiable restraints and necessary limitations—bounds that must be observed as a condition of real freedom. Man's actions must be "within reason." So long as man does merely what he likes, he is missing true freedom, not achieving it. Choice must be rational, and decision must be governed by reason. In all this we are, of course, using the language of metaphor. The point is that freedom as the absence of *all* restraint is meaningless; it is a condition that has never existed and never can exist.

Nevertheless, it is this conception that results in the interpretation of freedom as the absence of restraint. Man in the state of nature was free. The conception of this state of nature varies greatly as we pass from Hobbes to Locke and then to Rousseau, but what is common to all representations of a state of nature is the conception of man as free from the ties and relationships of organized society—free, that is, from constraint and restraint. In such a state there was indeed a law of nature, unwritten but universal. This law was not a restraint, for innocent man was not conscious of it; he did not know that he was observing it or obeying it. It was inherent in him, written in his heart, constituting his nature. The state of nature could be pictured as ideally happy or profoundly miserable, as a realm of perfect harmony or as a condition of utter anarchy. It was either a golden age or a realm of utter darkness. But whatever one's point of view might be, the characteristic conception of man inherent in the idea of the state of nature was that of a being naturally free, untrammeled and unrestrained.

It may be pointed out that this natural liberty was conceived in purely individual terms—in terms, therefore, that were entirely abstract and unreal. For man, as Aristotle said long ago, is by nature a social animal, and the *individual* apart from society has no existence and can have none. Even in the dim ages before history began, man was always a member of some organized community, however crude and rudimentary the organization may have been. He was always subject to the restraints of the tribe or to the customs of the clan even before laws were made. The primitive free man was an artificial creation which served a very useful purpose in the bitter struggle against entrenched and powerful evils. And yet it was man as an individual in this sense of the term that was supposed to have enjoyed freedom from any external authority.

This conception and the use made of it were determined by the conditions that prevailed in the eighteenth century and by the nature of the conflicts that were characteristic of the period. The liberal thinkers of the age were fashioning weapons to be directed against arbitrary political authority; repressive government was the arch enemy! Moreover, a new economic era was dawning; the forces of the Industrial Revolution had already come to birth and had begun to exercise a decided influence. The desire for the removal of those hindrances that curbed business enterprise and hampered industrial development was growing more and more powerful. The mercantilist system had exhausted its function but was being maintained because political power still rested in the hands of the landed class, whose interests had created it. Control was exercised by governments that in the main represented the waning power of the landed aristocracy. It was inevitable that the rising power of the merchant and of the industrialist should challenge the system, which was increasingly felt to be inconsistent not only with their interests but also with the new position of importance in the social order they were now demanding and in some measure achieving. The commercial and industrial classes were also conscious of new powers, of a new spirit of enterprise that demanded expression. Because this consciousness was being frustrated, they rebelled against what they now regarded as artificial restraints. Government authority was proving restrictive, and in many ways repressive. It was conventional and had no justification in "the nature of things." Regulations were shackles imposed upon the individual who by nature was free!

It is not surprising, therefore, that the democratic tradition arising out of this philosophy in the eighteenth century should have conceived of freedom in what we have called negative terms. Always it was freedom *from*. Laws had grown either to confirm rights or to escape anarchy; in either case the tendency was to regard them as necessities which, however, were regrettable. They were necessary, but necessary because man had lost his original innocence, or could not be trusted to observe a law that was neither written nor enforced, or was so constituted that his passions led to a war of all against all. Laws were the restraints that assured a moderate good in a world in which the supreme good had been rendered impossible. Government was the power that guaranteed limited rights, which man received in exchange for the fuller rights that he renounced in the compact on which the state was based. Natural freedom was exchanged for a more secure, but also a more restricted, freedom. The point is that in the climate of eighteenth-century thought it was inevitable that freedom should be conceived primarily as freedom from certain interferences—those in particular that limited and circumscribed the activities and energies of a forceful generation of men.

Not only was this implied in the dominant conceptions of the time, it was also a consequence of the development of historical events. From its birth in the Puritan Revolution through its growth and development in the French Revolution, the struggle for liberty was in the main a struggle against oppressive power. Its aim was emancipation from arbitrary authority. It is possible to argue that Cromwell's men knew what they were fighting for—although as a matter of fact the differences among them went very deep—but they knew much more clearly what they were fighting to destroy. What dreams the leaders of the French Revolution may have cherished and how different from one another were the dreams of the Dantons, the Mirabeaus, and the Robespierres can be gleaned from history, but no dream was ever as clear as were the convictions that condemned the *ancien régime* and determined its destruction. The exhilaration and exaltation of the struggles for liberty came from the clear realization of the arbitrary character of the power that imposed grievous limitations upon the activities and energies of resolute and passionate men. The revolutions of the eighteenth century were directed against the felt injustices of authority, which, so it was argued, had no justification in nature or in reason.

This explains, in part at least, the general temper and spirit of nineteenth-century liberalism. There was left as an aftermath of the democratic struggles of earlier days a distrust of government and a tendency to restrict its activities within the narrowest possible bounds. The state was regarded with suspicion as constituting a permanent menace to the liberties that had cost so dear in blood and tears. Laws were necessary no doubt, but the fewer they were and the narrower their scope the better. We have seen how this issued in the economic sphere in the general acceptance of laissez faire as the prime condition of freedom. It was not, however, confined to the economic sphere. The functions of government were conceived in the main as negative functions, and the state was less an engine of progress than a bulwark against unnecessary interference with individual liberties. Government existed for other purposes, no doubt, but none was so important as that of safeguarding the rights that in some sense or other were inherent in, and natural to, man.

Even the most fervent believer in natural rights, however, could not deny that laws are necessary. Freedom without limit is meaningless. Hobbes in his description of the state of nature was probably nearer the truth than Locke and Rousseau, or any of those who pictured it as a golden age of innocence and harmony. The colors with which Hobbes painted the picture of a life nasty, brutish, and short may have been too dark, and we need not believe for a moment that his leviathan was the only alternative to it. Still it remains true that law and authority are the conditions of freedom, and the organized state the only real alternative to anarchy. Apart from them each individual would enjoy only so much freedom as the force and strength he could command would secure for him. It would be a freedom perpetually challenged, perpetually in jeopardy, and man, therefore, so far from being free would ever be beset with fears.

Laws, then, are the restraints that guarantee freedom. They safeguard and enlarge our liberties. Governmental coercion, or the possibility of it, which is involved in the power of the state, saves us from a worse coercion, that of forces which unaided we cannot match or restrain. Government and laws are the guardians of liberty; far from restricting freedom, they enlarge it. Even granting this the liberals and democrats of the eighteenth century still maintained that there were some rights man could not give up, rights inherent in human personality and therefore, in the language of the Declaration of Independence, inalienable. No power on earth, neither the state nor man himself, could divest him of them!

Difficulty arises with the question of what these inalienable rights are. The Declaration of Independence declares them to be life, liberty, and the pursuit of happiness. The French Declaration of the Rights of Man lists them as liberty, property, and security. The fact is that once natural rights are asserted, what is to be included in them depends on the particular circumstances and convictions of those who assume the task of determining them.

The concept of rights, as we shall see later, does not provide any adequate basis for that purpose, for the appeal to the law of nature is necessarily inconclusive. Its precepts cannot be formulated or its content known in a way definite enough for purposes of judgment. This, however, does not mean that the concept of rights is entirely without significance.

The approach to the problem of liberty from this point of view leads to confusion because the concept of laws as restraints or limitations and of government as coercive power is not in accordance with the facts of experience. Generally, in a democratic country at least, the laws are not felt as restraints or as coercion by the great majority of the people. The average individual is as a rule unconscious of most of them. It is only on rare occasions that the question of obedience or the temptation to violate them arises. In doing what the law demands, the individual normally does what he ought to do and what he knows he ought to do. There is no consciousness of any limitation of, or interference with, choice, and no sense of opposition. The laws are forgotten, for the individual lives in accordance with them and has no occasion to break them. His reason approves of them—if indeed they are brought to the bar of his reason at all. If he belongs to the minority that opposes a particular law, he may still obey it, and unless he feels strongly that obedience is contrary to the public good or would violate a firmly held conviction, he does not feel that obedience involves any kind of coercion or subjection.

It is, therefore, only in the marginal cases that the issue of liberty arises directly in a democratic state. The state may make positive demands that individuals feel they cannot honestly and conscientiously meet. A man may feel that a "good" law—good in the lawyer's interpretation of the term, in the sense that it has been constitutionally made—is still a bad law. Bad not only because it minimizes his comfort or interferes with his material interest, but also because it conflicts with his profoundest moral convictions. This is the case with which Professor Laski is concerned when he writes: "The greatest contribution that a citizen can make to the state is certainly this, that he should allow his mind freely to exercise itself upon its problems. Where the conscience of the individual is concerned, the state must abate its demands."[1] This is an issue in the marginal cases and since it has already been discussed nothing more need be said about it here.

[1] Harold J. Laski, *Authority in the Modern State* (New Haven: Yale University Press, 1927), p. 56. The whole of Section 4 in Chapter 1 should be read for a profound and stimulating discussion of some of the points touched upon above.

Nor need anything be added to what has been said about minority rights and obligations in a democratic community. The right of the minority is the right to convert itself into a majority if it can, and the obligation of the state is to provide the conditions that will give it fair opportunity to do so.

LIMITS OF TOLERATION

Beyond this point the problem of freedom as absence of restraint may become acute, and the simple concept of liberty gives rise to questions that are far from simple. There is generally a consensus of opinion with regard to what are sometimes called the elementary freedoms: freedom of thought, of speech and writing, of worship, and of assembly. In principle none of these particular freedoms need much defense in democratic communities, but in practice, interpretation is far from easy and defense is often greatly needed. The price of these primary liberties is eternal vigilance. The fundamental question relates to the measure of restraint and the methods for imposing it that are consistent with, and conducive to, the general welfare. Very often opinions will differ sharply here, and still more often the public mind will be confused in particular circumstances, even when there is agreement in principle.

From the point of view of *direct* and *actual* restraint, freedom of thought may almost be assumed, for no government has devised any means for controlling the human mind. To *impose* a belief on anyone is a contradiction in terms. The appearance of consent may be enforced, the reality never; profession may be induced by threat of penalty or promise of reward, but such profession obviously is to the advantage neither of the power that forces it nor of the individual that makes it. Thought is free in the sense that no external power or coercion can determine its real character. To recognize this as a truism today must not blind us to the fact that it was established only after centuries of fierce contention. The Inquisition and the long story of persecution are evidence of that. Generally, however, we may assume that even the most timid advocate of freedom or the most rigid authoritarian will accept the position that a man's thoughts are his own and that no one can circumscribe or limit their flight. But when freedom of thought in only this sense is secured, the gain is a singularly barren one.

What men have contended for under the banner of freedom of thought has been freedom of speech and of writing as well, the freedom not only to think as they will but to *say* what they think. The arguments for this freedom constitute a part of the classic tradition of democracy and are enshrined in the literature of liberalism from Milton's *Areopagitica* to John Stuart Mill's *On Liberty* and beyond, so they need not be repeated here. "Give me the liberty to know, to utter, and to argue freely according to conscience, above all liberties."

Even here, however, unlimited freedom goes beyond what is practicable or justifiable. Speech that knows no bounds is clearly incompatible with the ordered freedom of any well-organized society. There is no modern state that has not some laws, however inadequate, against libel and slander. These are necessities because the protection of reputation against unscrupulous malice is one of the conditions of freedom for the great majority of men. Similarly, there are few states, if any, that find it possible to dispense altogether with censorships. Most states have laws prohibiting the publication of obscene and pornographic literature. The threats to liberty in these matters arise most frequently not from the laws, but from a narrow and rigid interpretation of them and from the tendency of the overzealous to appeal to them more often than circumstances and conditions justify. Beyond this there is some danger of yielding too readily to the dead weight of tradition or to the timidity that places too much reliance upon a "fugitive and cloistered virtue." Censorship in any form must be kept strictly on the defensive, lest the public good come to be interpreted in terms of established precedent. Restriction and restraint must never be resorted to for the maintenance of static mores, or as a hindrance to progress. "Let her and Falsehood grapple: who ever saw Truth put to the worse in a free and open encounter?"

So far the argument has followed familiar lines. It has not encountered the most serious wave, which must now be faced if not surmounted. Defining the limits of toleration in normal times will give rise to discussion that may often become acute, but in democratic countries a fair measure of agreement is always within reach. What if, however, times are not normal but critical? What if they are times of great social upheaval and revolutionary ferment, times of great international tension, or in the last resort times of war? Toleration is a virtue less easy to practice when danger threatens, and perhaps this is as it should be. At least there is good ground for the assertion that tolerance should be more carefully scrutinized and defined in times of grave public danger. A government that is insecure or a nation whose peace is threatened is less likely, and less able, to take those chances that under normal conditions it would take quite readily. But freedom of speech cannot be considered in a vacuum; it must be considered in relation to concrete situations.

The case of Czechoslovakia in 1937 and 1938 brings home the challenge of these considerations. That Konrad Henlein's movement had constituted since 1933 a definite threat to the state is clear at least in retrospect, whatever may have been thought at the time. In 1938 it had obviously become a propagandist movement, stimulated and encouraged by a neighboring power whose designs even then were open to suspicion. At what point would it have been justifiable to suppress the Sudeten agitation and to what principle could the government have appealed for justification? It can hardly be questioned that the refusal or the inability of the Prague government to apply coercive measures soon enough and effectively enough had a profound and perhaps decisive effect on the course of events and on the tragic outcome. Was the government too liberal? Certainly the result was not an extension but a vast curtailment of liberty for the majority of the people. Here, clearly, was a condition in which the application of the abstract principle of liberty was not justified in the event. Obviously what is required under such conditions is a careful balancing of the various factors of public interest, rather than indiscriminate and uncritical application of an abstract principle.

The case leads to the conclusion that under certain circumstances an apparent curtailment of liberty may be necessary for the preservation of liberty. This presumably is the justification for the limitations that are applied even by democratic governments in times of grave crisis. In a democratic state involved in war the people willingly relinquish some of their cherished liberties in order that these same liberties may not be imperiled more seriously than they are by a temporary abandonment of them. This involves no real sacrifice of freedom, although obviously there is danger to it. There is, for instance, the danger that a government may go beyond what is really necessary, impelled perhaps by an unconscious urge for power or an unrecognized distrust of democracy. There is the danger that liberties once relinquished may not readily be restored. In any democratic country, unfortunately, there will be interests only too ready to take advantage of a temporary suspension of the public will or any voluntary curtailment of recognized and established liberties. One of the safeguards in such a situation is an awareness of what is really happening when liberties are suspended or limited and a refusal to be blind to the real nature and necessities of the circumstances. Another, and in the last resort the only effective, safeguard is an awakened and vigilant public interest with a firm resolve that the exigencies imposed by conditions of crisis shall not be prolonged a moment beyond the necessity.

The Czechoslovak situation referred to illustrates a still more perplexing question. The Nazis of Sudetenland claimed freedom for themselves while making no pretence of believing in freedom for others. The Nazi creed, which they proclaimed as their own, was a denial of even the principle of freedom. There was not the slightest suggestion that in the new political order they sought to establish there would be any regard for the rights of minorities. Liberty was not a good to be sought generally, but a slogan to be used for their own advantage and abandoned when it had served its purpose. In fact, the *Gleichschaltung* which was the core of Nazi policy made respect for freedom impossible. The Sudeten German demand, therefore, involved aims clearly inconsistent with the basic principles of the republic of which the Sudeten Germans were citizens; principles, moreover, that unquestionably represented the opinions and beliefs of the majority of the people of Czechoslovakia.

What should a democratic republic do under such circumstances? It is not enough to say what is of course true, that the Nazi demand was inconsistent and therefore insincere, for the problem raised is not solved by such an assertion. Was there an obligation on the Czechoslovak government to permit the propagation of a demand that if effective would jeopardize the liberties of millions of its citizens, for whose safety and liberty it was responsible? These citizens outnumbered the Germans by many millions. The Sudeten demand, moreover, was a threat to the very existence of the Czechoslovak government. Is it a requirement of democratic principle that under such circumstances complete latitude be given to propaganda and agitation?

To state the question more generally: Must a democratic government grant to those who seek its overthrow by force the freedom to speak and to organize for that purpose? Suppose such a group clearly asserts, as fascists do, that if they succeed, democratic processes will not be tolerated in the new order; that once they have achieved power, they have no intention of permitting the use of methods of persuasion, appeal, and propaganda, which might secure the re-establishment of a democratic government? Must a democratic government under such circumstances resort to no measures save argument and persuasion?

The issue is not comparable to those raised in ordinary political contests in democratic countries. Victory by one political party does not destroy the chances of the opposing party to reverse the result. Here, broadly, is fair encounter waged under rules agreed upon in advance. But the totalitarian does not intend to permit opposition. He declares that he will not abide by the decisions of a majority or depend on public opinion. He relies on force and by force he will destroy opposition if he can. His triumph is more than a temporary setback for democracy. When he seizes power it is with the intention of using it to defy the popular will whenever necessary. This means the end of any possibility of re-establishing democratic government except by force. This removes the issue from the arena of political controversy as generally understood. It establishes the arbitrament of force, insists that this is decisive, and provides no opportunity of appeal. The condition created, therefore, is one in which the opposition of principle involves an ultimate conflict. Where one side frankly avows its intention to rely on force, the other has no option but to take measures to meet the threat. There is already an incipient state of civil war. A democratic government must meet the threat to its existence by a readiness to meet force with force. Argument and persuasion cannot be maintained with those who have abandoned them. Those who appeal to the sword cannot complain if the challenge is accepted. Those who deny liberty must not claim her protection when they are hard pressed on the field of their own choosing. It cannot, on the other hand, be the duty of a democratic government to consent to its own destruction.

The fact is, of course, that to advocate the overthrow of government by force is revolutionary propaganda. It is certainly possible to believe with Locke that under certain circumstances revolution is justified, but this must not blind us to the nature of revolution, in the sense in which the term is used here. Violent revolution is an appeal to force for the overthrow of what is regarded, rightly or wrongly, as arbitrary, oppressive, or unmerited power. It may be justified, but the resistance to revolution by those who are equally convinced that the government is legitimate and good is justified too. It is the duty of a government to prevent revolution and to suppress it if it occurs. It must use the means effective for that purpose. Revolutions do not succeed by argument, although argument is relevant in the judgments of history. The rights and wrongs of the question at issue in any particular case are not the point here, although whether a revolution is justified or not is decided ultimately by such considerations. Reason may, and in the long run will, decide the question of right and wrong in a given revolutionary struggle, but it does not determine success or failure. The point is that the appeal to force may make it necessary to resort to force in defense of what is threatened. A democratic government therefore will have to meet the revolutionary challenge, not on the ground it would choose if it could, the ground of reason, but on that which the opposition forces it to take.

Democracy must defend itself. Where the attack is by argument, it will meet the attack by argument; where the attack is by fire and sword, it must use—however much it hates to do so— the only weapons that are effective against such attack. Those who use force must be circumvented, those who organize plots must be frustrated, those who plan violence must be discovered, and those who advocate violence must be restrained. Hard saying though it may be, it is difficult to avoid the conclusion: "Of them we are not bound to be tolerant."

How this conclusion is to be interpreted in practice is a question of expediency and of political sagacity. It cannot be determined by an appeal to the abstract concept of freedom; it must be determined by interpreting freedom in the light of concrete situations. At what point in the struggle should restraints and limitations be placed on propaganda? When should agitation be suppressed or curbed? Concretely, at what point did the Nazi movement become so great a menace to the Weimar Republic that toleration became weakness which actually prepared the way for a betrayal of freedom? When and on what grounds should Prague have proscribed the Sudeten movement? Clearly the answers depend on the gravity and imminence of the danger that these movements created—in other words, on considerations of political expediency. The questions raise issues of policy. And both these cases are a warning against minimizing the danger of acting when it is too late.

Obviously where the revolutionary movement is weak and the government stable and secure, a wide latitude may be permitted and may even be wise. The government has little to fear, and if it is a democratic government it has much to gain by a generous interpretation of the principle of freedom. It can afford to take risks. But a government in crisis, whether at peace or at war, cannot do so, for then the "risks of liberty" may become actually the risk of losing liberty. The more secure the government, the greater the possibilities of freedom for its people. The ability to determine justly and wisely the precise limits of toleration and restraint is one of the supreme tests of statesmanship. It is also one of the crucial tests of democracy.

The practical application of the principle of freedom, therefore, is a question of policy, not of abstract right. In general it may still be necessary to insist that in times of crisis there will always be the danger of going beyond what the situation demands and to exceed, in restriction and restraint, the limits that dire necessity imposes. The wise and just balance is not easy to strike or to maintain. The general principle, however, that emerges from our discussion is that liberty in the sense of absence of restraint consists of reducing the restraints on individual choice and action to the minimum consistent with public safety. The principle, as we have seen, is easier to state than to apply, and it may seem too general to provide sure and clear guidance in government and policy. That is due, in part at least, to the inherent inadequacy of the conception of liberty as absence of restraint. Liberty is more than this; it is a positive good.

POSITIVE FREEDOM

It is a mistake, then, to think of law as a restraint on the individual's action or as a limitation of his freedom. It is rather a condition and guarantee of that freedom. Law represents the crystallized and formulated results of a nation's experience in the actual task of establishing and maintaining a harmonious community life. It contributes, therefore, in so far as it fulfills its function, to the enlargement and extension of individual liberty. As a matter of fact the good citizen when he reflects knows that this is so, although under normal conditions he takes law for granted. He observes and obeys the laws without thinking of them. When he does think, he knows that they represent a potential interference with his activities only to protect him from interferences infinitely more vexatious and dangerous to which otherwise he would be subject. Consciously or unconsciously he yields obedience to them, recognizing that his obedience is a positive advantage. He gives consent to them, and in giving willing obedience to them he is obeying his own will. The laws fulfill a positive function in securing for him a wider range of choice and a greater freedom of action.

The general distrust of government action so characteristic in the liberal tradition of the nineteenth century and in the thought of classical economists obscured this fact if it did not implicitly deny it. The extension of government activity does not in itself mean a corresponding restriction of individual freedom. This is obviously not the place to discuss the complex and difficult problems of government planning, but the fact is that government in democratic countries has increasingly extended the scope of its powers, invading regions that hitherto were regarded as lying beyond its proper province. Its controls have been established within what were once called the citadels of free enterprise. It has sought to achieve positive ends—social security for instance—to an extent that would have seemed dangerous or worse to the typical individualist of yesterday and that is still regarded with suspicion by the individualist of today. This suspicion is responsible for much of the opposition to governmental projects of a constructive character. Sometimes the assertion is made that the choice lies between, on the one hand, a planned economy with servility of the people and, on the other, a strict limitation of government activity with the continuance of such social inequalities as existed in the era of crisis that preceded the war.

That there may be dangers to individual freedom in the extension of government activities is admitted, for this is a danger inherent in government itself. Governments may be oppressive, but there is no necessary dichotomy between government control and individual liberty. If the controls are popularly demanded and popularly supervised, they may be expressions of community self-control. They need not involve any interference with individual initiative or any limitation of individual freedom. They may mean a more generalized sense of responsibility; they demand a deepening sense of responsibility. As government assumes new functions, it is important that public spirit as well as public interest should keep pace with the new opportunities and the new obligations that are inevitably created. To deny that this is possible is to be skeptical of democracy at a critical point. To be aware of the necessity for it is to recognize that democracy meets here a new and critical test. To assume that democratic government is not capable of meeting the demands, social and economic, of a complex and difficult era without impairing the traditional liberties is to admit its inadequacy. To be doubtful of its capacity to do so is to be doubtful of its future.

This is not an argument for or against a "planned economy."[2] It is an argument against the assumption that the extension of government control in a democracy is necessarily a curtailment of individual liberty or of private initiative. Initiative may be exercised and enterprise may be developed in obeying laws and in cooperating with such social controls as are necessary. The effective operation of a public health system, for instance, calls for a high degree of public and professional cooperation, but the observance of such measures as it prescribes or the avoidance of such practices as it prohibits is actually educative. It therefore enhances the freedom of the individual while at the same time adding to his responsibilities. It may also stimulate interest in problems of public health and so prove fruitful in research and discovery. Both employer and employee may cooperate in the application of factory laws imposed by government and which in a sense must necessarily be restrictive. In so far as they are desirable for safety and health, however, they do not really restrict freedom but enlarge it. They also stimulate the search for more effective devices and conditions to secure the ends at which the regulation aims. In these and in many similar cases liberty is enlarged and initiative encouraged by what may seem to be limitations.

In a democracy, therefore, the extension of government functions may also be an extension of self-government. The implied antithesis between government control and individual liberty is unreal. It implies what John Dewey calls "the essential fallacy in the elaborate political and economic theories of freedom entertained by classic Liberalism. They thought of individuals as endowed with an equipment of fixed and ready-made capacities, the operation of which if unobstructed by external restrictions would be freedom, and a freedom which would almost automatically solve political and economic problems."[3] It does not solve political and economic problems; it may sometimes prove a means of

---

[2] The term *planned economy* is used so loosely in current discussion that it is difficult to attach a specific meaning to it. It is sometimes used to mean a complete socialization of the economic system after the Russian pattern, and sometimes to mean merely an extension of governmental control and operation to certain limited areas of economic activity. Between the two extremes there may be wide variations of policy. Obviously, governments will always find it necessary to make plans, and no one would contend that such government plans must never involve changes in the structure of industry and commerce. They must always be judged on their merits and in relation to specific situations.

[3] John Dewey, "Philosophies of Freedom," in H. M. Kallen, ed., *Freedom in the Modern World* (New York: Coward–McCann, 1928), p. 247.

escape from the necessity of facing them! Against the conception of government as a police power we may set a more fruitful conception, that of government as the creator of social values and the active instrument of social welfare.

The fact that obedience and freedom are not incompatible is recognized in spheres where freedom is habitually interpreted in positive terms. Men have achieved and are achieving an enlarged freedom from natural necessity. They win command over nature's powers and resources by obedience to nature's laws. It is in recognizing natural laws that man makes nature and its forces his servants and ministers. Man has achieved in our own day, for instance, a new freedom, the freedom of the air. He now wings his way through vast spaces at incredible speed—something that for long was regarded as a vain dream. Suddenly the dream becomes reality and man's possibilities, both for good and for evil, are enlarged; his activities take on a new range. The boundaries of human activity are pushed back; what were once bonds imposed by nature are now utilized to secure a larger freedom.

The new freedom has been purchased at a price, the price of understanding and obedience. A law of nature has ceased to be a fetter and has been converted into something different by being understood. Certain conditions have been fulfilled, certain principles recognized, and with understanding and obedience has come freedom. The law of gravity remains, but man by adapting himself and his ways to it finds it now not a hindrance, but a condition of achievement. We send our ships through the seas and our planes through the air, not by repudiating laws, but by observing them and obeying them. This is positive freedom.

Every art has its rules, and every human enterprise implies conditions of achievement. The great painter must at first master the technique of painting. More than that is of course necessary in order to achieve greatness as an artist, but that at least is necessary. And once he has mastered the technique of his craft the painter finds a freedom that the amateur or the novice can never know. The principles and rules that were difficult to learn, when learned are difficult no longer. They are the conditions of his mastery over his material and of his ability to express in color and in form the inspirations that come to him. He is free because he knows the principles of the art he practices. He no longer needs to think of them; he observes them unconsciously. They are no longer felt as restraints; they have become means of self-expression. He can now achieve what without knowledge would have been impossible, but implicit in his achievement are the rules that embody the knowledge accumulated in centuries of practice and experience by past masters of his art. He works in accordance with certain laws, but he is not conscious of obeying laws; he is expressing his ideas in the best way possible for him. The extent of his mastery of the technique of his art is the measure of his freedom, although not necessarily of his greatness.

The freedom of the scientist and the artist illustrates admirably what is meant by positive freedom—the freedom to do, the freedom to achieve. It is not suggested, of course, that the laws of nature or even the laws of any particular art are similar in kind to the laws of the state. The laws of nature are statements of observed uniformities, and there is never any question as to whether they are good or bad. They are what they are. The laws of the state are positive enactments and they may be good or bad, from the point of view both of policy or of moral principle. They are made, and therefore subject to the imperfection that pertains to everything of man's making.

The laws and principles of a particular art approximate more closely to the laws of the state. They are the crystallized rules of practice, a real deposit of the experience of those who have mastered the art. They are statements of conditions that artists have found should be observed if certain desired effects are to be produced. They may be modified or discarded, enlarged or improved as experience grows and as experiment tests them. The laws of the state too, in a democratic nation are the deposits of experience. They are subject to change and to modification. Some that were regarded as good may be found to be bad; some put to the test in social experiment may be found unsatisfactory and must be discarded. In general, laws in a democratic country are the formulated rules for the achievement of social welfare. They need not be conceived merely in terms of prohibitions. As necessity arises they may be made for definite constructive ends.

The laws of the state must sometimes be used for the purposes of necessary restraint, for there are always some in any community who need restraint. But the great majority do not need the restraints of law, nor are they conscious of the laws as restraints. The average citizen never thinks of doing the things the law forbids. But government has other functions besides those of formulating prohibitions and providing penalties for their infringement. Liberty is the ability to do what we ought to do— not merely the abstract possibility of doing it, but the ability to do it. Surely it is one of the major functions of government to provide for its citizens the conditions that will secure for them the greatest measure of opportunity for doing the things that are worth doing. It must also help to create in its citizens the will and the ability to do them. Its real function is to provide both the conditions and the incentives that will stimulate its citizens to do and become the best that is in them. Its final justification is to be found in the development and enrichment of personality in which freedom is realized. "The peculiar quality of Athenian Liberty," it has been said, "is that it was productive." The Athenians were free in relation to the art of life somewhat as the painter is free in relation to his painting. Freedom is a kind of mastery. Government cannot grant it to citizens or create it for them, but it can create the conditions that are conducive to its development. This is in fact its supreme function.

It is this freedom that the discoveries of the eighteenth and nineteenth centuries seemed to promise. The optimistic philosophers of the Industrial Revolution believed that the machine would do for England what slave labor had done for the fortunate citizens of ancient Athens. The age of steam, and later of electrical energy, was to prepare the way for a new age of enlightenment. Freedom from drudgery, from too arduous toil, was to become the common heritage of men and women, and leisure beyond anything that human society had known before would be brought within the reach of the many. That men would know what to do with this leisure and would devote themselves to the pursuit of the higher interests of life was an assumption inherent in these philosophers' rather easygoing optimism. A world freed from the bonds of harsh, economic necessity was the dream they cherished. It did them credit, for this would have been real freedom. The dream has so far proved an illusion, but it was not as foolish as it may seem to us now. The discoveries and inventions of the age of science *did* result in an enormous increase of power and an unparalleled increase of wealth. The industrial order of the nineteenth century was amazingly efficient; the machine in its myriad forms enhanced the productivity of man's labor a hundredfold and more. From this point of view the Industrial Revolution ushered in an age of abundance and of continually repeated miracle. All that was necessary was to give free play to the forces that had been unleashed and to the men who now directed them!

During the latter half of the nineteenth century disillusion had already set in. It found expression in the rhetoric of a Ruskin or in the irony of a Samuel Butler. The machine was no willing slave that could be depended on to remain in subjection, but a power that threatened a new slavery. Men were not freed from drudgery and from sordid and degrading labor in the enervating routine of the new machine industry. The privations of the landless laborer had been no worse than the dreariness of the factories and mines into which the laborers flocked, and the squalor of homes under the old domestic system was hardly worse than the degradation of city slums. While some men spoke of the new freedom, others spoke even more vehemently of the new slavery. It was not entirely fantastic to suggest, as Capek did in his play *R.U.R.*, that the logical outcome of the transformation might be, not man with the "light of freedom in his eyes," but the robot with the threat of destruction in his brute strength.

Freedom must mean opportunity and capacity—the opportunity to live, to appreciate what is best in literature and art and music, what is beautiful in nature, what is true in the agelong quest of the human mind. But before it can mean any of these things it must provide the conditions that will enable men to live. Whatever interpretation we place on human rights, we may assume at least that the right that conditions all others is the right to life. And so far, in spite of our scientific and technological advances, we have not really established that right securely. As long as great multitudes live on or below the level of bare subsistence it is clear that there are vast areas in which the first condition of real freedom has not been achieved. It is still true—and this is a fact that condemns us—that in advanced industrial countries, England for example, more than one fourth of the population live in either "primary poverty" (conditions that do not provide adequate means for healthful subsistence even with the most economical living and the most efficient management) or "secondary poverty" (conditions under which any improvidence, accident, sickness, or unusual expenditure will reduce them into the condition of primary poverty). It would seem that the optimistic liberalism of the nineteenth century was unfounded even in those areas where it seemed to be most justified. The new industry did not produce "plenty," even though it did produce abundantly! This is the baffling paradox of our era. While depressions recur and want continues, it will be true that productive capacity, scientific advances, and technological triumphs all fall short of achieving freedom in the most elementary interpretation of that term.

And beyond this lie those higher reaches of human experience, the appreciation of what is fine and true and good in life, in nature, and in art—the freedom of the spirit, which is man's highest good. This liberty may be destroyed by censorship or it may be limited by unjust restrictions of various kinds. These, however, are not the most serious threats to the freedom of the mind that men have desired and for which they have fought. There is no ban on Shakespeare, for example; everyone is *free* to read him. But they are not really. For, to take the most extreme case, the man who has not the money with which to purchase a copy of Shakespeare's works or does not have access to a copy is not possessed of that freedom. And in spite of public libraries, a cheap press, and a vast improvement of facilities of all kinds, this extreme case is not inconceivable. It illustrates a point that has much greater significance than this case in itself would suggest. For every individual who is not free because he is denied physical access to Shakespeare's works, there are hundreds who are not free because the conditions of their lives do not give them time and leisure to read them or because they have not the ability to read them. For these, of what use is the negative freedom that is secured by absence of censorship? And there are many hundreds more who have not been given either the incentive to read him or the education that would enable them to understand and appreciate what he has to say. This is a freedom they do not possess and do not know!

The restrictions on human freedom that are most to be feared today are those that curb and limit opportunity. It is not government that needs most restraint today in order that the individual may be free, but the gigantic forces that have been set in motion by the processes of our vast industrial order. The most dangerous denials of liberty are those inherent in the cramped conditions and the harsh necessities that limit choice, circumscribe action, and stunt the growth of the spirit of man. "The notion that men are equally free to act if only the same legal arrangements apply equally to all—irrespective of differences in education, in command of capital, and that control of the social environment which is furnished by the institution of property—is a pure absurdity, as facts have demonstrated."[4]

It was as an instrument for the furtherance and the achievement of this positive freedom that government was suspect in nineteenth-century liberalism. Not only was its effectiveness

---

[4] Dewey in Kallen, *Freedom in the Modern World*, p. 249.

for this purpose doubted, but its right to assume this function was frequently denied. What was not realized was that the direct threats to freedom in our modern world have not come and do not come from governments; they come from those concentrations of power that are even less amenable to restraints than governments, that are not easily controlled by governments, and that may overthrow governments. In this modern world governments need to be strong, for it is a world of giant forces. Perhaps the outstanding problem of our era is to make sure that government shall be strong enough to control the concentrations of power that are a threat to the freedom of its people, and at the same time to make sure that a strong government shall use its strength reasonably and wisely. This assurance can be given and maintained only by a public opinion that is vigilant, enlightened, and wise. A strong government is to be feared only when it ceases to be responsive to public opinion. But what if public opinion is confused, distorted by considerations of selfish interest, and torn and divided by those interests? There, not in the extension of positive governmental functions, lies the supreme danger to human freedom.

Liberty is still an ideal. It beckons us from afar. Our vision of it is clouded by the rising dust of what we must hope is humanity's forward march, and we catch only glimpses of it. But something is gained if we feel the attraction of what we see and strive faithfully to understand what liberty means and what service it demands of those who seek it.

CHAPTER 8. Equality

"WE HOLD these truths to be self-evident,—that all men are created equal; that they are endowed by their Creator with certain unalienable rights; that among these are life, liberty, and the pursuit of happiness." So runs the familiar declaration that has been primarily responsible, not indeed for the formulation of the idea of equality, but for its popular acceptance as essential to the conception and practice of democracy. The words of the Declaration of Independence have become the symbols and watchwords of the democratic faith for vast multitudes who know little of the circumstances of their origin and less about the struggles that had raged around the concepts they embodied. The most debatable of these concepts and the most frequently challenged is that of equality.

As important in the development of the democratic tradition as the Declaration of Independence are the "Principles of '89," the declaration of faith that may be said to have been the marching orders of the French Revolution. The Declaration of the Rights of Man and of the Citizen of 1789 is, however, more measured in statement and more qualified in its assertion of the principle of equality. "Men are born and always continue free and equal *in respect of their rights*. Civil distinctions, therefore, can be founded only on public utility." In the later statements prefixed to the constitutions of 1793 and 1795, equality is given its place with the other "natural and unprescriptible rights," which are there stated as "Equality, Liberty, Security, Property." Thus the formula remained until the Constitution of 1848, where it became the familiar "Liberty, Equality, Fraternity."

These formulations in great historic documents of the principle of "a right to equality" reflect both a popular sentiment and an article of belief that go far back into the history of the past. Deep in the human spirit, manifest especially in the great religions, there seems to have been a feeling of revolt against the inequalities that existed in human society. It breathes, for instance, in the impassioned invective and the fiery denunciations of the great Hebrew prophets, and it finds even more definite expression in Christianity, which declares that in the eyes of God there is neither Greek nor barbarian, Jew nor Gentile, bond nor free; all are one. Where all are the children of the one Father, the distinctions that create inequality are difficult to accept and still more difficult to justify. In most of, if not all, the great religions thought is colored by some such sentiment and, generally, doctrine embodies that sentiment more or less definitely.

The sentiment finds expression, too, and on occasion not merely in words, in those movements of revolt in past ages in which men have been stirred to anger and indignation by the miseries of their lot, in contrast to the privileges of those who lorded it over them. It is implied, for instance, in the homely and familiar couplet that crystallizes the sense of inequality, as well as the resentment against it, felt by generations of men and women:

> When Adam delved and Eve span,
> Who was then the gentleman?

"The dream of John Ball," as William Morris interprets it, is that of a human society of equals. The inspiration of the Puritan Revolution was derived from many sources, but it is not without significance that one of the influential and forceful elements in the revolutionary movement adopted the name of the "Levellers," a name that carried with it an implicit protest against some of the more flagrant inequalities of the time. It is true that the Levellers were not as equalitarian as their name would suggest, but we find in them the same objection to privilege and its consequences that we find in most of the revolutionary movements of early times. Men at different times have rebelled against many things—hunger, misery, want—but what has given edge to their discontents and passion to their protests has been the apparent injustice that separated the fortunate few from the unfortunate many. The dynamic force in popular movements has been generally, if not always, resentment against the flagrant inequalities that have existed among men.

IN THE THOUGHT OF GREECE AND ROME

It is, however, not only as sentiment that the opposition to inequality has existed. In the tradition of Western civilization since the days of Rome there has been present a clear recognition of equality as an ideal. The interpretation of that ideal and still more its practical application have not been clear, nor have they always been consistent. But the significant thing is the persistence in Western thought of the concept of human equality, however it may be interpreted and however inadequate its practical application.

The idea is formulated in clear terms in the political thought of Rome, originating with the Stoics and transmitted by them to the great Roman lawyers, who incorporated it as a principle in their legal system. The idea is based upon a conception of the essential character, the uniqueness, of man as distinct from all other creatures. Man is a reasonable being and reason is his peculiar distinction. However much men differ from one another, they have at least one thing in common without which they would not be what they are; they are possessed of reason. There is only one ultimate definition of man: he is a rational being. And this one fundamental and common characteristic, which goes deeper and is more important and real than any differences that may exist among men, constitutes a principle of equality. For since men are rational they share a common life. Mankind is a family, within which there may be vast differences and innumerable variations of custom, talent, knowledge, and condition, but which is held together by the bond of reason. Cicero states the doctrine clearly: Man is the highest of created things; through the possession of reason he is distinct from all other creatures and like the Creator. By virtue of the divine element in human nature man participates in the ultimate principles of right and justice. Furthermore, all men possess by nature a consciousness of these principles, because all men are alike rational. "To whomsoever reason is given by nature so also is right reason, and therefore also the true law."

There is, then, according to Cicero and the Stoics no resemblance so great as the resemblance between man and man, and no principle of relationship so deep as that of reason. There is something in human nature so distinctive as to constitute a principle of equality. Men have more in common with one another than they have in distinction. "There is, in fact," Cicero declares, "a true law—namely right reason—which is in accordance with Nature, applies to all men and is unchangeable and eternal." In the light of this universal law all men are equal. Cicero here reflects the trend of men's thinking in the years that preceded the Christian era and makes clear that in this matter Rome had traveled far from Hellas. It seems a far cry from Aristotle and the twilight of Greek democracy to the characteristic ideas of the Stoics. It is a change, as Professor Carlyle puts it, "startling in its completeness."[1] The conception of a world community was dawning or had already dawned. It stood in marked contrast to that cherished ideal of the city-state that had absorbed the attention of Plato

---

[1] See Carlyle, *Mediaeval Political Theory*, pp. 6–9; and Sabine, *History of Political Theory*, pp. 163–65.

and Aristotle. Neither of them had thought of this "community of man" which now became the substance of dreams, and even something more than that. By contrast there seems to be a certain provincialism in the speculations that centered upon "that highest form of human community," the city-state. An old world had passed away; a new one had struggled to birth.

Nowhere is the transition so marked and the difference so pronounced as in relation to this fundamental conception of human nature. Firmly imbedded in Greek thought was the idea of essential and vital differences within humanity. The idea of a world community in however vague a sense would have been alien to the temper of Greek thought. Men were by nature essentially different and therefore unequal. Differences of race were not obscured, and certainly not transcended, by any essential similarity or sense of a wider community. There were Greeks and barbarians, and the essential inequality between them was assumed. If it was not always asserted, it was because there was no purpose in asserting the obvious. But, as a matter of fact, it *was* frequently asserted. There was a virtue natural to the Greek to which others might aspire but which they could not attain. It was not to be expected that others should live and act as Greeks lived in Athens, or as they had acted at Marathon and Thermopylae and in many another crisis of their fate. To the Greek the world was made up of "ourselves and others"—ourselves capable of greatest achievement and highest virtue; others outside the charmed circle, admirable no doubt in many ways, but apparently destined for a lower plane of existence. This was natural!

The social order of the Greek city-state reflected in characteristic fashion this fundamental conception of differences within the world of human beings. The institution of slavery was taken for granted as being in the nature of things; the citizen was made of different clay from that of the slave. Aristotle was not running counter to the accepted opinion of his day, and certainly not to that of the earlier days of the golden age of Pericles, when he frankly defended the institution of slavery on the ground that it was natural. Men were by nature different, and unequal. Some were fitted for subjection, others were capable of citizenship; some were born to be slaves, others were born to be masters. The slave was made for obedience and benefited by it; the master was made for rule and therefore exercised it. It was not government that drew the line of demarcation but nature—or government drew it because nature had drawn it first. There were, then, certain vital and natural differences running through humanity that constituted basic inequalities among men. The fact that the slave might win his freedom was one of those inconsistencies that hardly seemed to qualify, and certainly did not invalidate, the general principle.

This belief in vital inequality does not seem so strange if we remember the conditions that seemed to justify it and gave it a certain plausibility in ancient Greece. Greek culture was distinctive and Greek genius was pre-eminent. Greek civilization was a bright light burning in the darkness of what was in the main a barbaric world. The contrast was decisive, and the Greek, or at least the Athenian, had some excuse for thinking that his culture was a thing apart, that his civilization was the expression of a spirit and a genius that others did not and could not share. "Greek and barbarian" is a phrase that did not seem so utterly strange under these conditions as it does to us today.

With the rise and triumph of Macedonia, however, this unique situation disappeared, never to return. Alexander was a great soldier but not a superman in any interpretation of the term that would have satisfied a Greek, and his conquering hordes, whatever their other qualities may have been, were certainly not the conscious bearers of a new civilization. The world in which the city-state had flourished no longer existed. A new world was in the making, a world in which for a long time to come ruthless might and power would determine the course of empire and the fate of peoples. It is strange that Aristotle, living in this age of transition and in close contact with the forces that were responsible for the change, should have been so oblivious to the significance of what was happening.

It was not only the city-state that was passing; the mode of thought appropriate to it was passing too. When out of the chaos of the ages of disintegration the Roman Empire emerged and established its far-flung dominion, conditions had been revolutionized. In particular the old Greek exclusiveness was gone, and the old assertion of superiority and uniqueness could no longer be made with any seriousness. The words of praise which seemed so fitting as Pericles applied them to Athens in his Funeral Oration would have sounded extravagant and unconvincing if applied to Rome. The Roman by virtue of the conditions of his world had to be a cosmopolitan. The culture of Rome was a borrowed culture. The art of Rome was Greek art transplanted into a new environment. The Roman had his qualities, but they were not qualities that suggested a unique virtue. There was neither justification nor excuse for thinking that others could not participate in it. Others did share in it, and to bring them to an appreciation of it was one of the necessities of an expanding empire. Roman colonization had perforce to make this assumption, and it is proof of Rome's greatness that it proceeded to demonstrate the validity of the assumption in its colonial policy. Roman thought and policy were inevitably inclusive, where the Greeks had been exclusive.

A philosophy that assumed deep divisions within humanity, the assumption inherent in Greek thought, was inappropriate to these new conditions. A world order necessitated a world outlook, and a republic expanding into an empire could not accommodate itself to the concepts of the city-state. Those who realized the significance of the change even dimly began to speak, as they were impelled to do, in terms of humanity. The old walls of partition had crumbled and fallen. Men were citizens of Rome, but by virtue of their rational nature they were citizens of the world. Rome was not a rare or unique example; it was the bearer of tangible and precious blessings which others could and did appreciate, and in which others could be brought to participate. Rome could further the spread of order and justice and fairness among men, for in all men there was implanted both the desire and the capacity for these inestimable boons. Rome could lead only because there was in all men a natural desire for order and security and fair dealing. Men by nature were equal—not separate but, since all men had reason, united in a common destiny, fitted for a common life, and governed by universal principles. They could be expected to become, or at least could be expected to regard themselves as, members of the great human family, in which differences were merged in the common possession of a kindred nature whose law was reason.

These are the conditions that were favorable to the development and spread of the characteristic ideas of Stoicism. Men were citizens of the world, even though they were citizens of some particular city; and men were brothers, although the content of brotherhood in this connection was left exceedingly vague. At least it came to be the fashion to stress the essential sameness of men, rather than their differences, what all men had in common, rather than the distinctions among them. Men, so the Stoic insisted, were more like one another than they were different from one another. Despite all the varieties of creed, language, custom, or race, humanity was one. To be a man was a fact of greater significance than to be a Roman even. All men are by nature free and equal. "We all have the same beginnings, the same origin, no one is in truth nobler than another, except so far as his temper is more upright, his capacities better developed."[2] The fact of humanity implies a basic equality.

It is clear, of course, that all this constituted a challenge to the earlier tradition of the Greek city-state, as it did also to the traditions of that ancient world in general. It also involved a challenge to certain institutions and customs that were deeply entrenched in the social order, which was the heritage of that ancient world. It was, for instance, not only a denial of the racial exclusiveness of that ancient world; it seemed also to be incompatible with the generally accepted institution of slavery. This incompatibility was felt, although it did not result in any serious agitation for the abolition of slavery in the Roman Empire. The fact remains, however, that slavery was definitely on the defensive once the Stoic principles had been formulated and had gained a measure of general acceptance. Its existence had to be rationalized, as indeed it was by both Stoic and Christian. Slavery, so the argument ran, was a fact of merely external condition; it did not destroy freedom, which was independent of circumstances and conditions. The slave, in his subjection, could yet achieve a freedom that might be the envy of many a free man. There were no chains that could fetter the human spirit. Man remained man and a brother in whatever state he might happen to be placed.

It is not necessary to discuss here whether or not this rationalization was convincing even from the point of view of the Stoic; the important fact is that it constitutes a defense of slavery that was felt to be needed. It was a salve for a conscience that was beginning to need one. The old argument of Aristotle, that of a natural inequality, was no longer tenable.

The Stoic philosophy influenced the teaching of the early Christian church and was in turn influenced by Christian ideas. Paul, for instance, shows clearly some of the marks of this influence in his sweeping condemnation of racial exclusiveness. And his teaching in turn gave direction and character to the teaching of the church fathers, who became increasingly influential in the Roman Empire. Here too the Christian assertion that all men are children of the one Father and therefore brothers contained or implied a doctrine of equality that could easily be interpreted in terms con-

[2] Sabine, *History of Political Theory*, p. 21.

genial to the Stoic point of view. Paul too knew of a law of nature, as his Letter to the Romans makes clear. Like the Stoics, moreover, the church applied the principle, not to challenge and overthrow those institutions that were incongruous with it, but to ameliorate the conditions that existed within them. Paul could write to the owner of slaves urging him to receive Onesimus as "a brother beloved." Apparently it did not occur to him to suggest to Philemon that his Christian profession required him to do more than this. Onesimus, though a brother, would still be an obedient slave! Nevertheless, the teachings of the church gave plausibility to, and greatly reinforced, the Stoic idea of human equality. The "slaves of Caesar's household" could become members of the Christian fraternity while remaining in their condition of servitude. In that fraternity at least they were brothers and therefore equals.

LATER DEVELOPMENT OF THE PRINCIPLE

The idea of equality lived on. It is true that in neither church nor state in the Middle Ages was there any great practical recognition of the principle. The feudal system was based essentially on a principle of inequality, and serfdom was almost as incompatible with the idea of equality as was slavery. The authoritarian character which developed in the church, with its hierarchical system of orders, could hardly be regarded as an expression of any real equality. Neither the Holy Roman Empire nor the Holy Roman Church troubled itself overmuch with the obvious inequalities that existed both in the social order and in the church. And yet the idea of equality, although dormant, was not dead. The leaven both of Stoic philosophy and of Christian teaching continued obscurely to ferment, without, however, producing spectacular results. In the thought of the church particularly, and in some measure in its practice, the principle continued to be recognized, even though it was interpreted in a way that often left it little potency. "From Christianity was derived the idea of the fundamental equality of all men, and a regard for human individuality, which slowly transformed slavery into serfdom, and insisted, within the organization of the Church, on the invalidity of distinctions based on birth or class."[3]

The Protestant Reformation was essentially a revolt against authority, but it was also a revolt against privilege and inequality. In spite of the apparent antithesis between reason and faith in-

[3] A. F. Hattersley, *Short History of Democracy* (New York: Cambridge University Press, 1930), p. 76.

herent in the logic of Reformation doctrine, stress was laid on individual judgment, so that almost in spite of the reformers it assumed the rationality of man and declared the supremacy of conscience. The inner voice, not external authority, was the supreme guide in human decisions. When this was interpreted in terms of theology and church doctrine, it issued in the declaration of the real priesthood of all believers. This in itself was not quite a doctrine of human equality, since the equality it asserted was that of *all believers*—a limitation reminiscent of Wycliffe's earlier doctrine of Lordship. The assertion that "Every one in a state of grace has real lordship over the whole universe" implies that among those in "a state of grace" there could be no recognition of any essential inequality.

Nevertheless, there can be no doubt of the equalitarian corollaries of the doctrine of the priesthood of all believers. Nor can there be any doubt as to the deductions that were drawn from it in the course of time by some of the most influential religious leaders in the sixteenth and seventeenth centuries, who argued: "If all mankind were the sons of Adam, and if all might become by adoption the sons of God, distinctions of birth, and wealth, and power seemed a mere human invention."[4] The seeds of democratic tendencies found this sentiment a congenial and fruitful soil. It was here that the doctrine of equality received the nurture necessary for its growth and the characteristic form it was to assume more definitely in the eighteenth century. Equality now came to be regarded definitely as a natural right and soon received its appropriate philosophical interpretation in the political theories of the seventeenth and eighteenth centuries in England and in France.

It is a curious fact that this equality should receive its most realistic interpretation from one who is generally regarded as the least democratic of modern political theorists. Thomas Hobbes does not assert natural equality as a right but as a fact.

Nature hath made men so equal in the faculties of body and mind, as that, though there be found one man sometimes manifestly stronger in body, or of quicker mind than another, yet when all is reckoned together the difference between man and man is not so considerable, as that one man can thereupon claim to himself any benefit to which another may not pretend as well as he. For as to the strength of body, the weakest has strength enough to kill the strongest, either by secret machination, or by confederacy with others that are in the same

[4] Ritchie, *Natural Rights*, p. 8.

danger with himself. And as to the faculties of mind . . . I find a yet greater equality amongst men than that of strength.[5]

It is true that few perceive this equality, but that is merely because man's natural conceit blinds him to the truth and makes him incapable of seeing in others the qualities and excellencies which he would recognize only too readily in himself. In any case, so Hobbes declared, he has never found anyone who would willingly exchange his identity for that of some other!

We need not take this point of view too seriously, for although there may be some element of truth in it, Hobbes has found very few followers in it. What is significant is that he is here reflecting the temper of his time and is also stating, in exaggerated and extreme form, the belief in equality that was becoming prevalent.

More characteristic of this trend of thought is John Locke, who revives the ancient Stoic doctrine and expresses it anew in his characteristic fashion. Men in a state of nature are equal. They are born to the same advantages, they possess and use the same faculties, "they are equal one amongst another without subordination or subjection." This is the basis that makes possible the contract upon which society in the first place and government in the second are built. The civil state is an association of men who are free and equal. "Men being, as has been said, by nature all free, equal and independent, no one can be put out of this estate and subjected to the political power of another without his own consent."[6] The establishment of government does not abrogate or destroy this natural equality; it merely qualifies it for a specific purpose. Equality may be reasserted in practice at any time if the purpose is not being achieved by the instrumentalities created by the contract into which men have entered. Men do not and cannot renounce the right of equality, although they may limit its full expression for definite ends they may think desirable.

The emphatic assertions of the American Declaration of Independence are foreshadowed in the quieter and more measured pronouncements of the philosophers. Its ideas as well as its language can be appreciated in the light of the philosophy of the times. The Declaration echoes the philosophical battle cries of the eighteenth century, but it was no philosophical battle that the framers of the Declaration had in mind. They were determined to take those battle cries from the cloister and the study into the streets, from the world of speculation into the world of action.

---
[5] Hobbes, *Leviathan*, Chapter 13.
[6] John Locke, *Two Treatises of Government* (New York: Appleton Century, 1937), p. 63.

The ideas once used by Locke to justify a revolution could now be used to make and justify another and different revolution. The Declaration of Independence owes something to Rousseau and still more to Locke, but the fact remains that its ideas are inherent in the political thought of the Western world, and are a part of that tradition which goes back much farther than the Revolution of 1688 or even the Protestant Reformation. And this is as true of its positive assertion that all men are created equal as it is of the declaration of "unalienable rights."

THE REAL MEANING OF EQUALITY

Quite as important as the declaration of equality is its interpretation. What does equality really mean? To answer this question is less simple than to trace the history of the idea, for here there has been confusion and misunderstanding even beyond what may be expected in relation to most abstract ideas. Obvious as it seems, it is nevertheless necessary to insist that to say that all men are equal is not to say that all men are similar. Never in the long history of the doctrine has equality been interpreted in this sense by any responsible advocate of it. All men are not alike, nor are all men equal in physical, mental, or any other capacity. Few indeed have taken seriously Hobbes' assertion of positive equality. The objection to the doctrine of equality based on the contention "that anyhow men are not equal" misses the point. Everyone will admit that there are natural inequalities—physical, mental, and others—to be found in any community or in any chance group of human beings. The essential idea that has been enshrined in the doctrine of equality throughout its history, from the age of the Stoics to our own time, is that there is a similarity or a kinship which is more vital than all differences. Man is a being unique in nature, "bearing the stamp of the King of Kings." Nothing is so important about men as the fact that they are men; nothing so significant as the fact that they are rational beings. It is not that they are all alike but that they are all alike in the possession of a unique quality, the differentia that makes them men.

We may go farther and say that a true doctrine of equality is actually based on the recognition of dissimilarity, or to put it in more familiar terms, of individuality. It is individuality that gives significance to the idea of equality. The differences that exist among men make possible the cooperation of many men in a common purpose. Individuality is the necessary condition of social life. Where each person is distinct and different, each may be necessary and no one is redundant. And where all are necessary, although necessary in a different way, the question of degree, of more necessary or less, becomes in a sense irrelevant. Claims of superiority cease to have any real significance. We come back to the basic assertion that each human personality is unique, has a distinctive function and destiny, is in some way necessary to the life of the whole. It is the fact of individuality that makes men necessary to one another, and, as Plato suggests in his *Republic*, this is why society comes into being and continues to exist. The principle of the division of labor in economics has its counterpart in the principle of differentiation of function in social ethics.

If this is so, then the consideration of supreme importance is that each individual be true to himself, exert himself to the full, and contribute to the whole the particular service that he is fitted to render. Such services may not be equal when weighed in the balances of the economist, but here it is not the judgment of the economist that counts, for we are dealing not with material, but with social, values. All that society has a right to demand of any individual is that he live up to his capacity, that he do all he is capable of doing, and that he be the best he can be. Where this is recognized, who is capable of measuring or of evaluating the contribution that is made? And to what criterion of judgment should appeal be made? What are the absolutes that determine worth? "Democracy as an idea is therefore a society not of similar persons but of equals, in the sense that each is an integral and irreplaceable part of the whole. For although the contribution of each is not equal in value, each one who contributes is equally a source from which the common life is drawn."[7]

We can come back once more to the familiar analogy, which is perhaps the last word on this question, the analogy of the living organism.

For the body is not one member but many. If the foot shall say, Because I am not the hand, I am not of the body; is it therefore not of the body? And if the ear shall say, Because I am not the eye, I am not of the body; is it therefore not of the body? If the whole body were an eye, where were the hearing? if the whole were hearing, where were the smelling? But now hath God set the members every one of them in the body, as it hath pleased him. And if they were all one member, where were the body? But now are they many members, yet but one body. And the eye cannot say unto the hand, I have no need of thee; nor again the head to the feet, I have no need of you.[8]

[7] Burns, *Political Ideals*, p. 278.
[8] First Corinthians 12:14-21.

Differences of function in the body politic or in the social organism are not grounds of superiority and do not in themselves constitute claims to special privilege. If all are necessary and all fulfill an essential function, then that is all that need be said. The common life of all is dependent upon each.

There are, then, all sorts of differences within humanity, but human beings have a common life, a common purpose, and a common destiny. God is no respecter of persons. There is beneath all differences something deeper, something that constitutes our common humanity; it is what the Stoic called reason, what the Christian may call the divine image. There is a passage in Wordsworth's "The Prelude" which Canon Masterman calls "the marching song of modern democracy."[9]

> Alas, what differs more than man from man?
> And whence that difference? Whence, but from himself?
> For see the universal race endowed
> With the same upright form. The sun is fixed
> And the infinite magnificence of heaven,
> Fixed, within reach of every human eye,
> The sleepless ocean murmurs for all ears,
> The vernal field diffuses its delight
> Into all hearts.
>
> Gifts nobler are vouchsafed alike to all,
> Reason, and with that reason smiles and tears,
> Imagination, freedom in the will;
> Conscience to guide and check; and death to be
> Forecasted, immortality conceived
> By all.
>
> The primal duties shine aloft—like stars,
> The charities that soothe and heal and bless,
> Are scattered at the feet of Man—like flowers.
> The generous inclination, the just will,
> Kind wishes and good actions and pure thoughts;
> No mystery is here—here is no boon
> For high—yet not for low; for proudly graced—
> Yet not for meek of heart. The smoke ascends
> To heaven as lightly from the cottage hearth
> As from the haughtiest palace. He whose soul
> Ponders this true equality, may walk
> The fields of earth with gratitude and hope.

This is the equality of the Stoic and of the Christian. It is also the equality that democracy asserts.

[9] *Parliament and the People*, p. 54.

EQUALITY OF OPPORTUNITY

There remains one important question that must now be faced and if possible answered. The recognition of the bare principle of equality does not carry us very far; what is its practical significance? Or, what does the application of the principle demand in the form of social and political obligation? There are, it is admitted, natural differences among men; these differences are *inequalities* of a kind. How can we distinguish these natural differences from those developed or imposed by conditions of status or privilege, those differences which are a denial of *essential* equality? The question is not easy to state nor is it easy to answer.

However, some general principles may be suggested here that will receive fuller consideration later. Natural differences among men result in differences of function, fit them for different tasks, justify different conditions of living; but these differences must not be regarded as rewards for native ability as such. Nor must differences of condition be created merely as recognition of particular talents. Native ability in itself deserves no reward, and the possession of a particular talent merits no special recompense. It is difficult enough to establish a real correlation between the values represented by services rendered to society and the monetary recompense given for those services. It is still more difficult to see any correlation between the exercise of a rare skill or ability and the material recompense for it. In our present order of society it is the custom to reward, with monetary recognition, those who possess rare gifts. Is it possible to find any rational or moral justification for this custom? There is no virtue in possessing a rare talent or an unusual aptitude. Natural endowment is the gift of the gods. Why then should it justify the preferential treatment of those who may happen to have been particularly favored? There is no basis and no justification for the marked discriminations that are made.

This, of course, does not dispose of the question as to whether inequalities of wealth or income are compatible with essential equality. Moreover, it does not eliminate all the consequences of variations in native or original talent. The existence of rare ability creates special conditions. It is important, for instance, that special abilities be developed to the utmost and utilized to the full. How is this to be assured? What is involved here is not a question of individual claim or advantage but rather of social interest and advantage. Talent must not be lost; it must be cultivated. In order to make sure that it is trained, and used when trained, it is necessary to provide facilities for the training and perhaps to provide incentives to secure its fullest use. The incentives should be sufficient to achieve their purpose, and they must be justified by the social significance of that purpose.

The nature of the appropriate incentives that would be justified cannot be determined in the abstract; it must be decided in view of concrete situations. In a society where great importance is attached to conditions of material comfort or to those advantages secured by wealth, inducement will have to conform to that general condition and will be determined by the dominant social temper. Where public spirit is highly developed, material inducements will be less necessary or may hardly be necessary at all. It is obvious also that the need for these material incentives will vary greatly even within a given society in the case of particular individuals or groups. Fortunately, in any community there will be many who will do their utmost and give of their best without thought of reward and without the stimulus of personal gain. Unfortunately they are not numerous enough to enable us to base a general policy upon the fact of their existence.

In an ideal society no doubt the claims of public service and a consciousness of the obligations imposed by consideration for the common good would be sufficient incentives. But to discuss the question in terms of the ideal society is unreal and profitless. The men and women who compose human societies as we know them are far from the attainment of complete altruism. In the actual world of today it is necessary to provide sufficient inducements to people of average standards to do the best they can with the powers and abilities with which nature has endowed them. That these incentives will, necessarily, involve material inducements in a world like ours can hardly be open to question. Even in Russia, in spite of its communist professions and the principle of the Marxist creed—"to each according to his need and from each according to his ability"—the necessity for tangible incentives has proved irresistible. The practical question is what incentives are necessary to produce the desired results. That they will vary greatly both in nature and in extent in different social orders, as well as in relation to different abilities, is a safe assumption.

The problem, therefore, becomes one of social expediency. It still involves moral issues, but the judgment of the moralist must now be qualified by that of the economist, the sociologist, and the practical politician. The solution of the problem is found in the kind of compromise that an imperfect world so often imposes upon us. It is still necessary to insist that inequality in income or in possessions may be justified only if such inequality can be shown to be in the public interest; it must be shown to be socially necessary.

This certainly does not imply any justification of the actual inequalities that prevail in existing society. Later in our discussion we shall return to the point that many existing inequalities in even the advanced democratic countries do not serve any social purpose. Frequently they are both in character and in extent a positive frustration of social purpose and a hindrance to the general welfare. Even the principle "to each according to his ability," which we have already considered unsatisfactory, would be a considerable advance upon the actual practice of the world today. "To each in such measure as is necessary to secure from each the utmost in endeavor, in effectiveness, and in the utilization of his ability and capacity," would represent an approximation to the principle that a sound doctrine of equality implies, and the general acceptance of this principle would certainly mark a vast improvement on the recognized practice of our day. Are the very high salaries of many business executives justified on the basis either of ability or of public advantage? Is it possible to justify the enormous incomes of the stars of the screen or of the playing field? The point that must be emphasized continually is that the good of society, the furtherance of public interest, is the only consideration that should serve as the criterion of judgment in attempting to answer these and similar questions. Inequalities of income in a democratic society must always be kept under critical scrutiny. They should not go beyond what is socially beneficial.

Not only does the necessity for adequate incentives justify certain kinds of inequality, but the material and cultural conditions of life appropriate to certain kinds of activity and to certain types of employment are inappropriate to others. In this connection also, hard and fast rules cannot be established. But it is obvious that the development and practice of highly specialized skills will demand conditions that cannot be secured for all, and which perhaps it would not be desirable to try to obtain for all. That the physician or surgeon should enter upon his profession in his middle twenties or later may be very desirable and socially justifiable, for a long and arduous training is one of the conditions of efficiency. Obviously this does not apply to the occupations of the great majority of people. The life of the creative artist cannot be governed by the same rules or pursued under the same conditions as that of other workers. Inspiration is not governed by the clock, and an eight-hour day or a one-hour day will not suit his requirements. He will work how and when he can.

These may be extreme examples but they serve to illustrate the point that just as equality does not necessarily mean equality of material reward, so also it does not necessarily mean equality or similarity of condition. Social equality is a flexible concept that must provide for the infinite variety of human nature and the infinite demands of distinctive functions. Some will need more leisure than others, some will need more creature comforts than others, some will need more flexible conditions of work than others, and some will require longer training and the economic maintenance that makes this possible. What is important is the clear recognition that all this is not a matter of favor, not a matter of reward, but a matter of public policy directed to the general good. A strict application of the principle of equality does not preclude such differences; it does not seek to obliterate justifiable distinctions. It condemns *some* distinctions because they obscure and nullify those that really matter and that deserve recognition. It insists that distinctions must be socially beneficial if they are to receive social approval.

More than this, it implies a value-judgment on such distinctions as are made. Perhaps the simplest way to express this point is to say that the principle of equality asserts the significance of natural differences and denies the significance of artificial distinctions. *Natural* and *artificial* are ambiguous terms, of course, and yet the distinction they imply is not without meaning. Differences of character, for example, are more significant than differences of wealth, and a difference of intelligence has a higher degree of significance than a difference of social status. Wisdom is a higher distinction than the possession of an assured bank balance. There is a sense in which a bank balance is artificial as intelligence is not, a sense in which wealth is artificial as wisdom is not. There are some distinctions that are clearly based on the extraneous and the artificial, some distinctions that have little or no relation to worth. They are not evidence of quality.

If this is granted, then a true equalitarian society in the democratic sense is a society in which the right distinctions are drawn and maintained. Fundamental differences find free expression; conventional differences are minimized. Putting it more concretely, distinctions of class, of rank, of wealth, of social status are conventional in the sense that they bear little relation to qualities of character, intelligence, and wisdom. Not only have they little relation to them, but they are distinctions that assume different standards of value. The conceptions of rank on the one hand and of quality on the other have little in common. Where these conventional distinctions are stressed, distinctions of quality are obscured, and it is then that essential equality is denied. It is the assignment of places, offices, and functions on the basis of class, rank, and wealth that constitutes the flagrant repudiation of equality, and it is this that involves the defeat of democracy.

In a democratic society equality means that the highest character, other things being equal, will be accorded the highest esteem, that the wisest will have the greatest influence, that the intelligent will have the widest hearing and the greatest following. The principle demands that essential qualities should have a free field and that favor be granted to none. To man *as man* must be given the opportunity to make the most of himself and to make to the whole the best contribution of which he is capable. If economic hardship proves an insuperable barrier, if lack of social status defeats this end, if opportunity is denied, to that extent society is proved to be neither free nor equal, and to that extent it is not democratic. We may conclude that a social arrangement that hinders the individual from finding the place for which nature has fitted him violates the **principle** of equality; conditions that prevent him from using his gifts and doing the tasks for which he has the ability are a denial of that principle. It is only where equality of opportunity prevails that society can hope to utilize the qualities of its members or hope to benefit fully from their abilities.

ACHIEVING ESSENTIAL EQUALITY

The principle of equality implies a criterion of judgment in relation to the individual's place and significance in the social order. If a man does faithfully and well the work for which he is fitted, the particular nature of his work should not affect the question of merit or desert. Society demands from each his best; from no man can it demand more. If a man does his best, he deserves in return the best that society can do for him. It is not however merely a question of desert. Society will serve its own end by serving him, just as he fulfills his own end in the service of society. The relation is one of mutuality. No necessary work is menial work; labor that is socially necessary, whatever its nature, cannot demean the individual that does it. The honest laborer is not merely worthy of his hire; he is worthy of the recognition that honest labor always merits. This, of course, cuts across the conventional notions of a society that is still class conscious. There is no inherent dignity in a white collar job, no claim to superiority in the fact that one happens to be engaged in intellectual pursuits. The "soft-handed" labor, necessary though it may be, carries with it no badge of respectability simply *because* it is soft-handed. That the brain worker belongs to a superior order is a naïve superstition comparable to the pride of the government official in the old Germany who rejoiced when entitled to add *von* to his name. The superstitions of snobbishness die hard. Dignity lies not in the task that is done, but in the spirit manifest in the doing of it.

"Who will sweep the city streets in the ideal city?" The question need not be answered. All that need be said is that sweeping the streets will probably be quite as necessary in the ideal city as keeping the city accounts or presiding over the city courts. In the performance of socially necessary tasks there is no question of higher or lower; there is only a question of having them performed as well as possible by those best able to perform them. Merit will be determined by other criteria than the nature of the task. So at least the principle of equality implies.

So too with the question of government. Not all men will be fitted for the tasks of administration or of legislation. There will be delegation of authority and therefore governors and governed in any political order. There will be variety of function; some will command and others obey in particular fields of activity, but this is not a denial of equality. On the contrary, equality in a democratic order is the necessary condition of achieving government by the best, since it diminishes or rules out the influence of adventitious considerations. Equality demands not that quality be disregarded in choosing and electing those who must exercise authority, but that the right qualities be regarded—the basic qualities of intelligence and character rather than those of birth, social rank, wealth, or power.

The conclusion to which the whole argument points may be stated briefly. Equality is achieved where there is free play for distinctively *human* qualities, wisdom and virtue for example; where tradition is not permitted to fetter initiative and where convention no longer determines place and position in the social order. The significant distinctions among men become the decisive and operative distinctions. Differences of class, privilege, and status will be obliterated to make room for distinctions of quality, function, and service. The whole duty of man, it may be said, is the duty of doing as well as he can the thing that nature and society have fitted him to do. And the whole duty of society is to provide for each the fitting opportunity and the appropriate conditions for doing just that. This is real equality.

It will be recognized that in no country has equality in this sense been achieved. It will also be recognized that a decisive advance toward its achievement is one of the urgent necessities of our era. A democratic new order is inconceivable on any other assumption. The extremes of wealth and poverty that prevail in the industrial countries of the world are inconsistent with the maintenance of a stable social order. They involve a kind of inequality that threatens the foundations of democratic society; they flout the principle of equity and add bitterness to the grievances of the dispossessed. To bear the hardships of want and hunger is hard; to endure them in a society where extravagance is flaunted and spectacular displays of senseless luxury make the headlines becomes sooner or later intolerable. To be unemployed is a tragedy; to be unemployed while others have affluence and security is not only tragedy but an invitation to rebel against the regime that permits it. It should not occasion surprise if under these circumstances those who suffer most are not too discriminating when offered alternatives, however specious the alternatives may be. This is one of the lessons of the history of recent years.

Inequalities of income, of wealth, of condition may continue, and they may be justified; the point is that in a democratic society they will *need* justification. They must be shown to enhance social welfare and to increase the well-being of the whole. They must be compatible with *essential* equality. There is no social purpose served by unemployment, and there is no equality in any real sense between the jobless and the well-paid official who has both security of tenure and adequate provision for sickness and old age. It is foolish to expect a sense of independence and a consciousness of human dignity in the individual for whom society apparently has no place and for whose services it has no use. Democracy is based on the positive assertion of the worth of the individual and the inviolable sanctity of personality; it cannot be assured of survival except by demonstrating the reality and the sincerity of this assertion. Freedom from fear and freedom from want are corollaries of democratic liberty; they are also the implications of democratic equality.

The distinctive thing in the principle of equality is its emphasis upon the dignity of man as man; the distinctive aim of democracy is the enthronement of human qualities without regard to the trappings that are only incidental. A true democrat, it has been said, is a man who believes that he ought to be proud not to be a man of any particular class or of any particular rank or of any particular wealth, but to be a man at all. Rank and class and wealth are artificial and therefore secondary. To be an individual is to have a specific capacity and a distinctive gift. To be democratic, society must recognize the capacity and find a place and function for the gift.

> The rank is but the guinea's stamp,
> The man's the gowd for a' that,
> That though on hamely fare we dine,
> Wear hoddin grey and a' that;
> Gie fools their silks, and knaves their wine,
> A man's a man for a' that.

In these words Robert Burns caught the spirit that produced and keeps alive in the human spirit both the aspiration to equality and the faith in its ultimate achievement.

CHAPTER 9. The Rights of Man

It is significant that the name that first leaps to mind when the rights of man are mentioned is that of Tom Paine. In a way the title of his book symbolizes the spirit of the century in which it appeared. The book itself is the last ambitious and powerful defense of a doctrine which, during one of the most critical periods in modern history, had exercised an extraordinary influence on the minds of men: the doctrine of natural rights. Theories do not make revolutions, but by rationalizing the desires, resentments, and passions of men theories may give both direction and potency to emotions that would otherwise be blind and therefore ineffective. Men do not fight purposefully without a principle, nor are they likely to achieve far-reaching results if they have no conscious goal. It is doctrine that gives driving force to the passions and emotions that conditions and circumstances may have aroused. Resentments and grievances may flare up into angry protest, but an idea may focus them until they become powerful for destruction or for construction. It is this function that was performed in the eighteenth century by the idea of "the rights of man."

This idea, of course, is much older than the eighteenth century. It is implicit in those ideas of human equality that have been discussed in the preceding chapter; it is derived from the idea of natural law, which, as we have seen, goes back to the ancient world of Greece and Rome. There was a golden age in some far-off and distant past which the Stoics referred to as a "state of nature" and which the church fathers identified with the original state of innocent man. In this state of nature men were free and equal, governed by laws that were rational and therefore beneficent because man was so constituted that his reason conformed to them. The state of nature passed away, for the passions of natural man destroyed the harmony of nature. Government was necessary to restrain the conflicting desires of men, and in order to secure its benefits men relinquished some of their rights. They renounced some in order to be more secure in those that remained. They entered into a solemn pact, a contract that became the basis of civil society.

This idea of a social contract was an attempt to explain *why* civil society came into existence, rather than an account of *how* it originated; it was a logical rather than a historical concept. It was a familiar idea among the Sophists of the Greek enlightenment, many of whom used it as the basis of the argument that the state was conventional, not natural. Plato puts the argument into the mouth of Glaucon in the *Republic*. The idea lived on through the Middle Ages, influencing the thought of both church and state.[1] The interrelated concepts of a state of nature and of a social contract, therefore, are not peculiar to the eighteenth century; they are traditional. But it was in the eighteenth century that they became the characteristic and dominant ideas of a period. It was in the Age of Reason that they came into general acceptance, almost as axioms. In the same period the dynamic quality of the concepts became apparent and their revolutionary possibilities were exploited.

What was characteristic of the eighteenth century, therefore, was not the formulation and recognition of these concepts, but the stress laid upon them and the deductions drawn from them. With the Stoics and in the Middle Ages the idea of a law of nature proved an admirable, although not always an effective, safeguard against the assumptions of arbitrary power and the extravagant claims of sovereign authority. It was a defense against absolutism both in church and in state. In the seventeenth and eighteenth centuries, however, emphasis was placed not on the law that prevailed in the state of nature, but upon the rights that man possessed in it. No one doubted that natural man was possessed of rights; the questions now at issue—the answers to which distinguished the conclusions of Hobbes, Locke, Rousseau, and others—concerned the nature of these rights. What were man's rights in a state of nature? What became of them in civil society? How many of them, if any, did man retain when government was instituted? Hobbes and Locke differed fundamentally in their answers, as we know, and Rousseau differed from both. For Rousseau the basic problem was how to establish a civil society that would leave man "as free as before."

REVOLUTIONARY IMPLICATIONS OF THE CONCEPT

What is important is that it was common ground among the philosophers of the age of revolutions that man could not and did not relinquish *all* his natural rights when he became a member of civil society. He relinquished some in order to preserve and to secure others. Even Hobbes, purposefully creating his all-powerful

[1] See Chapter 4.

and all-embracing leviathan, leaves to man the one fundamental natural right for which he yields up all the others, the right of self-preservation. Rousseau, as we have seen, admits no relinquishment or renunciation of natural rights at all; the contract is entered into to preserve *all* man's natural rights. For man cannot divest himself of these rights, nor can he delegate them to representatives or governments. Locke, as we might expect, stands between these extremes. Life, liberty, and property are the rights that remain, and must remain, inviolate even in civil society, and for the defense and preservation of these rights government is instituted.

All these theories have one thing in common; they are all actually or potentially revolutionary. Where government fails to fulfill its function, where it ceases to live up to the obligations it has assumed in the contract, there its justification comes to an end. With Hobbes revolution of course is the last desperate expedient, to be avoided at almost any cost, since it involves a return to that awful state of nature where life is nasty, brutish, and short. Still, where government in spite of its vast powers does not provide the security for which it is instituted, there is no apparent alternative to revolution. With Rousseau revolution is a continuing process. His doctrine is one of permanent revolution, since sovereign power is never given to governments, but remains vital and operative in the people. Governments can be and are made and unmade in the normal exercise of the general will. With Locke, writing in defense of the Revolution of 1688, revolution is justified and will always be justified when government fails to safeguard the natural rights of life, liberty, and property. Always the doctrine of natural rights in the seventeenth and eighteenth centuries had revolutionary implications.

It is not surprising therefore to find that the doctrine was asserted most clearly and most forcibly in revolutionary situations. It was an idea convenient and ready either to justify a revolution in retrospect or to prepare the way for one. In England it was used for the one purpose, in America and France for the other. The Declaration of Independence bears all the marks of its period, not only in its ideas but in the positive character of its assertions. The truths asserted are "self-evident," the rights of life, liberty, and the pursuit of happiness are "unalienable," the purpose of government is unquestionable.

That, to secure these rights, Governments are instituted among Men, deriving their just powers from the consent of the governed. That, whenever any Form of Government becomes destructive of these ends, it is the Right of the People to alter or abolish it, and to institute new Government, laying its foundations on such principles and organizing its powers in such forms, as to them shall seem most likely to effect their Safety and Happiness.

Thus the doctrine passes into what may be called the political creed of the United States.

In France the assertion of the doctrine of natural rights is equally positive and the deductions drawn from it equally revolutionary.

The representatives of the people of France, formed into a National Assembly, considering that ignorance, neglect, or contempt of human rights, are the sole causes of public misfortunes and corruptions of Government, have resolved to set forth in a solemn declaration, these natural, imprescriptible, and inalienable rights.

The French declaration, however, is more exhaustive than that of the American Founders and for that reason is less logical. The inconsistency of later articles with the idea of natural rights is conspicuous and glaring, for here are enumerated a number of rights which are and must be the creation not of nature but of law in the ordinary and accepted sense of that term. It may be a sound principle that "No man should be accused, arrested or held in confinement except in cases determined by the law and according to the forms prescribed," but clearly it is a principle that had no meaning and could have none in a state of nature. Most of the rights enumerated by the National Assembly are in fact *civil* rights. This is perhaps why the Assembly was careful to frame the title of its declaration as the "Declaration of the Rights of Man *and of the Citizen.*"

As to the rights of citizens there need be no question, for they are defined and determined by the laws of the state. The idea of legal right is precise and clear, and no one would deny that every citizen is possessed of rights of this character. "Real laws," so Jeremy Bentham declares, "give birth to real rights." There may be differences of opinion with regard to the interpretation of a particular legal right in specific circumstances; there may be still greater differences as to whether the rights created or recognized by law are satisfactory in character and in extent; but there can be no question as to the existence of such rights. "A 'legal right,' in the strictest sense, is 'a capacity residing in one man of controlling with the assent and assistance of the State, the actions of others.' More briefly, though with somewhat less precision, we might say that a legal right is the claim of an individual upon others, recognized by the State. A legal right need not necessarily have been created by the State (e.g. by statute); but it must be such that the law courts will recognize it, and, in all orderly communities, the force of the State is at the back of all legal decisions."[2]

This has little relation to the assertion of natural rights. In the conception of natural rights there is neither precision nor definiteness, for there is no authority to decide what these rights are nor any criterion by which to judge their significance in particular applications. There is a profound difference, as we have seen, in the rights enumerated and recognized as natural by Hobbes, Locke, and Rousseau, and a very important difference also in the rights declared to be natural in the American and French declarations. "Life, liberty and the pursuit of happiness" in the one case and "Liberty, Property, Security and Resistance to Oppression" in the other certainly do not amount to the same thing. It is significant that these declarations have only one term in common. It would be hazardous to suggest that the differences in the remaining rights are merely differences of terminology. Why, for instance, did property rank as a natural right in France and not in America? And since the difference in this case is important, to what tribunal can appeal be made to settle the question as to whether the omission in the one case or the inclusion in the other is justified? The conception of a state of nature gives us no guidance in this dilemma. Even assuming the existence of natural rights, it is probable that no two people would agree as to the rights that should be included within this category. Personal preferences would determine what would be regarded as natural by each. As a basis for determining and asserting the rights of man, the theory of nature is inadequate, because the concept of nature is ambiguous.

BURKE'S DOCTRINE OF RIGHTS

This criticism adds nothing to those of Edmund Burke and Jeremy Bentham, whose devastating attacks upon the doctrine of natural rights discredited it at least in its eighteenth-century form. Burke did something more than bring out the essential weaknesses of the idea; he suggested, at least, the direc-

[2] Ritchie, *Natural Rights*, p. 78.

tion in which a more satisfactory conception of rights is to be sought. And for this reason it may be of some advantage to summarize a few of the points he made.

What are the natural rights of man? This question, so Burke declares, is a purely abstract one, interesting perhaps to the theorist and the speculative philosopher but of no practical importance. If we assume that a contract was entered into and made the basis of civil society, then man's rights are determined by the terms of that contract. What purpose is served by asking what rights man may have possessed before he entered into the contract? Man as we know him is man in society, and the only question that has real practical importance concerns his rights as a member of society. "Natural" man is a fiction, created by dealers in metaphysics! If he ever existed he certainly does not exist now. Burke would consider civil, social man and no other. No man, so he declares, can enjoy the rights of both an uncivil and a civil state. That social man has rights Burke is of course the first to admit, but they are rights created by society; they are the consequences of that complex of relationships in which man finds himself in his normal social life. Social rights are as important as natural rights are illusory.

It is true that these social rights may seem less extensive or numerous than the assumed rights of natural man. They will necessarily be limited by considerations of social expediency and of social purpose, but they are real, and natural rights are not. Man sacrifices nothing in becoming or in being a member of society. Whatever advantages the state of nature may have possessed, the enjoyment of rights was not one of them. In such a natural state man would be free neither to do what he liked nor to do what he ought. He would be limited and frustrated by the will of those stronger than himself whose desires and aims were in conflict with his own. What would his claim to liberty amount to under such circumstances? Compared to this empty freedom, which is in fact merely the freedom of the strong and ruthless to impose their wills on others, the liberty of social man is incomparably better. In society at least man is free to do what is right, which with Burke means that he is free to do all that is consistent with the true purposes of social life. Man in society sacrifices the illusion for the reality; he renounces the shadow for the substance. The only real rights are the rights of man *in society*.

Burke is as generous in his recognition of these social rights as he is emphatic in depreciating natural rights. In *Reflections on the French Revolution* he writes:

Far am I from denying in theory, full as far is my heart from withholding in practice the real rights of man. In denying their false claims of right I do not mean to injure those which are real. . . . If civil Society be made for the advantage of man, all the advantages for which it is made become his right. It is an institution of beneficence and law itself is only beneficence acting by rule. Men have a right to live by that rule, they have a right to justice. . . . They have a right to the fruits of industry and to the means of making that industry fruitful. They have a right to the acquisitions of their parents, to the nourishment and improvement of their offspring, to instruction in life and to consolation in death. Whatever each man can do severally without trespassing on others he has a right to do for himself.[3]

Here indeed is an impressive list of rights. What Burke apparently did not realize was that the rights he enumerated would have value and significance only according to the interpretation that might be placed upon them. No one permitted to interpret these rights for himself would wish to add much or perhaps anything to the number of rights included in Burke's list. "The right of men to the fruit of their industry and to the means of making that industry fruitful" is a statement that might well be interpreted to please Rousseau much more than it would please Burke. It might, indeed, have been adopted later by Karl Marx without any great inconvenience or any substantial modification of his teaching. The right of men "to the nourishment and improvement of their offspring, to instruction in life and consolation in death" involves the recognition and acceptance of far-reaching claims. It is more than doubtful whether Burke had such claims in mind as he was carried along on the tide of his splendid rhetoric. Generalization in discussing rights may be only a little less dangerous than abstraction!

Burke was on surer ground in stating the conditions under which a right should be recognized and exercised. These must be judged in the light of social purpose and the public good. Man, Burke declares, has no right to that which he has not the capacity to use. The claim to a particular right must be made good by evidence of capacity to exercise it; the right to a particular advantage must be justified by showing that its possession and use furthers the public good. Burke applied this principle to the grant of political power. The franchise, he argued, ought to be given to

[3] Edmund Burke, *Works* (Boston: Little, Brown, 1865), vol. 3, pp. 308–9.

those who may be presumed to possess political capacity. Burke believed that the number of those who were politically competent was very small, but the tests of capacity that he had in mind would certainly not be accepted today. His views on the franchise were those of a typical eighteenth-century conservative, and nowhere is his conservative temper more apparent than in his application of the principle that a right cannot be accorded to one who has not the capacity to use it to justify an exceedingly restricted franchise. His application of the principle, however, does not make invalid the principle itself.

Burke was more fortunate in the application of the second principle in his doctrine of rights. He argues that the possession of a right does not necessarily justify its exercise. Men, and governments too, may possess rights that it would be inexpedient and even unjust for them to assert. It is this principle that he states with magnificent eloquence and applies with remarkable insight in his speeches on the American Revolution. The contention of the British government of that day was logical enough. England had the right to tax the colonists; it possessed unquestioned sovereignty, and sovereign power certainly involved the right of taxation. If the right existed England was justified in exercising and enforcing it! So ran the argument, and in accordance with it the policy of England was determined. Burke does not challenge the logic of this argument. He declares, rather, that to possess a right, even an unquestioned one, does not alter the fact that to insist upon it may be an act of blind and disastrous ineptitude. It is possible in enforcing a right to perpetrate a wrong.

"Show the thing you contend for to be reason," Burke cries, "show it to be common sense, show it to be the means of attaining some useful end and then I am content to allow it what dignity you please." What was the use of talking about abstract rights in such a connection? "The question with me," says Burke, "is not whether you have a right to render your people miserable but whether it is not your interest to make them happy. It is not what a lawyer tells me I *may* do but what humanity, reason and justice tell me I ought to do. . . . I am not determining a point of law; I am restoring tranquillity, and the general character and situation of a people must determine what sort of government is fitted for them."[4] And this principle, it is clear, applies not only to those abstract natural rights upon which Burke was content

[4] Burke, *Works*, vol. 2, pp. 140–41.

to pour his scorn, but also to legal and constitutional rights. A man may have a perfectly legal right to foreclose a mortgage, but it is frequently inexpedient to do so, and under certain economic conditions it may be actually unfair and unjust. Under normal conditions the right of free speech may be constitutionally guaranteed, but there will be occasions when the responsible citizen feels that it would be wrong for him to exercise that right.

IDEAL RIGHTS

The point that emerges from Burke's analysis may be stated simply. Rights must be established not by appeal to an imaginary state of nature, but by an appeal to those essential purposes for which society exists and to those ends that social life must serve. To establish a right it is not sufficient to show that men had such a right in some dim past; that they once possessed it does not prove that it should be admitted now. The essential condition of recognition for any claim to a particular right is that it can be shown that this recognition will contribute to the advancement of social welfare and to the realization of desirable social ends—which is precisely the principle to which our discussion of liberty and equality has led us. Whatever enables man to contribute more fully to the happiness and well-being of society ought to be recognized as a right, and to such rights the individual may justly lay claim.

The term *ought* in this statement provides a clue to a sound doctrine of rights. The rights of man are not mere abstractions and the assertion of rights is not the barren dogmatism that it seems. If by rights we mean those opportunities for satisfaction and service which an ideal society would secure for its members, and which a society far from ideal must yet strive to secure in increasing measure for them, then the conception of rights becomes reasonable and fruitful in practice. It provides us with a criterion by which present conditions may be judged, and with an incentive to improve them when and where they are imperfect or inequitable.

The declaration of a right, then, becomes an appeal not to a past from which presumably man has emerged, but to a future toward which his course is set; it calls for the exercise of man's faith, not of his memory. It involves an ethical assumption that is basic to it. Human life has immanent in it a progressive purpose; humanity is moving—no doubt with tragic retrogressions and failures at times—with painful and uncertain steps toward a goal. We never see that goal clearly; we merely catch glimpses of it. But those glimpses are sufficient in days of darkness to kindle hope and to keep faith alive. They create that discontent with things as they are that is the mainspring of progress. In asserting the rights of man those who have caught a glimpse of the goal, or who believe they have, are declaring what changes must be wrought in conditions, in customs, in modes of thought, in order that another step forward toward its realization may be achieved. The argument for such change must be an appeal to reason; it must show that the change demanded as a right is possible, desirable, or necessary. Where the argument is convincing, there the right ought to be recognized. This is the demand that moral man makes on an immoral, or at least an imperfect, society.

This is why belief in rights has proved so persistent and why the idea of rights has shown such amazing vitality in spite of the grave defects of the theories and doctrines in which it has found expression. It is also the reason why we may safely assume that it will retain its vitality. It may be easy to dispose of the historic formulation of the rights of men in the declarations of America and France; it is not easy to dispose of the deep-rooted convictions to which these declarations give what may be imperfect expression. It may be easy to dispose of Tom Paine's theories, as Burke and Bentham do, but it is not so easy to dispose of his spirit. The declaration of rights is evidence not of man's august origin, but of man's enduring faith and unquenchable hope. It is true that interpreted thus the principle gives no ready formula that will enable men to decide which claims are to be recognized as rights and which are to be rejected. It has never served to settle disputes automatically, nor will it serve such a purpose today; it will not prevent disagreement, but it will and does provide a basis for reasonable discussion. It is a reminder that in discussing rights experience and reason must be the final arbiters and social good the ultimate criterion.

The argument for a particular right, therefore, must show that to grant it is possible, and that its exercise is desirable in the light of social purpose. Here obviously we have passed beyond Bentham's narrow conception of rights as the creation of law and nothing more. A great many of man's rights are indeed legal or constitutional, and in relation to these appeal is made to, and issues are decided by, the appropriate courts of law. But to declare that these comprise and exhaust the rights of man is to fly in the face of both experience and reason. The assertion of rights is the assertion of what ought to be, as opposed to, and requiring change from, what is. It is the challenge of the reformer! The success of his challenge proves that it was needed; thus what was asserted as a right becomes a *recognized* right. It receives the sanction of law or custom or both. A social right is of course established more securely by virtue of the legal sanction, but to argue that legal sanction created the right or made what was not a right at one moment into what was a right the next, is to strain language beyond what is reasonable. But what can reasonably be said is that a right which existed has at last received the recognition it deserved; those who asserted it have been able to persuade a majority of those who previously were indifferent or opposed to them to recognize it.

Real laws do not give birth to real rights. They inscribe them on the statute book: they provide machinery for their enforcement; but they do not create them. For rights do not emerge, Minerva-like, from the brain of the legislator. This is to invert the true order of things. They have a prior history. They enter his mind because he is able clearly to see that there are certain conditions of life which, in the name of justice and expediency, society ought to enforce. And if these conditions really ought to be enforced, they are virtually rights, though they may have to wait for enactment for a generation, or forever.[5]

It follows from this that there is always a time lag between the formulation of social rights and their recognition in terms of legal enactment or of constitutional practice. The legislator always limps rather painfully behind the reformer, and some of the strains and tensions of political and social life are due to this fact. Where legal or constitutional recognition is unreasonably hampered by restrictions and repressions, where popular recognition is not followed by recognition in law or custom, where change is made too difficult, the assertion of rights may still prove to be revolutionary. It is a mistake to minimize the explosive possibilities of "ideal" rights, in the sense in which the term is here used, merely because they are ideal! The appeal to the future may prove even more powerful than that appeal to the past which was used effectively to make and to justify the revolutions in America and France.

[5] John MacCunn, *The Ethics of Citizenship* (Glasgow: Maclehose, 1894), pp. 51-52.

AN ILLUSTRATION: THE RIGHT TO WORK

The argument developed so far may be made clearer and more concrete by reference to certain present-day issues to which its conclusions may be applied by way of illustration. The problem of unemployment, for instance, has in most industrialized countries become the crucial issue in social and political life. It is a problem for which no assured solution has yet been discovered. It is certain, however, that the social conscience of our age will remain uneasy and disturbed until a satisfactory solution is found. The feeling has been growing and is now general that it is intolerable that multitudes should be condemned to the misery and tragedy of forced unemployment.

This feeling has been responsible for the assertion of the right to work as a simple human right. A full and frank recognition of this right, it is urged, must be recognized as a basic condition of a progressive and healthy social life. We need not stop to consider the obvious objections to the phrase "the right to work." Work in itself may provide neither personal satisfaction nor social benefit, and if the problem were merely one of providing work it could be solved immediately. The provision of unnecessary work is at once easy and futile. The assertion of the right to work is really a demand for recognition of the principle that if a man is honestly prepared to do useful work, he has a right to expect society to provide him with the opportunity for doing it and to expect such recompense as will provide him with means to satisfy his needs and maintain a reasonable standard of living. Enforced unemployment, it is urged, is a violation and a denial of this human right.

It will be readily admitted that full employment for all those capable and willing to undertake necessary work is a desirable social end, but this is not sufficient in itself to constitute a social right. What is clearly desirable must also be shown to be possible before the right can be established. It is not only the will of society that is involved but its capacity to give effect to its will. It must be shown not only that most people favor a policy of full employment for all, but that resources are available to give effect to this policy. There cannot be a social obligation to do what is *not* possible. The first question to be faced, therefore, is whether society has the means to do what it recognizes as desirable.

Something indeed is gained by the recognition of an abstract right to work, but what is certainly not achieved by it is the provision of work to be done, or of adequate recompense for doing it.

The bare recognition may serve as a goad to stimulate governments and others to explore every possible means of securing the necessary resources and of providing the necessary conditions. It does not follow that they will succeed. Here too the warning of Burke is salutary: "The State is to have recruits to its strength and remedies to its distempers. What is the use of discussing a man's abstract right to food or to medicine? The question is upon the method of procuring and administering them. In that deliberation I shall always advise to call in the aid of the farmer and the physician rather than the professor of metaphysics."[6]

The conclusion to which this argument leads is that the assertion of the right to work raises questions not merely for the philosopher or the moralist but also for the economist and the statesman; they are questions of means as well as of ends. The practical man's judgment may be as important as that of the theorist. In one sense it may be even more important, for while ideals may give direction to policy, harsh necessity will determine the limits imposed upon it. It will be agreed that there is ground for gravest dissatisfaction with a system in which millions are workless and therefore hungry or in want. Everybody recognizes the desirability of eliminating unemployment. The vital questions now are whether or not this can be done and how. The "remedies to our distempers" may be beyond reach in a particular stage of social development or under the conditions of a particular era. A right cannot be assured of practical recognition unless the possibility of giving effect to it exists.

In the past this was an effective reply to the assertion of the right to work. The economy of the nineteenth century was an economy of scarcity; one of its major problems was that of providing "enough to go 'round." Great advances in production were made, and although the problem of production may not have been solved by the end of the century, it was well on the way to solution. Now our economy is one of abundance, and our major problem is not one of scarcity but of surpluses. The paradox of our time, as has been stated so often, is the paradox of want in the midst of plenty. Obviously the objection based on lack of means or insufficiency of resources has lost much of its force. The scientific and technological advances of the past fifty years have wrought an economic revolution comparable to that effected by the discoveries of Watt, Arkwright, Crompton, and the rest in the early years of the Industrial Revolution. What may have been

[6] *Works,* vol. 3, p. 311.

impossible in the nineteenth century is possible in the twentieth century.

We are, if we could but grapple with our fate, the most fortunate of the generations of men. In a single lifetime science has given us more power over nature, and extended further the range of vision of the exploring mind, than in all recorded history. Now, and now only, our material resources, technical knowledge, and industrial skill, are enough to afford to every man of the world's teeming population physical comfort, adequate leisure, and access to everything in our rich heritage of civilization that he has the personal quality to enjoy. We need but the regulative wisdom to control our specialized activities and the thrusting energy of sectional and selfish interest. To face the troubles that beset us, this apprehensive and defensive world needs now above all the qualities it seems for the moment to have abandoned—courage and magnanimity.[7]

The right to work must be considered anew in the light of changed conditions and new possibilities.

The truth that emerges is that the conception of rights is not static. What cannot be recognized as a right in one age may demand and receive recognition in another; it moves from the realm of ideals into the realm of practical policy, and this in particular is responsible for the marked change of attitude in relation to unemployment in our generation. What is inevitable must be borne, with whatever patience we are able to summon to our aid. But what if the evils once borne cease to be inevitable? And what if there is a growing realization that the necessity for bearing them is no longer imposed either by the niggardliness of nature or by man's lack of ingenuity in utilizing and mastering nature's forces? If the suspicion grows that the maladjustments of our social order are due to conditions that are of human contrivance, if the conviction deepens that it is the system, or lack of it, that is at fault, then the demand for change will become dynamic and may become threatening. People will insist that something be done, and they will be in a mood to experiment even where experiment means risk and danger. Men in such circumstances will respond to leadership only if it is positive—and, unfortunately, the fact that it is positive is not a guarantee that it will be wise. The leadership of Mussolini and of Hitler was *positive* enough! And because it was positive such leadership produced amazing results, but such results were and may be again as disastrous as they were amazing. But if leadership is not positive, if it offers no solutions to press-

[7] Arthur Salter, *Recovery* (New York: Century, 1932), p. 347.

ing problems, if it holds out no prospect of far-reaching change where change is clearly necessary, it will certainly not be wise, for it will inevitably be doomed to futility. No generation of men will remain patient when conscious of profound frustration; they will, if need be, resort to desperate remedies. If there is no prospect of guidance that is both wise and dynamic, the battle is lost by default. Because the dynamic leader without wisdom will find a following!

It is in this sense that our age and its conflicts have a revolutionary character. The assertion of the rights of man now challenges an economic order as it challenged a political order in the eighteenth century. But the challenge today is made on firmer ground. It is no longer based on a doctrine of abstract natural rights; it is based consciously on a conception of social rights. It is practical where Tom Paine and his followers were doctrinaire. It demands an economic and social system that will work, one that will convert what has now become a possibility, at least in the industrialized countries of the West, into actuality, one that will overcome whatever is responsible for condemning capable citizens to joblessness and hopelessness.

This is what lies behind the insistent assertions that unemployment such as we have known in our time cannot be allowed to continue, that there must be freedom from want, and so on. A society in which capable and energetic men have no scope for their capacity and no fitting outlet for their energies, in which the most tragic waste is the waste of human material, seems to have become intolerable to the social consciousness of our time. Men will not put up with it unless it can be shown that there is no remedy for it, and they will not believe that there is no remedy for it until they have tried all remedies. It is in this new temper that the right to work becomes something more than an abstract claim; it becomes a social imperative.

Naturally, the causes of our tragic social failure in this matter must be laid bare if the fitting remedy is to be discovered and applied. If want and need are not due to scarcity, as they once were, what is responsible for the privation and hardship that are the common lot of vast multitudes even in our "prosperous" democratic countries? A comprehensive review of the answers given cannot be attempted here, for the question carries us far beyond the limits and purpose of this discussion. But a few considerations are relevant to the main line of our argument, and one of the answers is significant in relation to the question of rights.

It is suggested that the disregard of social welfare as the end of all social activities, economic as well as others, is at the root of our troubles. Production is not determined in our economic society by considerations of social needs, but by considerations of profit possibilities, and there is no necessary or even probable coincidence between these two sets of considerations. The "harmony of interests" that Adam Smith asserted and upon which his system was based either did not exist or has ceased to exist so generally that it can give no assurance of social well-being. Private interest does not always work to public advantage; so much was admitted even in the nineteenth century, as a vast mass of social legislation which limited and circumscribed private interest bears witness.

In the twentieth century the position seems to have been reached that private interest cannot be assumed to work *generally* to the public advantage. Private interest may be consistent under certain circumstances with mass unemployment; it may dictate policies that must even aggravate that condition in a serious economic crisis. This is not because it is unscrupulous or selfish but simply because it is private. It may, for example, dictate a shutdown which is clearly justified by the orthodox economic principle that "it does not pay." Yet social expediency and social advantage might dictate a different policy. The concentration and integration of the steel industry in England in the thirties may have been economically justifiable. But it ruined the shipbuilding industry of Jarrow and left the town derelict with thousands of men workless and thousands of homes hopeless. It is very doubtful whether the policy which suited the steel industry secured or furthered the interests of England and its people. The destruction of surplus wheat may be necessary to maintain prices for wheat producers, but it is difficult to see how it can be a social benefit in a society where thousands are still hungry.

Even the general coincidence of private profit and public advantage can no longer be assumed. Implicit in the assertion of the right to work is the conviction that unemployment is neither socially necessary nor socially desirable, that the conditions responsible for it are neither inevitable nor justifiable. In short, it now involves a positive conviction based, not on any idea of a state of nature, but on considerations both of practical possibilities and of social ends. The criticisms of rights in the eighteenth century and of this particular right to work in the nineteenth are no longer convincing; they seem even to be irrelevant.

HOW RIGHTS WIN RECOGNITION

This argument does not prove the existence of a right to work, nor is it intended to. It is, rather, a significant illustration of what is meant by a right and of the considerations that must be taken into account in deciding whether the recognition of a right is justified. It indicates how rights win their way to recognition and illustrates the way in which the demand implicit in the assertion of a right may become imperative. Rights are rooted in social purpose; they grow and develop as the social conscience gains in clarity and insight; they are established and win recognition by the growth of a general conviction of the rightness and necessity of this recognition in the real interest of society. Assertion is not enough; demonstration is necessary and the demonstration must be reasonable. "Show the thing you contend for to be reason."

This same principle may be applied to other rights. The right of property was assumed in the eighteenth century to be a natural right, and, as we have seen, the assertion of that right was emphatic in the teaching of John Locke. In spite of the authority and prestige of Locke its recognition is no longer unquestioned. Even if we assume that Locke was right in declaring that private possession of those things "with which man had mixed his labor" existed in a state of nature, the right to private possessions is not established thereby. The question must be decided on other grounds. Does the recognition of that right still serve a useful social purpose? Does the institution of private property justify its existence by a positive contribution to social well-being? The fact that it did this in the past does not give us any assurance that it does so today or will continue to do so tomorrow. Institutions sometimes outlive their usefulness and exhaust their historic function. In some cases the recognition of rights may be withdrawn, just as in others it may be won after long denial. The "rights" of one age may be the wrongs of the next.

This does not prove that the right to private property exists or does not exist. It merely indicates that those who assert or claim rights must always be ready to show cause for their continued recognition or for a recognition never previously accorded them. Rights once established must forever be on the defensive, since the world does not stand still, with the thoughts of men widening and the habits of men changing. "Time makes ancient good uncouth." And the only defense of rights that will serve is the ability to convince the social conscience and the public mind that the rights are still creators of beneficence and that their recognition is still a condition of definite advantage. For this simple reason a right always implies a duty and the recognition of new rights always implies the creation of new obligations.

The advocacy of human rights is still necessary in a democratic order. It has not been outmoded as a result of the inadequacy of the ancient watchwords or the abandonment of the philosophy that gave them currency. If it is no longer possible to believe without qualification the ringing sentences of the Declaration of Independence, it is both possible and necessary to reinterpret them and in the new interpretation to reaffirm them. And it is both possible and necessary to find new watchwords in a new philosophy. In asserting rights today we know that we are appealing not to a past long-since dead, but to an unborn future; we are appealing from an imperfect present to a better future. The rights we may still claim will not be deductions from what man was or is supposed to have been long, long ago. They will be claimed rather on the basis of our conception of what man ought to be, and what some day he will be. They will be made explicitly and frankly as claims of the ideal. The conception of rights will not die, for the simple reason that men will never be content with what is, but will always be stirred by what ought to be. We may assert with Professor Laski "that one of the great mainsprings of human effort is the realization of a good greater than that which is actually existent."[8]

The rights of man, then, are the conditions and opportunities that man would have if society were what it ought to be. Man's rights are what man needs in order that he may help to the full in the task of making society what it ought to be. It is his obligation to use such conditions when they are secured and to seize these opportunities as they come. Rights and duties become the dual but complementary aspects of human motivation, for every right implies a duty and every duty a right.

[8] Laski, *Authority in the Modern State*, p. 64.

CHAPTER 10. Fraternity

THERE remains to be discussed the last of those concepts that have been traditionally regarded as the watchwords of democracy. If our treatment is brief, it is not because the idea is relatively unimportant but partly because it is *so* important. For the idea of fraternity carries beyond the realm of political expediencies and policies into the realm of spiritual values and religious doctrine. This is not to imply any recognition of the dichotomy between the two realms that is implicit in certain types of religious and social philosophies. The world of values is one, and truth is indivisible. Nevertheless any adequate discussion of fraternity would necessarily carry us far beyond the limits set by the purpose this book is intended to serve.

Ultimate ideals have certainly not been left out of account in our discussion thus far; they must be included in any consideration of democracy. But they have been considered with specific reference to the practicalities of social and political life; they have been appealed to where their immediate relevance to the problems of our time has seemed clear and in need of new emphasis, and where practical policy seemed to be dictated by them. We have been trying, not to sketch the outline of an ideal commonwealth, but to indicate possible lines of advance that we must follow if the promise of a new order is to be fulfilled in our time. The ideal of fraternity has indeed been assumed throughout, but we are so far removed from its realization that much needs to be done before we can profitably consider its stern and exacting demands, as well as its glorious promise. The brotherhood of man is a splendid vision; we must never lose sight of it or lose faith in it even when the whole aspect of our world seems to be a denial of it. It is a beacon that shines from afar.

THE IDEAL OF BROTHERHOOD

Fraternity is therefore at once the most exalted and the most difficult to discuss of all the ideals of the democratic faith. This is partly because it so far outsoars the actual achievement of even the most advanced democracies that there is a suggestion of unreality even in a bare statement of it. The world with which we are familiar is a world of deep antagonisms, of stern and ruthless conflict; it seems to be almost the antithesis of what is meant by brotherhood. If profession can produce no better result than this, it is perhaps advisable to avoid too loud and too fervent a declaration of it. One speaks with some trepidation of journey's end when we are only just setting out into untraveled country, knowing only that the journey will be difficult and arduous and that the end of it will be seen at last only by the eyes of faith. We are today in a mood to abate our high-sounding professions and to try as best we can to settle down to do the strenuous task that is immediately imperative and near at hand—perhaps just holding the clearing we have already made in the wilderness or pushing a few steps farther into the pathless jungle beyond. The "far-off Divine event" is definitely far off! We must still believe in it, but . . . !

It may be, too, that the difficulty in discussing this ideal is due to a feeling that fraternity is less a good to be sought directly than a condition to be realized in seeking other ends. It may be that fraternity like happiness is not found by seeking it, that to aim at it is to miss it. Actually, it is in cooperation, in the pursuit of common ends, that men find one another and the understanding that is real brotherliness. Sharing experiences and finding deep community of interest in mutual appreciations, these rather than pledges of fraternity surmount the barriers that ordinarily divide us from one another. A society that has achieved liberty and equality even, in the sense in which we have tried to interpret them, will probably have taken a long step toward the realization of fraternity. Both concepts assume the essential worth of man, and a recognition of the worth of man is a good basis for that love of men that is true fraternity. Certainly where this recognition is withheld fraternity can be nothing more than a pious sentiment or a romantic illusion.

The word *fraternity* suggests the family group as the type of social relationship that democracy aims to create. It is by the extension in ever-widening circles of those sentiments, emotions, and purposes that bind family members together and that constitute the essential characteristics of the family, that society will increasingly fulfill its purpose. This kinship, which even in the family is something more than the tie of blood, becomes in society a kinship of spirit, the tie of a common purpose and destiny. If we are to believe Paul, there is also in the deepest sense a mystical tie of blood among men, for "God hath made of one blood all the nations of the earth." The family, therefore, is the symbol of ideal social life; it is also the nucleus out of which that society may develop. It is, in germ, what human society will become when its growth is complete.

We see today, even in a world such as ours, the faint beginnings of this ultimate social relationship, foregleams and promises of a fraternal world order. Of these promises the family relationship is one among many, the most conspicuous indeed but fortunately not the only one. In spite of our social failures there are today associations of men and women in which fraternity is more than a mere sentiment and in which the bonds of mutual respect and common purpose are suffused with affection and strengthened by personal sympathies. Churches, fraternal orders, unions of all kinds, even political parties tend to become in many instances more than groupings united by some specific and limited purpose. There emerges a spirit of camaraderie, of understanding, cordiality, and mutual appreciation in such associations. There is in them also a tendency toward mutual forbearance, a spirit of give and take, a readiness to place the interest of the group before that of the individual. This, if not real fraternity, is at least a long step toward it.

Even within the system of relationships that we call the "competitive system," cooperation is more fundamental than competition. Nowhere is teamwork more essential than in the complex operations of industry and commerce. Adam Smith was wrong no doubt in his assumption that "an invisible hand," a benevolent Providence, had ordained a necessary coincidence between self-interest and the general good, and that if each sought his own interest, the interest of the whole would take care of itself. It is important, however, to discover how and where he was wrong. He did not take sufficiently into account the frailty of man, his lack of wisdom, and the strength of his desires and passions. In a world of perfectly reasonable men his principle might have been justified. Unfortunately such a world does not exist. Since perfect knowledge is denied us, there is not much use discussing whether "knowledge is virtue" and whether if men knew enough they would always act wisely. History and experience make it clear that they do not act wisely!

And yet, even in the fierce competitiveness that the doctrine of laissez faire justifies or even advocates, the basic condition of success and effectiveness is cooperation rather than competition. The subdivision of labor, as Adam Smith saw, was specialization for the purpose of securing fuller opportunities for cooperation. It made for efficiency because it made each individual necessary to the whole. Nowhere is the fact of interdependence more obvious than in the highly integrated world that modern industry has brought into being. "In civilized society," says Adam Smith, "man stands at all times in need of the co-operation and assistance of great multitudes, while his whole life is scarce sufficient to gain the friendship of a few persons. In almost every other race of animals, each individual, when it is grown up to maturity, is entirely independent, and in its natural state has occasion for the assistance of no other living creature. But man has almost constant occasion for the help of his brethren . . ."[1] Even economically, it would seem, we are members one of another.

There is a practical, if unrecognized, fraternity implicit in the organization of our world. We are debtors to multitudes whom we have not seen and whom we shall never know, men and women in far-off lands, whose labor makes it possible for us to be fed and clothed. Every breakfast table bears witness to the fact that without the aid of unnumbered workers in many lands we would not only not be able to live well, but we would probably not be able to live at all. "Our lives are gone out through all the earth." This is a commonplace of course, but perhaps even yet its significance is not appreciated as it should be. There is no self-made or self-sufficient man, and no nation that is or can be self-sufficient. The necessity for cooperation is inherent in the nature of things. Man is a dependent creature and never more dependent than in a society that has developed to the highest degree efficiency in producing the necessities of life. The greater man's mastery over nature's forces the greater the dependence of each upon his fellows.

Society exists, therefore, because men need one another and cannot do without one another. They are made for society; they can live only by cooperation and can live well only as cooperation becomes close and more and more general. The very differences of men, as we have seen in discussing equality, are the imperatives that make them necessary to one another and enable them to complement one another in achievement and in service. Cooperation is really the law of life, so fundamental that even in a society that sets out to be frankly competitive it cannot be dispensed with or ignored. Cooperation is at least the beginning of fraternity.

INTERNATIONAL FRATERNITY

Even in the realm of international life, which of all realms seems the most anarchic, there are beginnings which at least con-

---

[1] Adam Smith, *Wealth of Nations* (World Classics Edition, 1904), vol. 1, p. 16.

tain promise, assuring us that fraternity is not entirely an idle dream. Associations may and do extend their ties across and beyond national frontiers. The unity of the church is not yet a fraternal union except in idea; yet such as it is it does survive, although with difficulty, the terrific strains of war. More and more associations—religious, cultural, scientific—become international in character; more and more the interchange of ideas, of thought, and of sentiment is facilitated by such organizations in a rapidly shrinking world. This is obscured in times of war, but it is a trend that is always resumed when wars are over. Such intercourse, it must be admitted, will not always or necessarily create a sense of fraternity, and it may be a long time before it creates a sentiment strong enough to counteract the influence of nationalism where nationalism is particularistic and aggressive. Still, in many areas we seem to be on the way to the understanding that creates respect; to respect may someday be added regard and sympathy. Even today, however, fraternity is an ideal that finds at least some practical recognition amidst the clashes of national ambitions. Tomorrow, so these small beginnings seem to promise, it will find fuller and better expression.

There is encouragement also in the broadening sympathies and wider areas of loyalty that we find in the record of history. The loyalties of the family may be strong and unflinching, but they may also be limited and narrow in proportion to their intensity. The affection that does so much to make home the precious boon it is, is not without its possibilities of social disadvantage and danger. Plato saw this so clearly that he could think of no reliable and effective remedy short of the abolition of the family altogether. This is a cure that is worse than the disease, a safeguard secured at a cost greater than the danger itself. The danger does exist however. Nepotism, unmerited favor, taking care of one's relations even at public expense and to the detriment of the public service—these are not unknown in democracies, or, indeed, in any political order. They are the common perversions of the family relationship. The real remedy for such abuses is to be found, not in the abolition of the family or in the destruction of those fine loyalties that family affection at its best creates, but in the extension of those loyalties in wider and wider circles. The family may be the seedbed of civic virtues; its feeling may become the pattern and inspiration of community feeling. The more restricted, but at first at least the more intense, loyalty may be transmuted into public spirit that carries with it something of the devotion that is inherent in family loyalty at its best. In turn the larger loyalty may restrain the narrower at those points where the danger of narrowness is greatest and where it might become a group selfishness. Natural affection is thus given an ethical balance by the wider purposes of community life.

Thus the narrower ties merge into broader ones, losing nothing of their substance or of their value in doing so. The ties of family relationship pass into those of local community, of city, of nation, and at last of the world community. But this transition and transmutation is not achieved without difficulty and effort. A quick and sympathetic imagination is necessary for its achievement. As our sympathies broaden in this way, there occurs, of course, a definite dilution. They cannot be expected to have the same poignancy, the same vividness as do our more intimate sympathies. They will, however, have a moral quality of their own. They are achieved and developed by conscious struggle—the struggle to "lose one's life in order to find it." This is not easy, and because it is not easy we instinctively try to evade it. This is why the age of brotherhood tarries and why fraternity is still a dream, though a dream we believe that must someday come true. Meanwhile, it is necessary to insist that fraternity when achieved is not only compatible with the full maintenance of our more limited loyalties, but that it is both a consequence and an enrichment of these loyalties. "To be attached to the subdivision," as Burke puts it, "to love the little platoon we belong to in society is the first principle (the germ as it were) of public affections." No *good* family man can be a bad citizen, and no bad citizen can be a good father; no one can love humanity who does not love his own—his family, his neighbors, his countrymen. Conversely, no man can love his own worthily if he has no sense of the tie that creates a common humanity and no appreciation of the kinship that makes mankind one in spirit.

There is here a warning not only against group selfishness, whether of family, church, or community, but also against the cosmopolitanism that parades its humanitarian and worldwide sympathies with a fine disregard for its obligation toward family or city or nation. Patriotism may sometimes be "the last refuge of a scoundrel," but interpreted aright it may also be the first condition of becoming a worthy citizen of the world. A man does questionable service to his city or his state—although here exceptional cases may be quoted to the contrary—if he undertakes obligations that leave his dependents without provision or care.

We recall the force of the stinging words that Burke applied to Rousseau, that unnatural father of fine general feelings: "a lover of his kind but a hater of his kindred." Real fraternity is not a sentiment but a principle, and like charity it may be said to begin at home. A little exaggerated perhaps but nevertheless essentially true are Burke's words, "No cold relation is a zealous citizen." How can we love humanity whom, shall we say, we have not seen, yet hate the brother whom we have seen? Home, neighborhood, city, nation—these are the training grounds and the arenas where in the dust and heat of conflict we may prove ourselves fit and worthy to be friends of humanity and lovers of our kind.

Our sympathies have broadened and are broadening; they do create larger and larger areas of understanding and cooperation. The story of humanity's upward climb and the stages in its social development give evidence of this. The family developed into the village community, the village community into the city-state, the city-state into the empire. And out of the empire when it was no more, out of the ashes of ancient Rome, arose the dream of world order, the ideal of medieval unity. It was not achieved of course, in terms either of Dante's world empire or of Gregory's universal church. It bears witness, however, to something in human nature, an aspiration that may be long frustrated but cannot be eradicated or overcome, however long its frustration or numerous its failures—the aspiration for a wider unity and a broader humanity. World unity may still be a dream, but it is a dream that does not fade. The long distance that mankind has traversed on the way from savage tribe to nation-state and at last to the conception of something that lies beyond, is sure ground for hope that it will continue its journey. It may be halted for a time; it may be turned back in its tracks to seek other ways. There may be retrogressions as well as advances, but it seems certain that it will not abandon the quest.

> For a' that and a' that
> It's coming yet, for a' that
> That man to man, the world o'er
> Shall brothers be for a' that.

Robert Burns may be as true a prophet as he was fine a poet!

Part Three
REINTERPRETATION AND APPLICATION

CHAPTER 11. Democracy and Industry

DEMOCRACY, as we have said, is more than a form of government; it is an ideal which has implications for life as a whole. Its principles are significant in human relations other than political. The challenge of autocracy in the rise of totalitarian states has made necessary a reconsideration of the theory of democratic government, but it has also raised questions concerning the application of democratic principles in other fields of human activity. In the years immediately preceding the rise of totalitarianism the main argument concerning political democracy was regarded as decided. This assumption, as it turned out, was not justified. Still less justified was the further assumption that what remained was merely to give practical expression in the political systems of the world to the principles which that decision had established. This task, it was recognized, would probably prove long and difficult, but since there was agreement on basic principles, it would not prove insuperable. The triumph of democracy was a question only of time.

The twentieth century, however, brought a growing realization that the problem of democracy is far more complex than this expectation implied. Not only was the assumption of the triumph of political democracy shattered, but the question was raised as to whether that triumph, if achieved, would create or even further the realization of a democratic society. There was no general agreement as to whether democratic principles are relevant to social life in general, nor as to the meaning of democracy in this wider interpretation. Sharp divisions of opinion were apparent in relation to vital issues.

Was it possible, for example, to conduct business and industry on a democratic basis? Here, it was argued by many, the principles of democracy could not be applied. Self-government in industry was a denial of the basic principle on which industry was organized in a capitalistic order. Any attempt to realize democracy in business would result in chaos and disaster. On the other hand, it was argued that in the closely integrated world of today political democracy could not be achieved in a social and industrial order in which its basic principle was either denied or declared to be inapplicable. Society could not survive where division went as deep as this; it could not continue half democratic and half authoritarian. Would not political democracy in the long run fail in a society based upon principles and ideas incapable of being harmonized with it? Democratic government demands a democratic order of life through all the varied reaches of the social system as a primary condition of its own survival and effectiveness.

Point was given to this argument by the challenge of the totalitarian powers. It was a part of their charge against what they called "pluto-democracy" that its democratic forms—the franchise, the secret ballot, parliamentarianism, and so on—achieved neither liberty nor equality and did not even create a community of spirit; that they were, in fact, mere palliatives which reconciled the workers to a condition of servitude. In short, the fascists attacked democratic systems on the ground that they were not really democratic, that they were plutocracies with a thin veneer of political democracy.

The real point of this charge is that it fastened upon the discrepancy between democratic principles and the actual conditions that prevailed in democratic countries; it declared that where political democracy was practiced, it did not actually provide people with those elements of well-being that are necessary for independence and self-respect. Political democracy did not work effectively as a method of social and industrial control. It left the most dangerous twentieth-century problems unsolved and failed to meet the justifiable demands of the workers.

This challenge could not be met by the reaffirmation of nineteenth-century liberalism; to meet it would need a new interpretation of democracy, in terms other than those of political categories. The battle of democracy had entered a new phase; it would have to be fought on new ground.

A SHIFT IN EMPHASIS

What has happened is that a new age has brought with it its own distinctive problems, and for these the old solutions are no longer adequate. Before World War I the struggle for political emancipation, the main task of the eighteenth and nineteenth centuries, was over in many countries. But the struggle for democracy was not over! There were new worlds to conquer.

In the early years of the century interest had shifted from political problems to economic and social problems, and upon these problems it was now concentrating. Aspects of the democratic idea that had been regarded as unimportant or irrelevant now received increasing emphasis. Democracy, it was said, was more than a method of government; it was a way of life. If it was a way of life, then it must be applicable in all the multifarious activities in which men engage. Life could not be divided into compartments, in some of which the democratic principle could function, while in others it had no place or was dangerous. The democratic ideal did not permit such partial and divided loyalty. If it was denied in social and economic relationships, it could not be affirmed with conviction in the realm of politics.

This new emphasis was due to changes in the structure of society and in the conditions of life created by the Industrial Revolution. The keen awareness of the new problems was a consequence of the very success that had been achieved by the liberal movements of the past. Traditionally the democratic struggle had been a struggle for political rights, the chief danger to which was conceived as coming from arbitrary government. From its inception the democratic movement had developed in opposition to the absolutism of monarchies or to the oppression of other kinds of governments. Its primary challenge, as we have seen, had been to the exclusive exercise of power by a minority, generally the aristocracy of the landed interest. The battle was waged, or at least led, by the rising middle classes and was directed against the survivals of feudalism. It was a great struggle with heroic episodes, and it produced results of permanent significance. "Whatever may be the weakness of the bourgeois world in the present era of its decay, it cannot be denied that the middle classes played a creative role in the eighteenth and nineteenth centuries, and that the liberties which are now being extended beyond their interests were first established in conformity to their interests."[1]

As time went on, however, the conflict broadened in scope and produced results that went beyond the interests of these classes and indeed beyond their original intentions. By the middle

[1] Reinhold Niebuhr, "The Germans and the Nazis," *Nation*, April 4, 1942, p. 399

of the nineteenth century even, the battle for political democracy was well on its way to being won in some countries. Merchants, industrialists, and the professional classes were finding their way into positions of political influence, which had been the preserve of the aristocracy and the squirearchy, and were tending to achieve dominance in government.[2] They had won a victory that at least secured them against the hindrances that had proved a handicap to the growth of commerce and industry and that had curbed the spirit of enterprise. They were themselves now in the seats of power. But the very struggle they had waged successfully had helped to create the political consciousness of the artisans of the towns. These too had caught glimpses of the liberty for which the middle classes had fought. They had been allies in the struggle. Indeed, they were the fighting forces without which victory might not have been won.

Hence, in the moment of victory, it became clear that the triumphant bourgeoisie would have somehow to share the rewards of victory with those whose aid they had sought and whose hopes they had kindled. This was not too difficult at the time either in economics or in politics. It could be done without really sacrificing the power they had won, and even without jeopardizing the position of authority they now occupied. In both spheres concessions could be made that would be tangible benefits and that would not greatly prejudice the freedom of enterprise they prized so dearly and for which they had fought so well. They were prepared to share the fruits of victory!

In the economic sphere, for example, the expanding economy of the industrial era enabled them to grant tangible benefits to the workers without too much strain or sacrifice. Conditions of employment were improved, wages rose steadily, and a progressive limitation of working hours was effected. These were important steps in the general amelioration of the condition of the workers. And these concessions, fortunately, were in accord with the altruistic and humanitarian spirit that had been a feature of the liberal movement at its best. Those who were really liberal-minded did not consider these advantages as mere concessions; they were the appropriate concomitants of political democracy. Moreover, the urge of the principle that had constituted both the liberals' faith and their battle cry in the struggle for freedom predisposed them to view with favor the extension of political

[2] See Harold J. Laski, *The Rise of European Liberalism* (London: Allen and Unwin, 1936), for a vigorous and stimulating account of this whole movement.

opportunities to the masses. The logic of their principles clearly demanded the extension of the franchise to wider and larger classes of the population and led them also to advocate liberal reforms. The logical goal of this movement was universal manhood suffrage, and with its achievement one phase of the democratic struggle was accomplished.

In the field of economic life, however, sharing the fruits of victory led to the inception of a new phase in the democratic struggle. Liberalism in politics had become wedded to an economic theory that seemed to be the logical counterpart of the liberal philosophy. The classes that had waged the successful battle against political privilege found the doctrine of laissez faire congenial to their philosophy and, what is quite as important, to their interests. They interpreted the doctrine of liberty in the economic sphere in terms of free enterprise, and this interpretation issued in a belief that the free play of individual initiative would automatically achieve the fullest realization of the common good. There was assumed to be a happy coincidence between individual and public interest. If each individual was free to seek his own good, it was to be expected that the good of all would be secured—not certainly perhaps, but at least more probably than through any other practical expedient.

The basic conception implied in this view was the comforting one that a pre-existent harmony between individual good and the general good had been ordained by a wise dispensation of a benevolent Providence. Adam Smith was the high priest of this creed. The interplay of economic forces, therefore, might be expected to achieve a balance that though not necessarily perfect, would mean stability and provide conditions for ordered progress.

It was all too easy to draw from this the conclusion that the less interference there was with this "natural" play of forces the better. And since the struggle for liberty had been waged against governments, it is not surprising that those who had engaged in the struggle believed that the interference most to be feared would still come from the same source. The state existed to safeguard the unhampered activity of persons or of groups, and it would maximize benefit most assuredly by minimizing control. State action, made imperative by obvious abuses, was a regrettable necessity that did not, however, invalidate the general principle. The state must maintain the ring within which the competitive fight was waged and in which fortunately the best would always win! The state's function was "the removal of hindrances" to the good life and to full and free activity. "The freedom it emphasizes is freedom from constraint and indeed freedom from a particular kind of constraint, that is to say, governmental constraint."[3]

Even in the nineteenth century these expectations of optimistic liberalism were continually disappointed, for utopia was difficult to reach. Increasingly it was felt that the triumph of democracy in government had not achieved the good that had been assumed to be inherent in it. When achieved, the freedom for which the individualist contended so valiantly did not seem to secure substantial freedom for the great majority. State interference at various points where actual grievances and social ills became intolerable did not disappear, did not even diminish! The natural play of economic forces did not seem entirely beneficent, certainly not for poverty-stricken millions who failed to secure employment. Reluctantly approval had to be given to state action for the "removal of abuses" or for dealing with grave emergencies. This produced a modification of the orthodox view without forcing its abandonment.

The typical liberal of the old school, however, still looked upon the trend toward a wider sphere of state action with apprehension and distrust. He might retreat; he would not retract. By the end of the century, however, it was clear that vast numbers of people were unappreciative of the liberty they were assured democracy had won for them. They did not feel free. The world that emerged from the nineteenth century was not a cooperative society of men who were consciously free and equal. The social order of the twentieth century did not realize the dream of the idealist or fulfill the hope of the common man.

INDUSTRIAL AUTOCRACY?

There existed, therefore, a challenge to the assumptions of liberalism that could not be ignored. Was democracy compatible with this social order that had emerged out of the struggles of the past? The question became most insistent in relation to the industrial system, where the principles of liberty, equality, and self-government—those principles that were the vital elements in the democratic faith—seemed to receive scant recognition. It was not merely that freedom was not fully achieved, but rather that conditions in industry created a new kind of servitude. Oppo-

[3] Carl L. Becker, *Modern Democracy* (New Haven: Yale University Press, 1941), p. 62.

sition to governmental interference seemed like acquiescence in these conditions or a fatalistic acceptance of their inevitability. The grip of the economic system seemed to become tighter, its pressure more and more oppressive for great multitudes of people. Under these circumstances the achievement of political democracy seemed a Pyrrhic victory. Real freedom, it was asserted, was not enlarged but diminished in the new world that modern industry had created—in spite of the extension of the franchise and of political privileges to the workers. And meanwhile political democracy itself was being frustrated and enervated by factors that lay outside the realm of politics.

This incongruity seemed inherent in the structure of industry. The necessary relationship upon which this structure was supposed to rest was that of master and man, a relationship that seemed to imply a denial of essential equality and also of self-government. If this relationship was permanent and necessary, then it would seem that autocracy rather than democracy was the natural order in the industrial world. The axioms of this order seemed to be that control should be concentrated in the hands of the few; that authority should be exercised from above; that obedience is the primary duty of most people. The arguments that traditional liberalism applied in opposition to absolutism in government were denials of these axioms, but in the world of industry these arguments were held to be irrelevant. The function of the captain of industry was to plan and to give orders, that of the workman to carry out instructions faithfully and without question. According to this doctrine there were two distinct worlds, based on different principles and organized according to mutually incompatible ideas, the world of industry on the one hand and that of politics on the other. But the two worlds were not separate. People did not live in two worlds but in one. The men and women engaged in industry were the same people who voted at the polls, but they were not treated in the same way! Could loyalty to a principle be developed when the majority of men worked under conditions in which that principle was assumed to be irrelevant?

A further point was raised. Certain qualities are necessary for the development of democratic citizenship. Where they are lacking, democratic government cannot function. Among these qualities are independence, self-reliance, initiative, and a sense of responsibility. These qualities, it was argued, are discouraged by the autocratic organization of industry. From the standpoint of the business executive they are hardly the marks of a good workman; they are less desirable perhaps than subservience and unquestioning obedience. For the smooth running of the industrial machine the political virtues might seem to be undesirable. Could the qualities necessary for the effective functioning of political democracy be developed if these qualities were discouraged and repressed in that area of their life where the day's work was done? The qualities of the good citizen in a democratic order are not the qualities that the new industrialism produced; nor are they the qualities that were generally encouraged.

In reply to this argument it was sometimes asserted that these qualities, if not encouraged by the autocratic organization of industry, are at least stimulated in the rigors of the competitive struggle that is characteristic of the modern industrial system. (Incidentally, the danger of mitigating these rigors and of blunting the sharp incentive to effort was used as an argument against governmental interference.) These qualities, it was said, are the marks of those "fittest to survive"; they are also the qualities developed in "the struggle for existence." As a matter of fact, however, these qualities are not conditions of survival, but rather the means of rising in the industrial hierarchy. Whatever the qualities that make for success in business and industry, it is certain that they are not characteristic of the common man. They are qualities that enable the fortunate few to rise *from* the ranks. They are the passports into the autocratic groups rather than qualities that limit and qualify autocratic authority. They are a claim to participation in direction and control, which, however, must always be exercised by the few over the many. The personnel of the few may change as new men force their way upward, but they remain the few and they remain the rulers of industry.

These considerations seemed to make the idea of a broad democratic industrial society with democratic character as its foundation visionary and impracticable. The typical business organization was perforce hierarchical and nondemocratic. The characteristic relationship of the new industry was that of the *cash nexus*—that is, of the worker who sold his labor and the employer who paid for it in wages. The relation of employer and employee, of master and man, became much more impersonal than it had been under simpler conditions. It is true that in many cases the sharp antithesis implied in this was softened by the exercise of a benevolent paternalism on the part of employers. It was regarded as a part of the duty of their station in life to be considerate and kind to those whom they regarded as "their people." This frequently gave to the relationship an aspect of kindly humanity that is not suggested by the term *cash nexus*. It softened the asperities and did something to modify the nature of the relationship, but it did not change it fundamentally.

With the growing complexity of industrial organization, personal benevolence became less possible and less important an influence than it had been in the nineteenth century. Business organization, however, remained nondemocratic even as it became more impersonal. "In our modern practice of private capitalism and free enterprise the trend has been, in large measure, to divest those who administer the capital fund from responsibility for the employment and material well-being of the labor force as a whole. When this tendency goes far enough, the two parts of the economic process fall apart and its functional integrity is lost."[4]

These are the considerations, broadly stated, that have been responsible for the revolt of those who see in the principles of the industrial order a challenge to the democratic faith. The literature of the twentieth century abounds with expressions of this spirit of revolt. It is sometimes stated passionately:

The civilization we create, the social order we build up, must provide for essential freedom for the individual and for solidarity of the nation. Now essential freedom is denied to men if they are in their condition servile. In the new order the wage slave can be starved, and the fact that many of the rulers of industry use their power benevolently does not make the existing relation between employer and employed right, or the social order one whose permanence can be justified.[5]

This may be neither an adequate picture of the industrial order nor an entirely fair presentation of its characteristic relationship. It is quoted because it expresses the spirit of the revolt that has developed since the beginning of the century, with which in our age we must reckon.

THE INCREASING POWER OF LABOR

The question to which these considerations lead is whether the industrial problem of our age can be solved on democratic lines, whether industry by its essential character precludes the possibility of embodying democratic principles in its organization and

[4] E. G. Nourse, "Democracy as a Principle of Business," *Yale Review*, Spring 1942, p. 474.
[5] A. E. (George W. Russell), *The National Being* (New York: Macmillan, 1916), p. 73.

government. There are no ready-made solutions to this problem. There are trends, however, that justify hope and that may contain the seeds of promise. It is at least a good augury that the problem is at last being frankly stated and openly discussed, and while there are some who assert that revolution alone can cut the Gordian knot, there are many more who believe it is too early to assume that this desperate measure is necessary. Developments in the recent past have partially bridged the gulf between management and labor—to a greater extent in some countries than in others—and while it would be foolish to minimize the gap that still remains, it would be equally foolish to assume that it cannot be bridged. It may be well to survey some of the possibilities.

The rapid growth of the labor movement, particularly the organization of labor unions, has been one of the dramatic and significant developments of the last fifty years. Trade and labor unions, violently opposed during the greater part of the nineteenth century and distrusted and feared later, have gradually won their way to general recognition and acceptance in most of the industrialized nations of the Western world. It is true that suspicion is slow to die and tempers are slow to change. It may also be true that justifiable suspicion was sometimes created by the abuse of power newly won and by the belligerent tactics of which organized labor has at times been guilty. It is neither necessary nor possible here to attempt a critique of the labor movement from this point of view. It is sufficient to recognize that organized labor has become a potent force in the world of industry. There are few people today who are not prepared to admit that labor organizations have come to stay and that their influence as well as their power will increase as time goes on. Somehow industry must adapt itself to the new situation this creates.

In some respect at least labor's influence may serve to modify the more obvious limitations of democratic principles in the industrial system. Potentially unions may be instrumental in creating a new and more democratic relationship between management and the workers. Already their existence has helped to reduce the preponderance of power in the relations of capital and labor that seem inconsistent with real industrial democracy. The free play of competitive forces in the determination of most of the conditions that affected labor left an enormous balance of advantage with the capitalist. In theory the rewards of labor were determined by a bargaining process between equals; actually neither in power nor in resources was there ever an approximation to equality. Freedom of contract here meant little more than a guarantee of final authority and decision to the holders of economic power. No bargaining process could have meaning where the scale was so heavily weighted.

The organization of labor has to some extent remedied this inequality of bargaining power, and to this extent it has achieved an approximation to more democratic conditions. Unfortunately this result has been achieved in circumstances that have left an aftermath of bitterness which still tends to frustrate the development of satisfactory industrial relations. Not only was opposition to the trade-union movement in its early history stubborn, but repressive measures were resorted to that were unjust and frequently cruel. The unions had to fight for their very existence; therefore they had perforce to be militant organizations. This character once assumed is not easily changed. A war psychology was created on both sides in the long and bitter conflict between capital and labor. There are signs, fortunately, that this is passing. In the days that lie ahead it may pass at an accelerated pace. There is reason to believe that in democratic countries labor organizations will come to be regarded as normal and necessary components of the industrial order, and as the fighting psychology passes, the possibility of mutual understanding will develop. Moreover, we may hope for the growth of a sense of responsibility so that both parties will display a concern for the public good.

Meanwhile some other consequences are apparent. The very existence of the unions with their growth in power is a partial limitation of autocratic control and is a challenge to it. Over a wide range of activity negotiation and agreement may increasingly take the place of dictation and command, not only in relation to wage agreements but even in matters of policy. The sense of mutual interest may overcome the long tradition of opposition, and mutual trust may supersede mutual suspicion. The tempo of change in this direction will depend on the readiness of both management and labor to adjust themselves to new conditions, to relinquish power on the one side and to assume responsibility on the other. The idea of partnership may undermine that of master and man. If this happens the construction of agencies of industrial peace need not be an insuperable task.

If this end is to be achieved, however, the essentials of democracy must find expression not only in the relations of management and labor, but also within their respective organizations.

The labor union or the employers' association that is to be capable of furthering democracy in industry must itself be democratic. Here as in the political realm there must be leadership, but the leader must never be permitted to become the dictator. Too often, it may be feared, the labor leader or the industrial leader "emerges" pretty much as the "leader" emerges in the totalitarian state, and with very much the same results. The president of the American Economic Association makes this point effectively.

While labor organization has set greater democracy in the distribution of wealth as its goal, it has also kept its face turned backward towards aristocratic patterns of procedure. Faced by the opposition of the hard-boiled school of business which has asserted that policies are no concern of labor, the union movement has concentrated its efforts on an acquisitive struggle rather than on the constructive possibilities of a business partnership. Militant unionism has run true to the non-democratic tendency of all fighting bodies.[6]

This is unfortunate but not surprising. Forced to establish their position against determined opposition, the unions naturally became fighting organizations, and in such organizations leadership depends on fighting qualities. These are not usually found in conjunction with balanced judgment and wise statesmanship. A sense of responsibility and the spirit of compromise do not flourish on either side in an atmosphere of economic warfare. If experience is significant, it may be assumed that with labor's achievement of a more assured position in the industrial order, the character of labor leadership is likely to change, but only if antagonism disappears on both sides and if the spirit of conflict is replaced by one of mutual respect. A frank recognition on the part of management that the days of laissez faire and of paternalism are gone would do much to accelerate the movement toward this most desirable end. Leadership, wise and far-seeing, is as necessary on the one side as on the other. So far it has not been too conspicuous on either side.

The growing importance of leadership may create a new consciousness among the workers of the value of training for those who show signs of capacity for positions of responsibility in a democratic industrial order. Hitherto the labor movement has produced its leaders without much plan or conscious preparation. The leader has risen from the ranks. If we make sufficient allowance for this the quality of leadership in many countries may seem surprisingly high. Nevertheless, this method of supplying

[6] Nourse in the *Yale Review*, Spring 1942, p. 462.

leaders leaves too much to chance to be satisfactory. In England the Workers Educational Association has exercised a profound influence on the labor movement in general and has certainly helped to create a reserve of knowledge and experience upon which the trade-union movement there has been able to draw with good results. Certain American universities are now doing pioneer work in the same direction. Skill in negotiation and a broad appreciation of the complex problems of our economic life are not gifts that come by nature—nor are they qualities that can be created by any system of training—but they can be developed. They are the essential elements of sound leadership, and they can be secured only by a farsighted policy of education for the workers.

All this implies no disparagement of the educational values of the labor movement or of the trade-union as a school for leadership. Active participation in labor organizations has frequently been excellent training for men who would otherwise have had little opportunity for exercising their gifts in civic affairs. The contribution made by the trade-union movement to political life and to political leadership in England is evidence of this. Some recent cabinet ministers, for instance, had their earliest experience of administration in the local organization of the movement, and the labor lodge has been their most effective school. These men, however, would probably be the first to admit that their influence would have been greater and their tasks easier if wider opportunities for education had been open to them in the formative years of their lives. And this would not necessarily have meant any diminution of concern or any lessening of sympathy for the masses whom they are called to serve and to lead.

There is one further point. The organized labor movement constitutes one of those expressions of corporate life the existence of which in a democratic state is necessary for its health. Voluntary organizations in democratic countries may be schools of civic virtue. It is in the smaller groups that the qualities of cooperation and initiative are evoked and nurtured. It is in such organizations also that the first lessons in the art of government are learned. Public spirit appears first, perhaps, in the loyalties that are engendered in the pursuit of common purposes by groups that are only a part of the larger whole. It is true that if these purposes are themselves narrow, limited by considerations of mere group interest, for example, they may be divisive rather than unifying elements in the common life. But this is not necessarily, nor is it usually, the case. Teamwork and cooperation, like all else, may be directed to wrong ends, but this must not blind us to the fact that they are the essentials of sound democratic government. The labor movement has certainly helped to develop unsuspected capacities, public spirit, and self-reliance in large numbers of workers who have found in it their primary opportunity for self-expression and political activity. And these qualities are essential if self-government is to be anything more than a meaningless slogan.

We are, therefore, justified in believing that the labor movement constitutes an opportunity for extending the bounds and deepening the meaning of democracy both in politics and in industry. Whether that opportunity is utilized will depend on the wisdom and vision of employers on the one hand and of workers on the other. Both will need to free themselves from the prejudices of an era that is now dead. It is not too much to hope that in countries which profess the democratic faith both parties will prove equal to the demands of a new and critical age. If that hope is unfounded, then all the arguments in defense of democracy will not save it.

THE EMPLOYERS' APPROACH

Labor organizations have opened up new possibilities of modifying the autocratic character of industry; they have not yet fundamentally changed that character. The problem of giving workers a share in the direction and control of business and of giving labor a conscious part in the conduct of industry remains. Is it possible to give the workers a sense of partnership in the common enterprise, of making them partly responsible for policies, of giving them a voice in management? Probably few would suggest that this can or should be done by sudden and sweeping changes. The important thing is to recognize and admit the goal and by careful experimentation to discover ways of achieving it progressively. There is a growing realization that industrial unrest can never be satisfactorily settled until a broad measure of democratization in industry is realized. It is interesting to find an employer of labor declaring: "Some people think that so long as workers get reasonable working conditions, reasonable hours, and good pay, that is all they want. I believe this is a mistaken view and that the workers attach much more importance to the question of status than is generally realized, and that we shall find this out when the war is over."[7]

[7] B. Seebohm Rowntree, "Self-government in Industry," *Britain Today*, May 1941. p. 8.

Can this democratization be effected without impairing industrial efficiency? In view of recent history it is not wise to exaggerate the efficiency of the existing regime. The objection that had force in the nineteenth century, that autocratic control was justified by its fruits, is no longer convincing. In meeting the problems of an industrialized social order in recent years, industry has displayed a marked degree of inefficiency, judged by any standards of public good. The memories of the great depression and its consequences will not soon pass away. The experiences of this tragic era have impaired the belief that the maintenance of unfettered control for management is the sure path to plenty and prosperity. The loss of prestige the present system suffered then will make it less difficult to secure a hearing for plans that may involve definite if not sweeping changes. It will be necessary still to keep in mind that efficiency is important and that measures which endanger it will hardly remedy the condition of those who suffer most from failure. The problem is one of securing the benefits of free enterprise while at the same time achieving the maximum of equity for those engaged in industry and of social good for the community.

It is not necessary to consider here the many experiments that are under way for this democratization of industry. It may, however, give concreteness to this discussion if a typical experiment is briefly outlined. The project in question has been in operation long enough to justify some tentative conclusions, and in a factory large enough—it employs several thousand workers—to serve as a type. In discussing it Seebohm Rowntree states what he regards as the essential features of democratic government. "The people (1) make their own laws; (2) have a say (though often a very indirect one) in the appointment of those who administer the laws; (3) are protected by impartial Courts of Justice against unfairness in their administration; (4) are at liberty to express their views freely, either by word of mouth or in writing."[8] The procedure his company adopted to embody these principles may be summarized thus:

(a) Twenty years ago the working rules of the factory were submitted for revision and alteration to a committee of eight representatives, four from management and four freely elected workers. The revised rules were signed by a director and one of the workers' representatives, printed in a handbook, and supplied to all the workers. They can be modified or changed only by

[8] *Ibid.*, p. 9.

agreement between workers and management. This, Mr. Rowntree says, is a fulfillment of the first of his four democratic principles.

(b) The appointment of the overseers or foremen is made in consultation with the shop stewards. The name of the person proposed for a particular department is submitted to the shop steward. If he does not approve the choice, he submits an alternative name. No difficulty has been experienced in reaching agreement, and appointments under this plan have "given full satisfaction to both the management and the men." This fulfills the second of his democratic principles. The plan does not apply to the higher administrative officers, but apparently the workers do not regard this as a serious limitation.

(c) Differences that arise are dealt with by an Appeal Committee composed of two members elected by the workers, two appointed by the directors, and an agreed-upon chairman. The committee's decisions are final; it has the right "to override the decision of the management, including the Board of Directors with regard to any disciplinary action . . ."

(d) The fourth principle is implemented by the establishment of a Works Council consisting of "about thirty workers elected by popular vote and about twenty-five administrative officers." It "meets regularly and discusses all kinds of questions of interest to the workers as a whole." The chairman is appointed annually, the office alternating between worker and administrative officer. Suggestions, criticisms, and complaints are encouraged, and the council serves as the normal channel for the transmission of factory opinion to the management.

This plan obviously falls short of self-government after the pattern of political democracy. The directors are not elected, the final word on policy rests with them, and the final responsibility is theirs. But if the Works Council interprets its function broadly enough, and if it develops the necessary independence, this limitation may not be as important as it seems. In any case, the plan has been outlined, not as a pattern to be adopted or criticized, but as an illustration of the problem and of possible approaches to its solution.[9] Its successful operation for twenty years, and these far from years of industrial ease, may suggest that democratic methods and processes are not as incompatible with business administration and efficient operation as is generally supposed. Obviously,

---

[9] War conditions have already produced changes that foreshadow great advances along these lines. The Works Production committees established in practically all British factories are examples of such developments which have permanent significance.

such a plan, while not a solution of the problem of industrial democracy, marks a step in that direction.

It may be that the real difficulty that obstructs still greater achievements of this character is to be found not so much in the problem itself as in the attitudes and prejudices that are the consequences of the autocratic tradition of industrial government in the past. There are evidences that these are diminishing. "The economist, with eye single to the achieving of the greatest material well-being for the people as a whole, must reject whatever aristocratic pretensions have survived from earlier master-and-servant attitudes or have grown up amid the militant activities of swift and splendid industrial conquest."[10]

THE CONTROL OF CAPITAL RESOURCES

Beyond these problems lie others still more difficult and complex. The control of productive processes and of capital resources is now in the hands of relatively small groups. The tendency to concentrate financial and industrial government within ever-narrowing circles has been marked. It is difficult, sometimes impossible, to discern a coincidence in the interest of these groups and those of the public. Certainly there is room for doubt that the public interest has been a primary concern with these small groups, either in directing policy or in utilizing to the full the capital resources at their disposal.

These groups will naturally aim at a maximum of profits combined with security for the financial interests with which they are entrusted. It is not clear that these objectives are necessarily consistent with the achievement of the greatest economic good for society as a whole. The flow of capital into production in the modern age is largely controlled by the trustees rather than the owners of capital funds—banks, investment houses, and the large insurance companies. Under existing circumstances it is likely, indeed it is expected, that they will be prudent and cautious; it is more than likely that they will be most cautious when caution is least desirable: in periods of depression and crisis. They are precluded by their obligations and responsibilities from undertaking hazardous enterprise when this above all else is desirable, when it might moderate the psychology that either makes or helps to deepen depression.

What is true of financial control in industry is also true of managerial control. There will be a strong temptation for the

[10] Nourse in the *Yale Review*, Spring 1942, p. 474.

executives of a large corporation to adopt a policy of retreat and retrenchment at a time when bold ventures might help to change or modify the course of economic events. "Safety first" is a dangerous principle in periods of economic crisis, yet it is the most alluring and the easiest to adopt. It may not be the wise policy from the point of view of public interest. Here, however, the public interest is not vocal, nor is it capable of exerting any effective influence. Control rests with the few, and neither workers nor consumers share in it to any appreciable degree.

In times of comparative prosperity this undemocratic condition will not be recognized, nor will it give rise to serious criticism or complaint. When crises occur, however, and still more when they recur with alarming regularity, questions will be raised with regard to the efficiency of the system as a whole. The swings of the business cycle involve tragedy and loss, miseries of unemployment, and a sense of insecurity; naturally these arouse a deep distrust of the economic regime that permits them. Is there any reason in the nature of things why these fluctuations should continue? There is no longer a blind acceptance of inevitability, no longer a dumb resignation under the grievous burdens these conditions impose. Economic laws are no longer sufficient to explain, or at least not to justify, the fluctuations that bring chaos and hardship in their train. There is a feeling that something must be wrong with the system, and that this wrong must be righted. And the feeling is justified.

In the decade of the 1930's we saw enormous amounts of capital which had been accumulated at great sacrifice and which were capable of great addition to our national productivity, lying idle or being given only intermittent or partial employment. The reason for this novel phenomenon ascribed by those who had in their hands the administration of such capital was that the funds could not be so used as to secure a proper rate of return or enjoy necessary security. This assertion, it should be noted, involves two issues—one as to *how* capital may be used, and the other the criterion by which to decide *whether* it shall be used. Can the democratic principle be involved in either of these questions? It lies, in fact, at the very heart of both.[11]

It is at this point that the realization of the real nature of industrial control becomes clear and disturbing. Issues vital to society are in fact determined by a few and on principles that have not secured social approval. If the policy that results actually

---

[11] Nourse in the *Yale Review*, Spring 1942, p. 467. For a fuller discussion of this problem the whole article merits careful consideration.

works—that is, if it provides prosperity and plenty—neither the nature of the control nor the principle on which it operates is likely to receive much criticism, because it will receive little attention. But when it fails it will receive both.

The fact that stands out in our day is the failure of autocratic government in industry to modify these conditions of recurring crisis or to remedy them. It is not enough, therefore, to point to the earlier successes of the system in a period of expanding economy. The system must be justified, if justified at all, by its fruits in the present; it must give evidence of its ability to break the vicious and disastrous business cycle. Unless it can prove its capacity to do this, some other method of control will certainly be sought. It will be of little avail to cry out against governmental interference if industry itself gives little promise of relief from the disasters of depression and panic. Autocracy may be borne if it works satisfactorily, if it gives some assurance of stability; it will hardly be tolerated if it shows signs of weakness and incompetence. Its bulwark against the advancing tide of democratic feeling will be undermined. It endured during the nineteenth century because it could point to its actual triumphs and the progressive improvement in material welfare that these secured. In the twentieth century, too, it has amazing triumphs in the realm of technology, but these have not produced the same happy results. They have not enhanced the security or improved the conditions of the workers to any appreciable degree. Nor have they produced stability or plenty for the people. Clearly something has gone wrong.

What is new in our day, therefore, is not so much the fact of autocratic control in industry, although undoubtedly this has become more marked and more general, but the general awareness of such control and a sense of its unsatisfactory character. This is the result, in part, of the spread of general knowledge; still more it is the result of the critical temper that the failures of the system have engendered. The public has become more critical and less patient as industrial power has become more and more concentrated and as the reins of industrial governance have come increasingly into fewer and fewer hands. This feeling has also been deepened by the cleavages between employer and employee and between producer and consumer that have been created by the growth of great corporations, which seem so impersonal and so unapproachable. These it would seem are beyond the reach of any appeal that may arise from public need. The sense of responsibility, both to the workers and to the public, that tempered the exercise of autocratic power under simpler conditions has been diffused and diluted. Where it survives, it is in a form so vague and impersonal that it can hardly be appreciated by a public so far distant and so sharply separated from the springs of power. Autocracy is no longer intimate, nor can it be consciously recognized as benevolent. Under these conditions the democratic challenge has been enormously strengthened.

THE TRANSFER OF EFFECTIVE POWER

Beyond all this there has been a silent revolution that has transformed another aspect of our industrial organization, emphasizing its autocratic structure. Not only has there been a concentration of power; a transfer of power has been going on steadily for some decades. The ruling class has changed. No longer is the government of industry a government of owners. The capitalist has abdicated and has been succeeded by the manager and the executive, even though the outward form of industrial organization has remained unaltered. The system is indeed still called capitalist, but this is merely a tribute to the persistence of customary usage. There is today a remarkably wide diffusion of ownership. The stockholders of a large corporation are numbered by tens of thousands. It is sometimes assumed that this in itself represents a partial democratization of industry. Actually it represents something entirely different. There has occurred a remarkable and decisive separation between owning and controlling, a divorce between ownership and direction. Stockholders no longer govern the corporations they own. The stockholder provides the funds necessary for industry; he receives once a year a proxy to sign, but he will probably forget to return it. Whether he returns it or not, he knows that this does not give him a voice in shaping policy. His right to participate in the election of the officers of his company is more abstract than the most abstract of natural rights. Even the restricted franchise of the property owner has disappeared.

This is the paradoxical result of a measure intended to broaden the basis of industry and to secure some measure of democratization. The creation of the corporation, or joint-stock company with limited liability, is one of the decisive events in the economic development of Western nations. In conception the corporation was organized on what seemed to be a thoroughly democratic basis. The stockholder had power proportional to his financial interest, and policy was in theory subject to his control and direction. Meetings were held periodically at which past policy was subject to review and decisions for the future were made. Majority vote, the typical device of representative government, was the accepted practice for giving effect to the democratic principle. Ownership would presumably be widely distributed and the owners would be able to control and to govern their own business. Actually the results have been entirely different. The wide diffusion of ownership has paralyzed the power of owners to control and direct or even to criticize with any hope of effectiveness. The authority of the stockholder is now diluted to the point where it no longer operates. The concern of the stockholder is to receive the dividends in sufficient amount at the appointed times. He will rarely be tempted to look beyond this consideration.

If his conscience is sensitive and another and higher concern sometimes gives him moments of disquietude, he will be overwhelmed by a consciousness of his own helplessness. If the policy of his company, whether in business, in labor relations, or in public relations, disturbs him or violates his sense of right, he will feel that he can do nothing about it. The feeling will probably be justified. He will have neither the means nor the time to consult those who may share his concern, and still less will he see any real possibility of organizing them for action. The normal means of appealing to those who might be like-minded are practically beyond his reach. He will know neither the names of his fellow stockholders nor their views. They are, however, easily accessible to the executives who have all the resources and the machinery of the corporation at their disposal.

That the stockholder should yield to the conviction of his own helplessness under such circumstances is natural. He has the obvious remedy, indeed, of disposing of his holdings, but this may not always be easy, and in any case it is escape from responsibility rather than a fulfillment of it. From the individual's point of view this is a method of purchasing ease of conscience by handing over the problem to someone else with every presumption that it will remain unsolved. The result is that the effective government of industry is an uncertain blend of oligarchy and technocracy.

The problem of broadening the bases of control and of returning to the stockholders the government of the concern they own is a vast and difficult one, and, as we have seen, it is not the most vital one. It is complicated still further by the fact that consumers also have a vital interest in industrial policy. In short, the task that confronts democratic society is the task of restoring the vast and complicated organization of industry to its proper position of subservience to the common good, of bringing it into harmony with the fundamental principles of democracy. Whether this can be done without conflict is a matter of opinion. That it will impose a strain upon normal democratic processes is probable. That it is vital to the achievement of democracy seems certain. Therefore it must be regarded as one of the challenges to democracy that can be evaded only at the cost of compromising the democratic faith. "The true solution of the problem of the government of industry has not yet been discovered. It is in process of being worked out. But we can say that it is becoming more and more of a commonplace that business has somehow to be made responsible to the democratic state, and that its internal constitution has got to become more democratic. . . . Unless we somehow make our industry more democratic, our politics must become more oligarchic. But it depends on ourselves which of these two things shall happen."[12]

[12]Lindsay, *Essentials of Democracy*, p. 70.

CHAPTER 12. Social Democracy

INDUSTRY is an exceedingly important sector of the life of society. We have already seen that the form of its organization and the principles on which it is based have a profound bearing upon the structure and relationships of society as a whole. The most decisive lines of cleavage between social classes are determined by the essential character of the industrial order. The relationship of employer and employee, of capitalist and wage earner, is generally regarded as corresponding roughly to the distinction between the "haves" and the "have-nots" in all industrialized communities. It is also generally assumed to be the dividing line between the bourgeoisie and the proletariat. These distinctions are somewhat blurred in the actual structure of society, but they are apparent enough to be significant. Lines of social stratification tend to follow those that are implied in the industrial relationship.[1] The employer-employee relationship may be regarded either as the characteristic manifestation of the inequalities of wealth and status or as the main cause of these inequalities. In either case these inequalities have a vital bearing upon the distribution both of power and of opportunity in any society.

It is asserted, therefore, that these inequalities inherent in capitalistic society are in practice incompatible with the full realization of both liberty and equality—two vital elements, as we have seen, in any adequate conception of democracy. Sometimes the argument is advanced that liberty and equality are mutually exclusive and contradictory. A society must choose one or the other; it cannot have both. Obviously, this depends on the interpretations of the terms. We have made the point that in any true interpretation the concepts of liberty and equality, far from being incompatible, are mutually complementary. Here it is sufficient to recognize that if liberty is conceived in the traditional manner, as absence of governmental restraint, economic inequality at least is its necessary corollary. In any case, such inequality is a characteristic of capitalistic society as we know it. The questions raised by this fact are many, but among them the most important is whether this condition is reconcilable with both the spirit and the ideal of democracy.

[1] For an analysis of the concept of *class* see R. H. Tawney, *Equality* (London: Allen and Unwin, 1931), Chapter 3.

INDUSTRY AND POLITICAL POWER

The argument that demands first consideration states that this inequality not only is inconsistent with the social implications of the democratic principle, but that it makes the achievement of real political democracy impossible. In a measure it nullifies the achievement of the nineteenth century, or secures the benefits of that achievement to a relatively small and restricted class. Liberalism has not secured for the people as a whole either freedom or effective self-government. It has meant a change in the character of government and in the ruling class, but it has not secured for the common man an effective participation in the exercise of power. Political authority in the last resort, it is stated, is based on economic power. The real government in a capitalist society will never be that of the freely chosen representatives of the people. In spite of appearances authority will be exercised by the "invisible government," which will consist of powerful interests in whose hands rest the mechanisms that shape and determine dynamic policy.

It is not necessary to assume that this authority of powerful interests will be exercised by direct rule or explicit command. The fact is, rather, that in a society where wide disparities of wealth exist and where economic power is concentrated in the hands of the few, vital issues will depend upon the control of social processes, and conditions will assure to those who possess wealth and privilege an effective monopoly of these controls. Democratic government is government by public opinion. Public opinion, however, does not grow in a vacuum. The idea that it is the product of calm and considered discussion, assumed all too easily by the advocates of democracy in earlier times, is a rationalization that is far from being the whole truth. Public opinion is *made*, and the agencies for making it in recent times have multiplied rapidly, but the possession and control of these agencies have been concentrated in a few powerful groups. Moreover, public opinion, if it is to become effective, must not only be made; it must be directed and organized in a highly technical manner.

At this point the most serious consequences of the concentration of wealth become critical. In any political community the agencies of propaganda are available to the wealthy few but not to the vast majority of the people. Under the conditions of modern industrial society these agencies will be directly controlled by groups that have at their disposal vast aggregations of wealth. They will tend to be quasi monopolies. They will also be profit-making corporations conducted upon the principles and with the characteristic managerial government already described. Policy will be determined by the ordinary considerations of large-scale industry. Considerations of public interest will not be absent, but they will not be primary.

The techniques and arts of propaganda have been developed to a high degree of perfection and will be utilized to the full by those who have mastered their use and control. The agencies of propaganda include the press, the radio, and the motion picture—all powerful instruments for shaping and influencing public opinion. These agencies are now in the hands of the relatively small minorities that govern industry and finance. The result is a monopoly of the sources of information and of the agencies of dissemination. Where public opinion rules, this control over the agencies that are most effective in making it is decisive. Those who lack wealth cannot hope to overcome the disparity of power that results, nor can they exercise much influence upon the character or the operations of these strong corporations. Controlled propaganda, rather than the reasonable discussion or the calm deliberation of informed citizens, is the maker of public opinion. And makers of opinion are the real rulers in a political democracy!

Some considerations modify this argument though they do not entirely refute it. It may be pointed out, for instance, that the corporations that operate in this field are themselves dependent upon the public, since the public is the source of the revenues that make profits possible. This constitutes an automatic check upon the abuse of their power and also limits it. They cannot disregard what the public wants or what the public will stand; sales or box-office receipts are factors in deciding the policies they must adopt if they are to achieve success. The public, therefore, exercises an indirect influence, real although not obvious. How far the press, the radio, and the motion picture exist to provide what the public wants and how far they are responsible for creating these wants is an interesting subject for speculation, but not one about which there can be any positive conclusion. It is probably true that a policy which ran counter to a strong trend of opinion would have to be revised or discontinued, but trends are rarely of such decisive character. Powerful interests with adequate resources can modify trends or even on occasion reverse them. A nationwide newspaper trust, for example, can be a powerful creator of opinion, and it can certainly arouse emotion and stimulate passion. This power may be, and frequently is, exercised with restraint and with a sense of responsibility, but this does not alter the fact of its existence. Its extent and the nature of its control seem anomalous in a democratic order.

This power is relatively irresponsible in the sense that it is not amenable to social direction and control. It is, as we have seen, one of the fundamental tenets of the democratic faith that irresponsible power tends to corrupt those who exercise it. The independent community newspaper was an "organ of opinion" voicing community opinion, modifying and sometimes changing it. The editor was known and his policy could be judged in the light of personal knowledge. He was responsible for his opinions. The growth of the news syndicate and the newspaper trust has created a different situation, in which real community control seems impossible. Society is not master over the huge aggregations of power that exist, theoretically, to serve its interest. Nor can public or voluntary associations supply the corrective that might be provided by effective competition. It is true that labor or a cooperative movement may establish its own press, but only under conditions in which inadequate resources are a serious and often crippling disability. The vast scale of industrial operations makes it almost impossible to assure success for any enterprise that does not command large resources of capital.

All this applies obviously to the press, but perhaps even more to the radio and the motion picture. Immense outlays are necessary at the inception of enterprises in these fields. Individuals or voluntary associations attempting to establish effective competition are faced with almost insurmountable difficulties. Prospects of success are so dubious as to discourage and prohibit even the most adventuresome spirits from the hazardous enterprise. Here the possibility of any significant limitation of the power of concentrated wealth, which is able to command the highest technical ability, seems small.

The agencies of public information and propaganda not only follow the pattern of the autocratic organization of large-scale industry, but they are largely dependent upon that industry and will be integrated with it. Their revenues are derived in the main from the industrial and commercial interests that are able to pay adequately for their services. That this is so in the case of press and radio is too obvious to need emphasis. They depend upon the sale of space or of time to other concerns that are organized on the same general principle and form a part of the same general system of capitalist enterprise. Where interests coincide, opinions and policies tend to coincide also. The public interest is not likely to be the primary factor in deciding policy under these conditions. The groups that control these vast enterprises are small in number, but they are sufficiently united in objectives and in purpose to constitute a united front against any agency or body of opinion that may challenge them. They are powerful primarily because of the enormous resources they have at their command and the strategic position they hold.

Added to this is an important psychological factor.[2] There has developed in industrial society a characteristic and pervading sentiment that may be defined roughly as the worship of success. The industrialized society creates its own characteristic ethos. Accumulation of wealth and achievement of economic power tend in such a society to be regarded as evidence of worth. Esteem for the captains of industry gives them and their opinions a prestige that carries far beyond the limits of industry. The successful businessman becomes the object of emulation. His word has weight in relation to social and political issues that may lie quite outside the world in which his success has been achieved. He carries into other realms the qualities and points of view of the world of business. He applies its standards and its objectives to social issues. It is not at all improbable, therefore, that the influence of his opinions will be out of proportion to their real worth, his business qualities carrying a weight in politics to which on their merits they are not entitled.

In politics, objectives and purposes frequently are, and ought to be, different from those that are presupposed in business and industry. But this is not likely to diminish the advantage the position of the successful businessman gives him. There is always a disposition to regard wealth as evidence of capacity and intelligence, without regard to the distinctive qualities that are needed for its accumulation or the motives that usually operate in the economic struggle. Indeed there is some tendency to regard wealth as proof of virtue. The man of wealth has "made good." In any community "the responsible citizen" is apt to be the man who has achieved something more than a comfortable security. Added, therefore, to the fact of wealth, is the prestige that attaches to success in its accumulation.

Under such circumstances it is to be expected that political life will be colored by the characteristics of industrialized society.

---

[2] The psychologist calls it "halo effect" and defines it as "a tendency when one is estimating or rating a person with respect to a certain trait to be influenced by an estimate of some other trait."

Public opinion develops in an atmosphere that determines its color. It is shaped by the interests and characteristics of a dominant class. This, it is argued, is responsible for the curious uniformity in class displayed by the membership of popularly elected assemblies in democratic countries. Recently an examination of the British House of Commons purported to show from the composition of that body that it was still in essence an aristocratic-plutocratic assembly. The aristocracy, old and new, landed and industrial, with the professions associated with it, still contributed the great and effective majority to that House. Business and the professions are in practice dominant in the political party organizations of the democratic countries. Does this concentration of political power correspond to the actual distribution of ability, or public spirit, or disinterested political wisdom? Or does it suggest that the machinery of election and of government is so constructed as to give privilege and opportunity to the successful, the affluent, and the powerful?

INEQUALITIES OF OPPORTUNITY

Here the issue broadens, leading directly to a more vital challenge. The inequality of economic power not only limits the possibility of political democracy; it is also responsible for the great inequalities of opportunity that exist in democratic countries. The vote and the ballot have not achieved positive freedom because they have not achieved real equality. The right to walk to the poll periodically is far from being the achievement of real democracy.[3] The freedom that has been achieved is no boon to those for whom in practice it means freedom to be insecure, to be unemployed, to be needy.

The individualist may answer that the underprivileged and the dispossessed have freedom to rise from their unfortunate condition—if they can! The qualification vitiates the contention, for it implies that the opportunity to rise is present and that the failure to seize it is due only to lack of those qualities on which success depends: initiative, perseverance, determination, frugality, and so on. The suggestion is that the condition of the underprivileged is due to their own personal failures. The competitive struggle is free for all; it is unfortunate that it involves failure and defeat for those who are either ill equipped for it or who do not enter the conflict with the necessary zest, but this cannot be helped. The

[3] Even the right to walk to the poll may be denied by the establishment of devices—such as poll taxes, for example—which disfranchise large numbers of people.

costs of the competitive struggle have to be taken along with its gains.

Whatever force this contention may have had in the heyday of laissez faire, it is not accepted as convincing today. Nor indeed is it often seriously advanced in clear and explicit terms even by the convinced individualist, although its implications survive. The fact is that the competitive struggle is not free for all, nor is it a struggle in which conditions are fair and the rules of the game equitable. At best it is a struggle in which only a minority can be successful. For the great majority of people opportunity is limited; for many it is nonexistent. No one doubts that vast numbers are ill equipped for the struggle, but many do not realize that differences of equipment are as important as variations of natural ability in deciding success or failure.

For those who are actually precluded from the preparation necessary to take advantage of it, opportunity is quite illusory. Many are not in a position to know of opportunities or even to recognize them. Opportunity is real only if it is within reach; rights are of value only if they can be used. Freedom to use the British Museum, it has been said, is of very little use to the uneducated man. "Freedom before the law is of very restricted benefit to the man who cannot get himself defended and perhaps cannot even afford to attend the court; freedom to vote is of very restricted use if active membership of a particular party can prejudice a man's chances of gaining a livelihood, or if uncontrollable economic powers can deliberately make desirable reforms so expensive to the nation as to be prohibitive."[4]

The limitations in the application of democratic principles in our social life largely nullify the freedoms the liberal movement has won. It is clear, for instance, that in the matter of education we are still some considerable distance from the achievement of real liberty. Lines of social and economic stratification reappear in the educational institutions even of those countries where the greatest measure of political democracy has been achieved. In theory the "public" schools in England and the private academies of the United States are open to anybody and everybody; in practice they are class institutions. There is no reason why the poorest boy in England should not "go up" to Oxford or Cambridge, but except in rare cases he does not because he cannot. This, it may be granted, is much less true in America, but the difference is still

[4] J. S. Fulton and C. R. Morris, *In Defence of Democracy* (London: Methuen, 1935), p. 193.

only one of degree. It is not an adequate reply to say that education in other schools and colleges, which *are* freely available, is as good as that provided by the exclusive schools. This may be true, but social prestige counts. It is still unquestionable that "the old school tie," whether in Great Britain or in America and whether of school or college, symbolizes the privilege of the few and the disadvantage of the many. The personnel of the government of Great Britain—in Parliament, still more in the civil service, and most conspicuously in foreign service—notoriously has been recruited from members of privileged classes trained in institutions of privilege.[5]

This, however, is not the most serious limitation on positive freedom. Even in countries that take genuine pride in their systems of free and universal education there is still a gulf between actual conditions and the democratic ideal. In no country has the broad highway been substituted for the "educational ladder." This substitution has been more nearly achieved in the United States than elsewhere, but it is far from complete even here. There are still tens of thousands who are prevented by harsh economic necessity from availing themselves of the educational opportunities that exist. There is a wealth of native ability that is never discovered, or that if discovered never has a chance of adequate development. The poor are still handicapped in the struggle and are not able to enter freely into the kingdom of knowledge. There is, even in democratic countries, a waste of human resources— capacities that are not developed, talents that are not utilized— more tragic than any waste of natural resources. This is a part of the cost of our economic "freedom." It is also one of the most serious limitations of positive freedom.

But we must go farther than this. The Four Freedoms have not yet been secured, nor do they seem to be within measurable distance. Freedom of speech and of worship have been attained within broad limits in many countries, but freedom from want and freedom from fear cannot yet be reckoned among the achievements of any democratic country. Insecurity is still the condition of the great majority in every industrialized community, and reaction against this condition has become so definite that even the individualist has had to acquiesce in state action for dealing with it. This has forced democratic countries to accept the "social service" state and to abandon definitely the simple faith in free enterprise.

[5] Tawney, *Equality*, pp. 92-95

Where multitudes lack assurance of the means of subsistence, political freedom is compromised and limited. Abandonment of the unemployed to the tragic fate of becoming the unemployable is no longer tolerable to the social conscience. The victims of the machine age have to be saved. It is too much to expect the man vainly seeking for work to develop the qualities that the democratic faith insists are the prime conditions for responsible and enlightened citizenship. There are more dangerous restrictions of liberty than those governments may impose. Personal freedom for men and women, certainly beyond what has yet been secured for them, is necessary before we can hope to develop the qualities that will enable them to participate freely, wisely, and fully in the affairs of the nation. All this may be stated positively: The inequalities that are characteristic of modern society are incompatible with the attainment of real democracy. Freedom must be freedom to live a full life.

It does not necessarily follow, as some assert, that *all* inequality is incompatible with democratic principles. We have found reason to conclude that democratic equality means the elimination neither of differences of material condition nor of diversified functions.[6] In any society there will be differences both in the measure and in the nature of individual capacities and aptitudes. Different aptitudes mean fitness for different tasks, and different tasks may make desirable or necessary differences of condition suitable to their performance. These conditions may be determined or secured by differences of wealth or of income. The case for equality of income must be established, if it can be, by demonstrating that such equality would contribute to the well-being of society. This demonstration has been attempted, for example by George Bernard Shaw, but it has never seemed generally convincing. Many, perhaps most, people still believe that there must be differences of reward, since society has long been habituated to a system that makes reward the incentive to effort. Whether this is ideally justifiable or desirable is not immediately relevant to our discussion. A democratic social order leaves room for necessary differences, but the democratic principle demands that these shall be based on ability and worth, not created or enlarged by the ability of some to use privilege and position to coerce others. Differences must be the result, not of tradition, but of social necessity; they must be productive of beneficence, not of privilege.

[6] See Chapter 8.

A society which values equality will attach a high degree of significance to differences of character and intelligence between different individuals, and a low degree of significance to economic and social differences between different groups. It will endeavor, in shaping its policy and organization, to encourage the former and to neutralize and suppress the latter, and will regard it as vulgar and childish to emphasize them when, unfortunately, they still exist.[7]

LIMITATIONS OF FREEDOM

The argument brings us face to face with a vital challenge. Whatever may be the justification for differences such as have been mentioned, it does not apply to most of the differences that actually exist. In advanced industrial countries today the inequalities have become so great as to raise doubts about the reality of their democratic character. Private property may not have exhausted its historic function, but its concentration in vast aggregations of wealth is a different matter. That rewards for services rendered bear a justifiable relation to the value of those services to the community is more than dubious. "The fact that men are prepared to pay for something is not sufficient guarantee that the satisfaction of the demand for it is socially necessary."[8] Nor does the industry that accumulates wealth by satisfying demand necessarily benefit society. Some demands obviously are not socially desirable, and all demands have differing social quality. In brief, the inequalities that exist are unjustified frequently in their origins and still oftener in their consequences; they may be neither just nor beneficent. The inequalities of wealth have now reached a point where they constitute a definite menace to social well-being.

Some arguments bearing upon the issues raised have sufficient currency and weight to deserve careful consideration.

It is urged that the inequalities that now exist actually restrict the freedom of the majority and curtail both opportunity and choice. A democratic society is one in which natural ability, acquired competence, and, other things being equal, personal preferences shall have as free play as possible. This is particularly important in relation to the choice of a vocation.[9] It is desirable, both for the individual and for society, that men should be able

---

[7] Tawney, *Equality*, p. 64.
[8] Lindsay, *Essentials of Democracy*, p. 73.
[9] A good deal is being done in this field through the development of mechanisms for vocational guidance and through efficient personnel work. These fulfill a democratic function.

to serve in the capacities for which nature has fitted them. It is true that any automatic device to secure the placing of persons in the tasks for which they are fitted is beyond the range of possibility and cannot be guaranteed in any social order. There will always be misfits; it will never be possible to eliminate entirely the tragedy of square pegs in round holes. But the important consideration is whether the structure of society minimizes or increases the probability of maladjustments. What may be reasonably demanded is that artificial barriers shall not interfere in the utilization of human qualities to the work for which they are suited.

This contention is implied even in the classic tradition of democracy. It was one of the major premises of nineteenth-century liberalism, as we have seen, that the free competitive struggle provided the conditions for this adaptation; that ability found its congenial expression as a result of the free play of competing talents—not perfectly indeed, but with a sufficient measure of accuracy to justify the system. Men, it was assumed, chose their work and by trial and error discovered whether or not they were fitted for it. If not, they found some other occupation.

This assumption has been rendered untenable. Where there is a great concentration of wealth accompanied by great disparities of economic power, the margin of choice becomes more and more restricted; for the majority it may be said that possibility of choice has disappeared. Personal preference operates in the choice of vocation only where there is a considerable measure of economic independence. But economic independence is precisely what the typical wage earner lacks. Generally he takes, not the job he would choose, but the job he can get, and his children will probably be confined in both their expectations and their choice to the same type of occupation or to one within a narrow range of alternatives.

This is less true in the United States than in the older industrial countries of Europe, although even there the number who have risen from the ranks is not inconsiderable. But in America too, since the disappearance of the frontier, the trend is definitely toward restriction of opportunity. And in any case, striking exceptions do not invalidate the general rule that where there are concentrations of economic power and disparities of wealth, there are definite restrictions of equality of opportunity and definite limitations of occupational freedom. Social contacts, the "pull" that social status gives, the training that wealth is able to secure, the wider knowledge of conditions that prevails in the dominant social class—all these constitute factors of advantage for some and handicaps for others. When disparities of wealth and power become obvious, these limitations become serious. Natural ability then seldom has free play.

The argument may be carried farther. The wage earner is handicapped not only at the outset of his career; his condition tends to crystallize into one of dependence, one of more and more restricted choice. Not only is his freedom in choosing a job restricted, but the possibility of his holding jobs becomes more and more precarious. To change jobs becomes more and more difficult. The wage earner is at the mercy of vast changes—changes caused by technological developments in industry, the shift of impersonal economic forces, the whims of public demand, and the necessities of rationalization. By all these factors he is profoundly affected, but he has little appreciation of the causes of his changing fortunes, and still less chance to control or mitigate the consequences. Those at the top presumably know what is happening and why, and they may be able to adjust their policies in accordance with their knowledge; control, direction, power are concentrated there. For the worker there is little more than the knowledge of what actually happens to him, frequently the bitter knowledge that his services are no longer needed. He knows there is a shutdown, but not why it is necessary; nor has he had any voice in determining what might have been done to prevent it. The power of dismissal may be exercised with a sense of grave responsibility, but the worker often is not conscious of this, nor is he generally asked to share in the responsibility. What he feels is that some power, in the exercise of which he has no part and against which he is impotent, has ordained what has befallen him. Under such conditions he cannot feel free.

There is also danger that the freedom of the consumer will be limited as a result of the concentration of wealth and power. The consumer, so traditional liberalism assumed, had the benefit of a free market. He bought what he wanted without let or hindrance. Here at least power was his, for it was he who determined the effective demand to which business would always respond. But monopolies can seriously interfere with the consumer's freedom of choice, and the necessity for curbing monopolistic interference has been recognized. The agitations of the trust-busting era were the result of a growing consciousness of the manifest evils that resulted from the exercise of concentrated power in restraint of trade. Monopoly could be used, not only to provide what the public might want, but also to determine what it should get and on what terms. The trust could withhold supplies, make possible the exploitation of the consumer, and eliminate the competition of the free market. The general realization of this fact inspired the Sherman Antitrust Act of 1890 and Theodore Roosevelt's antitrust campaign ten years later.

The trust-busting campaigns did something to retard the development of monopoly, but they did not curb it effectively. The concentration of economic power was only slightly halted by the application of antitrust laws. What was not realized clearly enough was that combating and eradicating abuses would not eliminate the tendencies making for monopoly. Concentration of power went on because technological changes and the conditions under which the new methods were utilized made concentration inevitable, and concentration created monopoly or quasi monopoly. These forces have since operated across national boundaries. Cartels, international in personnel and in scope, control the production and distribution of certain vital commodities over vast areas. Interlocking directorates, quota agreements, the exchange of patents and of secret processes, the fixing of price limits—these are the general features of economic development on a world scale and some of the mechanisms that concentrate control in fewer and fewer hands.

The result is the disappearance in large measure of the free market and the automatic consumer control of an earlier and simpler industrial order. Supplies can be effectively curtailed or withheld; new processes may be introduced or withheld; patents may be exchanged on conditions that do not conform to the public interest or even to national interest. Some of the consequences of these agreements in relation to war production have startled the general public into awareness of actual conditions. But the discussions stimulated by this new awareness of the facts have sometimes obscured the fundamental issues involved. The real question is not whether the particular agreements brought to public notice run counter to public interest. Here there may be differences of opinion. The vital question is whether in such agreements the public interest is or can be a primary consideration. The public has no real opportunity or power to exercise control over the terms of such agreements. The purposes for which they are made may be justifiable, but the public certainly has no effective means of passing judgment upon them.

Here then is power actively exercised. To what or to whom

is this power responsible and whose interests are to determine its use? It is no longer possible to believe that large-scale industry is concerned merely with the simple but vitally important task of satisfying wants. At present it can stimulate wants or refuse to stimulate them; it can also create them. It can determine how and when improved means of satisfying wants are to be withheld or made available, and on what conditions. The business world has developed a government of its own; and it is not responsible government, nor is it democratic. The belief that consumers still enjoy the freedom that was one of the alluring attractions of laissez faire can no longer be accepted. If it has not already passed away, it is passing.

INEQUALITY AND SOCIAL UNITY

The final point to be considered is perhaps crucial. It too may be put in the form of a question, the form in which one meets it most frequently: Does the present order justify us in the belief that it is capable of securing and maintaining that sense of unity which is the essence of public spirit and which is the necessary condition of real community life? Is it conducive to, or consistent with, the realization of fraternity? "If a house be divided against itself, that house cannot stand" is an ancient truth. Society today, so the charge runs, is a house divided. Any nation in our modern world is, in fact, two nations, one of the rich and privileged, and one of the poor and dispossessed. Inequalities that go too deep and involve burdens too heavy exist in combination with a conscious demand by the workers for a better life. It is a demand that the democratic achievement itself has helped to create. The masses have caught a glimpse of a land of promise and will not be content until they have possessed it. The question that confronts us is whether democratic processes are capable of resolving these divisions and of finding a solution for the problems underlying them. The alternative is revolution.

Unfortunately, *revolution* is an ambiguous term. Sometimes it is used loosely to denote any considerable change of habit, custom, or mode of thought. With more justification it is used to mean any far-reaching social change that involves a fundamental reconstruction of the social order, such as occurred during the Industrial Revolution. In this sense the conflicts of our age are revolutionary both in their character and in their probable consequences. That our era demands far-reaching social changes is clearly suggested in our argument up to this point. It seems certain that we must face the necessity of creating a new order. Having succeeded in preventing the imposition of a totalitarian new order upon the world, and upon ourselves in particular, it is now our obligation to develop a social order worthy of that achievement. In this sense our choice has been determined for us. Men will not make the utmost sacrifices for a return to the world as it was in the "locust years"; there is neither incentive nor inspiration in such a prospect. Nor, as our argument implies, will the doctrines of nineteenth-century individualism and of laissez faire be adequate as bases for a new and better social order. At what point change passes from what may fairly be described as evolution and becomes revolution is a moot point, which need not at the moment be decided.

There is another sense, however, in which the meaning of the term *revolution* is definite. It is change brought about by extralegal or unconstitutional methods and by a resort to force that is not provided for in the processes of ordinary government. This is the traditional and specific interpretation of the term, and it is the sense in which it is used here. From the point of view of this interpretation the question with which we are concerned is this: Can the far-reaching changes that are necessary in our time be effected by means of the normal processes of democratic government? Or are they of such a character that resort to force is probable or perchance inevitable? Is democracy destined to prove inadequate to the task which at the crisis of our fate confronts us? To put the question paradoxically: Can we achieve the necessary revolutionary changes and still avoid revolution? Will democracy prove capable of resolving the conflicts inevitable in a time of critical transition, so that the ultimate use of violence is neither necessary nor probable?

The most positive answer to this question is that of the orthodox Marxian, who insists that conditions of class warfare are inherent in industrialized society and that the collapse of this society will be effected by revolution. It is not necessary to discuss this dogmatic assertion and certainly not to accept it. It will be more profitable to consider the modified form in which a similar but more cautious judgment is stated, and in which the same general point of view is implied: Democracy is in crisis and the issue of the crisis is uncertain. It may be that capitalism, a necessary phase in the economic development of the world, has fulfilled its historic function. The extreme unsettlement and the chronic unrest of our time are the symptoms of a decaying social order. We may be witnessing the beginnings of the end of an era. There is at least the threat of violent revolution and it may be that revolution alone will be sufficient to resolve the tensions and antagonisms of a society sick almost unto death. It is not a consummation to be desired; it is a tragedy to be feared.

This argument, therefore, is in no sense a plea for revolution. The view does not imply any opposition in principle to democracy; it expresses rather a deep skepticism with regard to the efficacy of its methods and the adequacy of its processes. The achievements of democracy in politics are recognized. But these achievements have not been enough, and they may not enable democracy to survive the crucial test. This test comes when the issue of the ultimate possession and exercise of power is raised, and the determination to retain power is as stubborn as the resolve to seize it. Power may be lost in defeat, but those who have possessed it have never yielded it up without a struggle. There is no reason to suppose they ever will. Rulers may be dethroned; they never abdicate. Revolution, like war, is always tragic, but peoples will be as unlikely to avoid the one as they have been unable to prevent the other merely by recognizing its tragic character.

Before rejecting this pessimistic conclusion, it is important that we at least attempt a realistic appraisal of the facts that seem to make it plausible. It has been suggested earlier that the division of society into two clear-cut classes is too sharp; actually the line of demarcation between classes in present-day society is not so clear and deep as is implied in this argument. The propertied class is no longer the small segregated class that it was in the middle of the last century. That there are extremes of wealth and poverty in every country is manifest, but in between the extremes there are infinite gradations. In the middle rather than at the extremes are to be found the great majority of the people.[10] Moreover, the disparities have on the whole diminished rather than increased. The number of people who now have an interest of some kind in the maintenance and security of property is greater than ever before in the world's history. Relatively few of the workers are entirely without possessions. Most of them exercise ownership of some kind, even if it is only in the form of insurance, shares in

[10] Hitler realized the inadequacy of the Marxian division of society into the simple categories of bourgeoisie and proletariat. He found his greatest following among the "little men" who were definitely not prepared to regard themselves as proletarians, and to these in particular his appeal proved extraordinarily effective. His movement was in large measure a movement of the "white collar" class, suffering from a sense of grave insecurity and frustration and yet almost completely immune to the communist appeal.

the cooperative, or a meager balance in the savings bank. The concern of the owner whose property is small is commensurate not with the magnitude of his possessions, but with its vital importance in relation to the hazards of life. The "little man" may feel his dependence on the little that has cost him so much, more keenly than does the millionaire upon the much that has cost him so little. He may fear and resent any threat to his scant margin of security with a fiercer intensity than will the rich man in relation to his fortune.

That this circumstance has tended to counteract the dangers which threaten wealth and also to weaken the appeal for revolutionary or even radical change has been made clear on many occasions in recent years. It has to some extent blunted the edge of the weapons of attack upon inequality and even upon privilege. The average worker, so long as he has a competence and a modicum of security, is naturally conservative. This seems to be proved by the traditional moderation of typical workers. They have always needed a strong lead before undertaking hazardous political action. In general, the leaders of labor movements in most, if not all, countries have had greater difficulty in combating apathy than in resisting extremism. In the British labor movement it is generally the intellectual who favors the drastic policy, and it is the trade-union official who, partly because he is closer to the great body of workers, usually advocates moderation and restraint. The masses are likely to serve as a drag upon decisive and far-reaching proposals for radical change. The man who has but little to lose may be keenly aware of the fact that this little is his all.

Diffusion of ownership, therefore, has had and still has an influence far greater than is suggested by statistics, which stress merely the disparities that exist. This spread of ownership has gone on steadily and over a considerable period of time. It was steady and almost continuous during the second half of the nineteenth century. The rich may have become richer but the poor certainly have not become poorer, and the gulf between rich and poor, if it has not been narrowed, has at any rate changed its contours. It does not seem so deep, and it is not quite so visible as it was. So long as it continues, this diffusion of ownership has the effect of creating at least a presumption of common interest among those who share in it, even though the shares may be vastly different. Here, certainly, the Marxian prediction has not been fulfilled.

This, however, does not dispose of the problem; nor does it

alter the basic facts. Inequalities are still great. That the disparities are not justified even on purely economic grounds, that they are not always or even generally the fruit of services rendered, that they are not conducive to public welfare, material or other—these are among the considerations that have gradually found their way into public consciousness. It is no longer believed that these inequalities have a sufficient justification, either in equity or in utility. Consciousness of this fact, generalized and at the same time deepened, has become characteristic of our time. The bases of these inequalities are no longer unquestioned. The result is a resentment that may be in part unreasoning or at worst a product of envy. Social resentment gains its strength, however, from a sense of its essential justice. It is not necessary to argue the question as to whether in fact this sense is sound. For the purpose of our argument its existence alone matters.

It is this rather than "dialectical materialism" that makes the consciousness of class division dangerous to the development of that sense of unity without which public spirit will not and cannot develop. Community feeling is corroded by the infiltrations of suspicion and misunderstanding. Cooperative action is hampered, or worse, as a result of internal strains and tensions. Social life tends to deteriorate into a struggle for the retention of privilege on the one hand or for its destruction on the other; for the maintenance of status or for its abolition; for the defense of power or for its seizure. It is not necessary to believe that these conditions actually constitute a class war, still less that they must necessarily and inevitably result in violent conflict. It is sufficient to recognize that they threaten the essential character of a social democracy. There is a large and growing consensus of opinion that something must be done to remedy these conditions, but there is no comparable agreement as to the measures that should be adopted to meet the situation.

The question that remains, therefore, is whether the processes of democracy can be relied on to effect the changes that are necessary. Obviously these changes will need to be far-reaching.

Thus our democratic houses are divided on fundamental issues. They cannot forever stand thus divided. Can the possessors be sufficiently dispossessed and the dispossessed sufficiently reinstated without resorting to violence—to revolution and the temporary or the permanent dictatorship? The communists say no—the totalitarian state is the only solution. The socialists say yes—the democratic method, but only if employed to abolish private property in the means of production. The great majority say yes—the democratic method; but the great majority, still clinging to the traditional system, are divided and uncertain as to the measures that must be taken to make it work.[11]

There is some ground for hope in the actual unity which, in democratic countries, is achieved under the pressure of grave crisis. *Esprit de corps* emerges in communities and nations in the face of dire threats to their existence. Crisis, as in the case of war, does not create this unity; it does, however, remove the inhibitions that usually prevent its manifestation and its effective operation. In normal times divisions are sufficient to curb the democratic spirit and may seem definitely to threaten it. The divisions disappear when they are merged in a supreme common purpose, but differences are not forgotten, and disparities do not disappear, although there is a sense in which war conditions are great levelers. It would be an exaggeration to say that in wartime there is an equality even of sacrifice, but there is at least a greater approximation to it than in normal times. And it is a psychological fact that when conditions impose hardships that are universally shared, they are easier to withstand, even for those who are called upon to bear the heaviest burdens. The restrictions of wartime also make the advantages of wealth less conspicuous. Inequalities remain, but the cleavages they create are at least blurred. These are some of the factors that help to inspire a common effort and create a spirit of cooperation. The sense of community is heightened.

Beyond this and even more important is the fact that common danger reveals the common interest. But this common interest is never quite strong enough to eliminate the divisive influence of selfishness, greed, and personal desire for power. It does, however, mitigate this influence and modify the antisocial activities that result from these vices. There is developed a more sensitive public conscience, and activities that are tolerated or excused under other conditions become the objects of sharp public condemnation. In wartime there is also a shift in the generally recognized scale of values and a modification in the standards of conduct. In a great crisis the conception of public welfare and of the common good stands out more clearly. Public spirit now becomes a condition of survival in a way too obvious to be ignored. Public duty and public service come to have the imperative character which the democratic ideal presupposes as the essential condition of

[11] Carl L. Becker, *New Liberties for Old* (New Haven: Yale University Press), pp. 110–11.

its own realization but which is not ordinarily appreciated. War conditions do not create public spirit; they do, however, make manifest its fundamental importance; they do help to make clear that by it communities live and for lack of it they perish. Under such conditions the sense of social unity, the feeling of communal solidarity, is quickened; public spirit emerges and grows.

This is democracy's alternative to that submergence of the individual that totalitarianism demands and strives to impose upon its peoples. The democratic ideal, as we have seen, does not admit a cleavage between society and the individual, nor does it admit an ultimate antithesis in their interests. It declares, rather, the ultimate identity of those interests. But the individual remains an end in himself, and the achievement of his destiny depends on his ready acceptance of the larger purposes of the common life as his own. The moral demand that the democratic ideal makes is not the submergence or obliteration of self at the dictate of state or government, but the sublimination of self in the willing recognition of purposes that go beyond self. This is the paradox of self-denial upon which the social theory of democracy rests.

In this sense and for this reason the heightening of social consciousness that crises or war conditions produce is significant. In a true democracy this consciousness is accompanied by, and itself produces, an enhancement of human qualities, an enlargement of individual capacities—for endurance, for sacrifice, and not infrequently for heroism. And while this is no solution of the problems of a society sick from the artificial inequalities that privilege creates, it does at least indicate the direction in which solutions must be sought. It suggests that the cure for our ills will be found not in less democracy but in more; not in abandonment of the democratic faith but in a fuller measure of devotion to it and a more thorough and realistic application of its principles.

For its becomes clear that the lack of public spirit, the prime condition of democratic effectiveness and well-being, is at the root of our trouble. Only the growth of public spirit can make possible the readjustments that are necessary and that will be still more necessary later. The need for far-reaching changes is clear; they can be achieved peaceably only in an atmosphere of willing subordination of private interest to the public good, of ready abandonment of privilege that serves no social purpose. These are democracy's alternative to the subjection of the individual demanded by the advocates of totalitarianism.

Let it be admitted that the moral attitudes which are implied in the democratic demand cannot be produced by feats of magic. They tend to appear, not perfectly but in a measure, in times of gravest crisis. Is it possible to carry them over into normal conditions when the crisis has passed? History has its sober warning against easy assumptions. Tradition is strong, deep-rooted prejudices are not easily uprooted, and there is still in human nature a love of power that is not always governed by motives of beneficence. Still there is no reason to believe that things need always remain as they are. Men and nations learn slowly, but they do learn, and not all the lessons of tragic experience are lost. Something is gained if the goal becomes clearer and if the difficulties of the path that lead to it are more fully appreciated and understood. The vision may wane, but it need not be forgotten.

Meanwhile, it may be said that one gain has already been achieved in our time. In those countries that have professed the democratic faith there is a deeper conviction than ever that none of the alternatives to the democratic way of life holds out any hope or prospect of permanent human betterment. It is significant that those who have been most critical of the actual achievements of democracy in recent times have now become the most ardent defenders of it. Political democracy is imperfect in achievement and partial in the realization of its earlier aims, but its defense deserves and justifies the utmost sacrifice. Its preservation is the first and essential task. The gains of yesterday are too precious to be surrendered at least without a mighty effort. In spite of the fact that the realization of political democracy is still incomplete and its achievement would not in itself guarantee a democratic social order, its preservation as it exists is necessary to provide the opportunity to pursue the ideal, the chance to fight better. This and this alone can keep alive the hope that the elementary freedoms will not have to be won again, as they were won before, through blood and tears.

We may cherish another hope. In striving for the preservation of the liberties that have been won for us, we may see the way to the achievement of new freedoms. It is an encouraging augury when those who have been most apprehensive of conflict and violence become less pessimistic. Resort to violence will always be a temptation to men of impatient temper and of extremist views, but it is no longer the fashion to exaggerate this danger. It is still less customary to assume the probability of revolution, much less the Marxist concept of its inevitability! Revolution in this sense has lost its potent appeal in an age that has witnessed the strange and tragic forms revolutions may take and the grim results they may produce. The old assumption, born partly of the tradition of the French Revolution and partly of the optimism of the Victorian era, that a revolution must always imply a liberal objective and always achieve a progressive end, is dead.

Revolution is always tragic. It is doubly tragic if, in spite of its cost, it leaves men, not with liberties enlarged and multiplied, but bound in heavier chains, as was the case in Italy after 1922 and in Germany after 1933. The democratic way is better. Revolution is the retribution that falls on those who stubbornly refuse to follow this way. This may be the supreme lesson that the experience of this tragic era has taught this generation. It remains to be seen how well the lesson has been mastered.

CHAPTER 13. Democracy and Nationality

THROUGHOUT the nineteenth century there was in the liberal tradition a definite assumption that the realization of democracy implied a recognition of the "principle of nationality." This carried with it the implication that the existence of a nationality constituted a claim to self-government. Where a demand for independent statehood existed in a national group, the argument ran, the democratic principle involved a presumption that this should be granted. "It is in general," said John Stuart Mill, "a necessary condition of free institutions that the boundaries of government should coincide in the main with those of nationalities."[1] This statement, it will be noticed, is qualified, for Mill was conscious that the general rule could be applied only within definite limits. Nevertheless, the statement is characteristic of the main trend of nineteenth-century liberal thought. State boundaries should run coincident with nationalist lines of demarcation. A homogeneous population was a condition of peace and stability for the state; a heterogeneous population meant trouble! As we shall see, there were, even in the nineteenth century, some writers, Lord Acton for example, who were unconvinced and who stressed the grave dangers of this doctrine. They were, however, a minority.

This belief survived. In the twentieth century it found its most definite and practical expression in the principle of self-determination enshrined in the Fourteen Points and advocated in the speeches of President Wilson. The word caught the imagination of the world and was made the formula to be applied in the readjustments and realignments that the peace settlement would accomplish. National consciousness was to be satisfied and embodied in new political arrangements, and presumably this would result not merely in a more stable world order, but also in a more democratic world. Subject peoples would be freed from alien domination, and minorities would be incorporated into those states with whose peoples they had national affinities. This was necessary in order to make the world safe for democracy; it was also a practical recognition of the rights of small nations. Nationality apparently constituted a claim to self-government, and the boundaries of each national group should as far as possible coincide with state

[1] *Representative Government*, p. 313.

frontiers. Political independence was equated with freedom and the satisfaction of nationalist aspirations was regarded as a condition for the achievement of liberty.

That this belief should have developed with the growth of the liberal movement in Europe is not entirely surprising. For, as we have seen, the struggles of that movement had been in the main directed against arbitrary governments. Frequently these were alien governments; not infrequently they were imposed upon unwilling peoples as a result of conquest. In most cases the struggle for independence was also a struggle for more liberal and more democratic government. Nationalism and liberalism were so frequently associated that the association came to be regarded as logical and natural. Both nationalism and liberalism received their greatest impetus in the French Revolution, and the association of ideas this suggested seemed to be confirmed by later events in Europe. This was particularly true in some of the most dramatic episodes of nineteenth-century history. The Greek war of independence had a romantic appeal, not merely because the very word *Greek* carried with it associations of a distant but glorious past, not merely because it represented a resurgence of national spirit, but also because it was a revolt against the power of a decaying and oppressive empire. This cannot be said about all the nationalist struggles of the Balkan peoples, but at least they had in common the character of revolts against rule that was at once alien and corrupt.

The struggle for the unification of Italy is the most striking illustration of the association of national sentiment and idealistic liberal aims. Here a movement produced not only a soldier-leader and a shrewd statesman; it produced also a prophet. Rightly or wrongly, Mazzini identified his patriotism with his democratic faith. For him the sacrifices he made and the sufferings he endured were justified partly by the possibility of a united Italy, but still more by the possibility of achieving a democratic Italy. For him the *Risorgimento* was as definitely a liberal movement as it was a patriotic one. In his glowing faith the two aspirations were fused. And it was Mazzini and not Cavour who, for the liberals of his time, really expressed the essential spirit of a revolt that was also a crusade. Nationalism had come to have definite ideal attributes.

NATIONALISM IN THE LIBERAL TRADITION

We may find in the conditions that marked the emergence of the modern sovereign state at least a partial explanation of the association of the ideas of nationalism and liberalism. Liberalism and the national state had their birth in the same era and came into being together as a result of the complexity of causes that created the Renaissance. When we look back to the medieval world, we are impressed by its unity, which certainly was in marked contrast to the diversity and the divisions that prevail in the modern world of sovereign states. There was not only the unity of a distinctive social system in feudal Europe; there was also the unity of a civilization that still maintained, or professed to maintain, the traditions of Rome. That this unity was good, that it should be preserved and developed, was a presupposition of medieval thought. The ideal was given practical expression and universal significance in the church. Within its fold peoples of different races and of many tongues found a bond that united them in a common faith. In the empire the concept of unity was symbolized rather than achieved, but the symbol was taken seriously. Dante believed that European civilization would find its security as well as its fitting consummation in a universal empire. Others believed that unity would be achieved only by the subordination of states to the universal authority of the church. Imperialist and churchman were at one, however, in believing that the world should have one "Head," at once the sign and the guarantee of unity. The dream of world unity realized in a universal organization, whether the church or the empire, was not destined to come true, but it did reflect the general character of medieval thought and aspiration.

In the fourteenth and fifteenth centuries new forces were already making the ideal of a united world order obsolete. Even when Dante was writing his *De Monarchia*, an eloquent plea for a world empire, the possibility of realizing his dream, if it had ever existed, had forever passed away. The unity of Europe, such as it was, was becoming less and less real. New lines of cleavage had already appeared, and from the mass of European life new groups were emerging. Among the peoples of England, France, and other regions of Europe, there was a growing consciousness of affinity corresponding to geographical divisions and involving a sense of their own distinctive character. Men might still be proud of the fact that they were European, because that meant participation in a great tradition, but now they had still greater pride in the fact that they were English or French, as the case might be; and certainly this new consciousness was deeper and more intense than that of European unity. The result was the rise of nation-states.

Soon the lines of division were accentuated by influences set in motion by the Protestant Reformation. Nationality had emerged; in the course of time it became the dominant factor in European affairs. In the nineteenth century a world of independent sovereign states was the presupposition both of political thought and of policy. This world order was an expression of a basic principle, the principle of nationality.

The new states had achieved and maintained their new separateness and independence against the opposition of external authority—particularly the authority of the pope in the case of England and that of both emperor and pope in the case of France. The struggle was long, and involved in it were many forces besides that of the dynamic sentiment of nationality—especially that engendered by the felt need for strong government. Feudalism was in decay and its passing was marked by strife, the invariable consequence of social crisis. The bonds of social unity were wearing thin, and as they snapped disorder and local wars ensued. Noble fought against noble; the feudal lord took up arms sometimes against his fellow and sometimes against his overlord. On occasion the result was anarchy. If civil wars were to be prevented, a strong hand was needed to restore and maintain peace and order, and governments, therefore, must be strong enough to control turbulent factions and to curb the ambitions of powerful barons.

How could governments be strong, or at least strong enough, if the king was subordinate to another power? Subordination either to emperor or to pope weakened the authority and endangered the prestige of the king and therefore prejudiced his ability to fulfill his most necessary function. Hence the long struggles of the kings, particularly of France and England, against the interference of emperor and of pope, struggles that may be said to have come to a head in the Renaissance and the Reformation. The theory of sovereignty was the counterpart in political thought of this struggle and of its result. Never again would it be possible for any external authority to impose its yoke upon the independent ruler of a sovereign state.

In this long struggle the sense of nationality was a decisive factor, but it was itself, in part, a product of the struggle. The king found his surest defense against the pretensions of alien power in identifying his cause with that of his people. It was not merely a king that resented interference and claimed the right to manage the affairs of his kingdom; the claim was that of a nation of which he was both the head and the representative. It was not merely King John or King Henry who resented interference and claimed independence; it was England! It was a nation that was asserting its right to develop its own institutions, to arrange its own methods of government, to exercise its own authority over its people. There was a distinct and progressive development in a line of thought that began with John of Paris, a Dominican but also a Frenchman, and culminated in the doctrine of sovereignty. This doctrine was the formulation in political terms of the growing consciousness of nationhood. Certain peoples had come to regard themselves as distinct and united, with special interests of their own and with distinctive characteristics as a people.

It is not surprising, therefore, that the successful assertion of nationhood came to be interpreted in terms of freedom. Independence for national states had been achieved through struggle against alien power and by successful resistance to authority which, it was now declared, had no justification in the nature of things. The struggle against emperor and pope had been a struggle for liberty. This seemed a perfectly logical interpretation of this phase of history, and it influenced the course both of thought and of events. It created the presumption that passed over into the liberal tradition of the nineteenth century, the idea that nationality constituted a just claim to political recognition—a claim, that is, to statehood. It was assumed that the triumph of nationalist movements in this sense constituted an enlargement of liberty and therefore that the growth of national spirit contained the promise of an extension of democracy. This belief was reinforced by the characteristic ideas of the French Revolution and was greatly strengthened, as we have seen, by the historic developments of the nineteenth century.

THE MEANING OF NATIONALITY

What is nationality? The concept seems simple and the historical facts are clear. Definition, however, is not easy because so many diverse factors contribute to the common consciousness that is the essence of nationality. Language, religion, the assumption of a common origin, living together in a particular geographic area, participation in a common historic experience—all these and other factors help to create a sense of kinship and of community. It is difficult to determine the relative importance of these various factors, and definitions of nationality, therefore, will vary according as the emphasis is placed on one or the other of them. A comparison of two such definitions will make this clear.

Let us begin by regarding a Nationality as an Aggregate of men drawn together and linked together by certain sentiments. The chief among these are Racial sentiment and Religious sentiment, but there is also that sense of community which is created by the use of a common language, the possession of a common literature, the recollection of common achievements or sufferings in the past, the existence of common customs and habits of thought, common ideals and aspirations.[2]

This may be compared with the more famous definition of John Stuart Mill.

A portion of mankind may be said to constitute a nationality, if they are united among themselves by common sympathies, which do not exist between them and any others, desire to be under the same government, and desire that it should be governed by themselves, exclusively. This feeling of nationality may have been generated by various causes. Sometimes it is the effect of identity of race and descent. Community of language and community of religion greatly contribute to it. Geographical limits are one of its causes. But the strongest of all is the identity of political antecedents, the possession of a national history and consequent community of recollections, collective pride and humiliation, pleasure and regret, connected with the same incidents in the past.[3]

Mill, in marked contrast to Bryce, stresses the political implications of nationality, and to this point we shall have to return. What is common to both these definitions is the recognition of the importance of sentiments, emotions, and sympathies in creating a sense of nationality.

Can any of the factors mentioned be regarded as fundamental? This cannot be said of race, of religion, or of language, important as any one of these may be in the case of some particular nation. The English are a mixed race; the Swiss are divided into three national groups by language; and both in England and in Switzerland there are fairly sharp religious differences. On the other hand, in certain cases one or more of these factors may be pre-eminently important. There is a Jewish nation in which religion is a primary factor in maintaining a strong common sentiment; racial origin also has a striking and unmistakable importance. It is clear, therefore, that the importance of these different elements varies greatly.

[2] James Bryce, *International Relations* (New York: Macmillan, 1922), pp. 116–17.
[3] *Representative Government*, Chapter 16.

In some cases, indeed, the assumption of a common racial origin is absent; in others a common religion has little if any significance. Clearly neither of these factors is important in the case of the United States.

The attempt to analyze the concept of nationality so as to determine the essential factor is probably futile. Even so plausible a suggestion as the following is not convincing.

A nation is a body of people united by a corporate sentiment of peculiar intensity, intimacy, and dignity related to a definite home country. Every nation has a home, though some nations such as the Jews, the Irish, the Norwegians, and the Poles live for the greater part in exile. If the Jews ceased to feel a peculiar affection for Palestine or the Irish for Ireland, they would both cease to be nations as the gypsies have ceased to be a nation, and when an individual Jew ceases to feel affection for Palestine, or an individual Irishman ceases to feel affection for Ireland, he ceases to be a Jew or an Irishman.[4]

There is some force in this contention, but it is doubtful whether the subjective element is as fundamental as the author suggests. Poles are intensely nationalistic, but the feeling of a Pole for Poland may become exceedingly attenuated after some years in the United States; frequently it is no longer a "sentiment of peculiar intensity." And a Jew need not be a Zionist in order to be a good Jew!

We may therefore abandon the quest for a specific factor responsible for, and entirely explaining, nationality. It may not be possible to explain why this "corporate sentiment" exists, but it is not difficult to see how it comes into existence. It is always the product of historic experience. People live together, having relationships with other groups but definitely separate from them. The causes that brought them together may be discernible in the historic record, as, for instance, in the case of the Britons, Angles, Saxons, Jutes, Danes, and Normans, who became fused into the English nation. Or the causes may be lost in the mists of the dim ages that preceded history. The members of a nation may be drawn from the four corners of the earth, as in the case of the United States. The supremely important fact is that they do come together and pass through experiences that are specifically those, not of individuals merely, but of the group. They live together, fight together, and endure together, sharing common ex-

[4] A. E. Zimmern, *Nationality and Government* (London: Chatto and Windus, 1918), p. 52.

periences of danger, suffering, exaltation, and enterprise. A nation is a human community that has its own distinctive history.

In the course of time the consciousness of a common destiny emerges. There are certain memories held in common that cease to be the memories merely of a generation; they become the heritage of succeeding generations. Certain words—such as *The White Mountain* for the Czechs, *Valley Forge* and *Gettysburg* for Americans, *Trafalgar* for the British—come to have an emotional and even a mystical connotation. They do not merely recall events; they suggest a tradition, and they also serve to express and enrich that tradition. The memories that are cherished are those of a people, and the emotion they invoke is a collective one. They denote experiences that have been crises faced and lived through, and that have left their impress upon the mind and spirit of the group. Generally in the great crises individuals emerge from the common life who express the spirit and purpose of these experiences. They become the revered heroes, the representative men of the group. They seem in a sense to incarnate the spirit and embody the ideals that are gradually and unconsciously being molded into a tradition. Something is born and grows which, perhaps even in more than metaphor, becomes "the soul of a people" or "the genius of a nation." It finds typical utterance in Wordsworth's ode:

> We must be free or die, who speak the tongue
> That Shakespeare spake; the faith and morals hold
> Which Milton held.—In everything we are sprung
> Of Earth's first blood, have titles manifold . . .

A similar sentiment could be found in the literature of all peoples who have a clear national consciousness. A living tradition has come into existence, and as it grows into self-consciousness, it creates what may be a justifiable pride in, and love for, the national being.

Where this has happened, differences of race, of language, of religion, and of a homeland even, will not be strong enough to impair or certainly not to destroy this corporate sentiment or to deprive it of its "peculiar intensity, intimacy, and dignity." These various factors will still be important, but they may be much less so than the consciousness of participation in a common tradition and in a corporate life. The United States is both proof and illustration of this particular fact. There is here a nation, in spite of differences of origin, of race, of religion, and in a measure even of language. It has its own tradition in which differences have been or are being fused, as the metaphor of the melting pot suggests. A common loyalty absorbs the older loyalties, and a corporate sentiment overwhelms the particular sentiments of men and women drawn from other lands. They retain some measure of sentimental attachment for the "old country," but it is not comparable to their dynamic loyalty to the nation to which they now feel they belong.

The main explanation of this sense of community is not far to seek. There is a way of life implied in the national being and the stamp of a particular tradition on the national character. The peoples of the United States have passed through the fires of great crises—the War of Independence, the Civil War, the great depressions and panics; they have engaged in great common enterprises—the conquest of the wilderness, the spanning of a continent, the harnessing of mighty natural resources. And in their great crises and their great enterprises they have produced their representative men: Washington, Jefferson, and Lincoln in politics; Longfellow, Emerson, and Hawthorne in letters, to mention only a few. Such men are not only great men, they are great Americans, bearing in their lives and thought the impress of the land that gave them birth. They both express and help to make the culture that is distinctive of their nation. The peoples have become a people!

Nationality therefore implies a culture, and this gives color to the thought and aspirations of the people who in greater or less degree share in it. This too becomes clear, even in the case of one of the youngest nations, the United States. Walt Whitman might have been born in another land, but he would not then have sung the particular songs he sang. Carl Sandburg would have been a poet in any clime, but he would not have been the poet of broad spaces and of a broad humanity except in the Middle West. This is true of music too. American folk songs bear the imprint of their origin in the life of this people. Many races, white and colored, have contributed to its musical heritage, but in spite of this it has its distinctive American color. Literature, art, music, poetry, ideas, the political tradition of freedom and equality—these are vital national possessions and bear the marks of their national origin in spite of the fact that the arts speak a universal language. This is still more obviously true in the case of the older nations—so obvious that it is not necessary to stress it.

This, then, is what we mean by nationality: a corporate sentiment implying something distinctive in the matter of character, tradition, and culture, and created in the historic experiences of a particular people. It issues naturally in a desire to cooperate for common ends and to live together in common understanding. It involves for the individual the sense of belonging to the group, a sense of obligation in relation to certain loyalties, and a feeling of kinship with others of his own nation.

A WORLD OF VARIETY

The human world is a world of nations and of nationalities. It is, therefore, a world of variety—a variety beyond even that implied in the fact of individuality. There is a principle of universal unity that binds together our common humanity, but it is a unity in diversity. It is not unreasonable to assume that this diversity has meaning and purpose, that it makes possible the enrichment, rather than the impoverishment, of the world's life. Nations, like individuals, are different from one another; they may, therefore, be complementary to one another, all equally necessary to the achievement of the purpose of the whole. They are necessary in somewhat different ways. Ideally the variety of peoples and of nations provides at once the condition of, and the necessity for, cooperation. Each nation by virtue of its distinctive genius and character is fitted for some special function that it alone can perform. There is, therefore, nothing inherently divisive, nothing exclusive, in a full recognition of the fact of nationality. Humanity, to use a worn but nonetheless useful metaphor, is a body that has many members, all of which are necessary for the fulfillment of the body's vital functions. Nations are different, not in that any one of them may claim superiority over others, but in that each may rightfully claim that it is necessary to the others, with a distinctive contribution to make and a definite service to render to the whole.

Nationality, then, may be interpreted so as to imply the concept of specific vocations for different groups, tasks to which particular nations are called, as does individuality for persons. It is not necessary from this point of view to deny that any particular nation is chosen; it is sufficient, rather, to assert that every nation is, in a sense, chosen. Israel was really chosen, as its great leaders and prophets believed and declared, but not in the exclusive sense that popular interpretation gave to that word. It was chosen, rather, to give to the world its ideal of ethical and universal religion. But Greece too was chosen, and Rome! The great task of civilization is a cooperative task, divided among the nations according to their genius, their traditions, and the historical conditions of their life. To each there is entrusted a work peculiarly its own and in so far as it is faithful to this trust, each may justly claim that it is fulfilling the purpose ordained for it. There is therefore a real sense in which we may speak of a nation's destiny.

History, marred as it is by conflicts and wars, still bears witness to the valuable contributions that nationalities, by virtue of their distinctive characters, have made to the culture of the world. It is the variety of national character, of customs and habits, of institutions and thought, that gives color to the human scene. Few indeed would desire a world of drab uniformity, even if such a world were conceivable. Besides, this variety and the interplay of differing points of view which it has made possible, have enriched both the thought and the achievement of the human race. Western culture is a stream with many tributaries; or, to change the figure, the pattern of our civilization has been woven of many strands, differing in color but all contributing to the design.

How disastrous [writes John Morley] would have been the gap if European history had missed the cosmopolitan radiation of ideas from France; or the poetry, art and science of Italy; or the science, philosophy and music of Germany; or the grave heroic types, the humour, the literary force of Spain; the creation of grand worlds in thought, wisdom, knowledge,—the poetic beauty, civil life, humane pity,— immortally associated with the past of England in the world's illuminated scroll. It is not one tributary, but the confluence of all, that has fed the waters and guided the currents of the main stream.[5]

Clearly there is nothing divisive or disruptive in nationality conceived in this sense. National loyalty need not be incompatible with the larger loyalties, whether to a state in which there are a number of diverse national groups, or to humanity as a whole. Loyalty to the lesser group, as Burke pointed out long ago, is not incompatible with loyalty to the wider community; rather is the lesser loyalty a condition of the greater. The man who fails in his loyalty to the state of which he is a member is not likely to be a true humanitarian. Similarly, loyalty to a particular nationality within a state, carrying with it an appreciation of its culture and regard for its tradition, is no bar to good citizen-

[5] John Morley, *On Politics and History* (New York: Macmillan, 1914), pp. 119–20.

ship or to sound patriotism. It may and ought to mean an enrichment of both. This diversity, as Lord Acton pointed out, is also "one of the chief instruments of civilization; and, as such, it is in the natural and providential order, and indicates a state of greater advancement than the national unity which is the ideal of modern liberalism."[6]

THE PRINCIPLE OF SELF-DETERMINATION

At this point, however, we pass from the idea of nationality to some of the problems connected with it. They are the result, not of the existence of nationality, but of the claims that are frequently based upon it. Some of these claims are implied in the definition already quoted from John Stuart Mill. Do members of the same nation necessarily "desire to be under the same government, and desire that it should be governed by themselves, exclusively"? And is the claim that this implies to be admitted without question? Mill, as we have seen, had little doubt of the answer. He believed that the existence of independent governments for national groups was a necessary implication of democracy. "One hardly knows what any division of the human race should be free to do, if not to determine with which of the various collective bodies of human beings they choose to associate themselves."[7] In this, Mill is fairly representative of the thought of his time. Self-determination meant just this, and the application of this principle, so it was believed, would tend to remove the tensions and help to secure the stability of the world order.

It is clear now, however, that this assumption was not entirely justified even in the conditions that prevailed in Mill's own day. There were, and there still are, many nationalities incorporated within states and forming parts of larger political unities in which the desire for independence does not exist. In Great Britain, for instance, there are still at least three well-defined nationalities that are content to retain their political unity. In both Wales and Scotland there have been, and still are, movements that aim at the achievement of home rule, but the demand has never been for independence, nor has it ever led, in responsible quarters, to the advocacy of secession. The fact is that these movements have made slow progress as far as politics are concerned, and they have been inspired by sentiment rather than by clear-cut political ob-

---

[6] Lord Acton, *The History of Freedom and other Essays* (London: Macmillan, 1909), p. 290.
[7] *Representative Government*, p. 310.

jectives. They have not evoked a deep and general response except in their cultural aims. Moreover, the practical objectives of such movements, when these have passed beyond the cultural domain, have been for devolution and the decentralization of administrative functions. The demand for a nationalist government as such is something different. The Bretons too have their own national consciousness, but it has not involved any great threat to the political unity of France.

These cases prove that the existence of a national consciousness does not necessarily create a demand for political independence, but they are also significant in another sense. They suggest one reason, perhaps the chief reason, why demands for independence have not arisen in these and in other countries where similar conditions prevail. In the case of Wales and Scotland, for example, the peoples involved do not feel that the government under which they live interferes with the full expression of their national temperament and character. They are free to maintain their customs and habits, free to develop their cultures and to pursue their characteristic ways of life. Their particular genius is not frustrated and repressed by political restrictions. They may speak their own language, worship in the way that seems most fitting to them, observe their feast days when they please. They are content, in short, because the government under which they live is not repressive, and therefore they are not conscious of any serious limitations imposed upon them. Hence they participate in government, share in determining its policies, and find their place naturally in its activities. If they were conscious of interference or were subject to intolerance, or if their national consciousness was curbed by arbitrary authority, the situation would change rapidly. Then, indeed, they might demand independence and be prepared to fight for it. At present there is nothing to fight for!

What is true of Wales, Scotland, and Brittany, is true generally. The Scandinavians of Minnesota and the Germans of Wisconsin may miss many associations to which they were accustomed in their homelands, but they probably do not miss the governments and the political activities of the countries from which they came. They are content because they have, and they know they have, essential freedom.

The significant conclusion to which this points is that nationalism, as distinct from nationality, is frequently, perhaps generally, not the natural expression of national feeling, but the profound human reaction of a subject group against intolerance. It is the protest that arises when the spirit of a nation is curbed and repressed, when there is a consciousness of unpleasant and arbitrary interference. It is a reaction not so much against political unity as against political domination.

If a group of people have a corporate sentiment, they will seek to embody it in a common or similar mode of life. They will have their own national institutions. Englishmen will make toast and play open air games and smoke short pipes and speak English wherever they go. Similarly Greeks will speak Greek and eat olives (if they can get them) and make a living by their wits. There is nothing in all this to prevent Englishmen and Greeks from being good citizens under any government to whose territory they migrate. The difficulty only arises when governments are foolish or intolerant enough to prohibit toast or olives or football or national schools and societies or to close the avenues of professional life and social progress to new classes of citizens. Arbitrary government, by repressing the spontaneous manifestations of nationality, lures it into political channels: for it is only through political activity that oppressed nationalities can gain the right to pursue their distinctive ways of life. Between free government and nationality there is no need, and indeed hardly a possibility, of conflict.[8]

The assumption that nationality constitutes a claim to statehood would seem to be due in part to ambiguity in the use of the term *nation*. It is customary to speak of nations when, as a matter of fact, the reference is clearly to states or even to governments. This ambiguity is perpetuated, if not to some extent produced, by the use of the term *international relations*. What is considered under this term may have, and often does have, some bearing on the relations of nations as such, but what the term usually denotes has much more to do with the relations of states. As we have seen, a unitary state may be multinational, and this need not endanger its stability or diminish its inherent strength. On the contrary, the existence of diverse nationalities may give it a virility and a capacity that it would otherwise lack. The most perfect states are not those in which minorities do not exist but those in which minorities are no longer conscious of themselves as minorities, where many nationalities are present but without discrimination against any of them. When this happy condition prevails, a higher nationalism is achieved, based not on race or

[8]Zimmern, *Nationality and Government*, p. 55.

language or any other accidental fact, but upon loyalties and obligations that are the product of a moral process.

If we take the establishment of liberty for the realization of moral duties to be the end of civil society, we must conclude that those states are substantially the most perfect which . . . include various distinct nationalities without oppressing them. Those in which no mixture of races have occurred are imperfect; and those in which its effects have disappeared are decrepit. A State which is incompetent to satisfy different races condemns itself; a State which labours to neutralise, to absorb, or to expel them, destroys its own vitality; a State which does not include them is destitute of the chief basis of self-government.[9]

Where the existence of a multinational state is imperiled, it will be found that this is due not to the inclusion of a number of nationalities within it, but rather to the existence of political conditions that create national grievances or that convert national differences into national antagonisms.

This is obviously true where a government aims deliberately at denationalizing its minorities. It may use many different policies for achieving this end, and unfortunately Europe provides too many examples of all of them. It may, for instance, place serious limitations upon the use of a national language by insisting that the language of the dominant group be used in schools, in courts of law, and in all the official branches of its administration. It may engage in a propaganda drive against the use of a national language. It may also penalize the minority nationality in the matter of religion, perhaps by imposing religious tests as a condition of public office or even of employment. Poland under the czarist regime used to be the outstanding example of this policy. It is no longer outstanding, because similar policies have been all too common in the twenty years between the two world wars. Sometimes the same end is sought by encouraging the infiltration of members and groups of the dominant nationality into the regions where the minority nationality is strong. Planting settlements and displacing the native peasant peoples was the familiar German policy in Poland after the partitions. More subtle methods may take the form merely of favoring in every possible way the members of the majority nationality and creating for them a position of privilege.

Wherever any of these or other methods have created a sense of discrimination among the minority nationalities, or where a

[9] Lord Acton, *History of Freedom*, p. 298.

sense of cultural frustration has arisen, nationality naturally assumes political forms. Nationalism becomes vehement when it is threatened or attacked. Even cultural associations and recreational movements may then become imbued with political implications and with nationalist aims in the narrower sense of that term. This has been conspicuously the case in central Europe, both before and after World War I. It has also been a powerful and disturbing factor in the Balkans. It is clear in these cases that the political demands were not the natural outcome of the coexistence of nationalities within the various states concerned, but were a logical issue of governmental intolerance, of political measures that were felt to be unjust, and of policies that involved unfair discrimination. Grievances festered and at last produced the feeling that relief could be found only in the severance of political bonds. It is under such conditions that the spirit of nationality gives birth to extreme political nationalism. "A healthy nation is as unconscious of its nationality as a healthy man of his bones. But if you break a nation's nationality it will think of nothing else but getting it set again. It will listen to no reformer, to no philosopher, to no preacher, until the demand of the Nationalist is granted."[10]

Obviously the cure that is suggested by the nationalist demand for independence is in the nature of a desperate remedy. As a matter of fact, it is a remedy that cannot be applied, as the experience of the last twenty years makes clear. At the Peace Conference at Paris and later it was discovered that liberating some minorities meant creating others. The creation of Czechoslovakia meant liberation for the Bohemians, Moravians, and even for the Slovaks—liberation from subjection to the government of Vienna —but it also meant, among other things, the inclusion in the new state of more than three million Germans. But if these Germans had been permitted the right of union with Germany, it would have meant the inclusion of a million Czechs in what they would probably have regarded as a new and worse bondage than that from which they had escaped. The same insoluble problem was presented by Transylvania, where Hungarians and Rumanians are mixed beyond any possibility of simple separation. The new state of Yugoslavia created what was regarded at the time as a new freedom for the Southern Slavs. They desired this and had demanded it during the war, and there was every reason to hope

---

[10] George Bernard Shaw, "Preface for Politicians," *John Bull's Other Island* (New York: Brentano, 1928), p. xxxvi.

that it would mean a new and better era for them. Yugoslavia, however, never achieved real unity, not because it was a multinational state, but rather because its government did not possess the political experience and wisdom necessary to meet the demands of a new situation. The possibility of unity was real, but it was not achieved. If a federal government had been formed with a large measure of autonomy for the minority groups, particularly for the Croats, the history of Yugoslavia might have been happier. The highly centralized state that was established was entirely unsuited to the situation, and the initial sense of grievance felt by the Croats was not overcome by wise concessions or by any real attempt to satisfy their national aspirations within the framework of the new state.

But it is clear that to divide Yugoslavia into three or four independent states would have rendered the Balkan problem more hopeless and insoluble than ever. And this is true of most of central Europe. Whatever solution the future may hold for the problems of that part of the world, it is certain that the creation of a large number of small independent states on racial lines is the least promising. A casual glance at any ethnographic map of Europe is sufficient to indicate the chaos that would inevitably result from an attempt to impose any arrangement of this kind. National minorities would not disappear; there might be fewer of them and the minorities of today might be the majorities of tomorrow, but the problem would not be solved. The conclusion is inescapable:

One of the most difficult problems of present-day Europe is that which results from the mixture of heterogeneous populations within the borders of a single State. Centuries of conquest, migrations, partitions, and dominations of one race by another have produced a tangle so inextricable that it is impossible to make political boundaries coincide completely with racial divisions.[11]

If this were not impossible, it would still be in perhaps most cases undesirable. Lines of economic unity cut across the lines of racial and national groupings, so that self-determination would involve a heavy cost in terms of material and social welfare. The Austria of the third decade of our era was homogeneous, as the old Austria-Hungary certainly was not, but it was also from the moment of its creation doomed to economic inefficiency. To be nationally united at the cost of being poverty-stricken is a dubious

[11] L. P. Mair, *The Protection of Minorities* (London: Christophers, 1928), p. 17.

boon! The old adage that if Austria-Hungary did not exist it would have to be created, had more truth in it than the peacemakers of Paris were prepared to recognize. And the failure to provide a satisfactory substitute for the old "ramshackle Empire" was one of the primary causes of the chaos in which central Europe found itself during the twenty-years' armistice. It may be important that people of the same nationality should live together under the same government, but what if this means inability to live at all? What if it results in the destruction of adequate means of subsistence and the impoverishment of a people? There may be those who would say that they prefer poverty with freedom to prosperity without it. Actually the issue is not so simple, for unfortunately poverty is the breeding ground of unrest, of revolutionary passion, and too often in the end neither freedom nor prosperity is achieved. The history of the past two decades makes it unnecessary to stress the point.

Czechoslovakia is an excellent illustration of another phase of the problem. It was impossible for the Paris Peace Conference to fix the frontiers of the new state on the basis of self-determination, for this would have meant the certainty of its early collapse. The Sudetenland was an economic necessity for Czechoslovakia, for without it the new state would have been a petty vassal state, possessing the semblance of independence without any hope of achieving its reality. Sooner or later it would inevitably be dominated by one or another of its stronger neighbors, with whom it would have to make such terms as it could; such terms, that is, as would enable it to redress the lack of balance in its own economy. There may have been an abstract case for permitting the Sudeten Germans to unite with Germany if they wished to do so. Unfortunately, if that wish had been granted and the choice had gone in favor of Germany, it would have meant the end of Czechoslovakia, as the aftermath of Munich was to make clear later. All this is true, quite apart from the important question of strategic and defensible frontiers, which also influenced, and rightly so, the decisions of the Peace Conference in this particular issue. Czechoslovakia presented a problem that did not permit the application of a simple solution.

It would seem, therefore, that where the demand for independence exists, it is not always desirable that it should be granted. Even if, as a result of historic circumstances, as a result of bitter memories of oppression and domination, the demand is determined and passionate, it is still not certain that to yield to it is necessarily the wisest course. It is not possible to isolate such a demand and consider it in a vacuum. The question becomes one of expediency, to be determined by many varied and conflicting considerations. The detachment of a territory from an existing state may have all sorts of complicated repercussions. What if the territory in question contains the chief sources of the coal and iron supplies of the state? What if the nationalist group seeking independence occupies and controls the seaboard and is actually in possession of the ports that provide satisfactory access to the sea? These are only two of many similar questions that obviously have a profound bearing on the issue.

In many instances, perhaps in most, separation would be a doubtful policy and nationalist sentiment an untrustworthy guide. Certainly it would seem that compromise solutions should be attempted before definitive decisions are reached. A federal plan for Yugoslavia might have healed the breach between Serbia and Croatia at any time up to the death of Stephen Raditch in 1928. In a much more doubtful case autonomy for the Sudetenland in 1928, on the lines drawn up and offered ten years later by the government at Prague, might have saved the situation, which did not become critical until some years later.

But there is not much profit in considering the might-have-beens of particular cases of this kind. These are mentioned not to imply a criticism of what was actually done—in the case of Czechoslovakia that would be unjust—but because they suggest that compromises, accommodations, and concessions may avert crises, while unyielding and unsympathetic resistance and repression merely invite them. The nationalist demand becomes intransigent as a rule only as a reaction against intolerance and arbitrary authority. The remedy is not to be found in the multiplication of states or in the quest for a magic formula, whether of self-determination or something else. In recent times the small states of the world have had bitter experience of the consequences of smallness and of the weakness that must accompany it. It is possible that they will be less jealous of political independence and more ready for cooperation. Even for the sake of a dubious independence, the dangers of a weak neutrality will seem too great to be risked again for some generations at least. We may be witnessing, not the passing of nationalism, for nationalisms may even be strengthened as a result of the war, but the beginning of less emphasis on its restrictive interpretations.

SUGGESTED REMEDIES

How then shall democracy be harmonized with the existence and continuance of a real spirit of nationality? We cannot desire a world of drab uniformity, of an undifferentiated culture. Is it possible, perhaps, to untangle the ethnic complex that history has created? There have been attempts to do so within limited areas and for specific purposes in our own time. The exchange of populations between Greece and Turkey proved feasible and on the whole worked satisfactorily, or at least it helped to alleviate the agelong tensions in Asia Minor and Thrace. It is difficult to estimate, much less appreciate fully, the personal suffering that is involved in such an undertaking even under the most favorable circumstances. And even with the aid of the League of Nations the enterprise involved a burden for Greece that was not easy to bear. The uprooting of Germans from the Tyrol and from the Baltic States was actuated by pressing political necessities. These transfers were carried through with little regard for the wishes of the peoples involved, and still less for their interests and feelings. No one will ever know the cost in human suffering that these operations involved. It is clear, however, that while the exchange of populations may be possible in some limited areas, it is a procedure that cannot possibly be applied to Europe as a whole. For the ills of a world so complex as this, it is a remedy as fantastic as it is tragic.

A more promising method of approach to the problem is found in the guarantee of minority rights by an international organization. It may be admitted that the minority treaties included in the peace settlement after World War I proved in practice to be of very limited value to the minorities they were supposed to protect. It is open to question, however, whether this proved that the idea was wrong. It is possible to argue, rather, that it was grave faults in the application of the idea that were responsible for the failure of the League system. Weakness permitted the disregard, and ultimately the virtual repudiation, of the provisions of the minority treaties and of various later declarations and conventions. The chances of success were reduced to a minimum by the circumstances under which the treaties came into existence. They proved unworkable because the machinery for giving effect to them was inadequate and the will to enforce their provisions was not present.

Without going into detail, it may be recalled that special minority treaties were concluded between the Allied and Associated Powers and five of the lesser powers of Europe—Poland, Yugoslavia, Czechoslovakia, Rumania, and Greece. Later declarations and conventions extended the general provisions of these treaties to a few of the smaller nations, Albania and Esthonia, for example, and to a few special areas, notably Upper Silesia and Memel, where definite changes of political status had been effected in the early postwar years. Thus it was that the

... States established, restored, or territorially enlarged by the treaties of peace, as well as Austria, Bulgaria, Hungary, and Turkey accepted certain obligations concerning the position of racial, linguistic and religious minorities in their territories; these undertakings which were recognized in general as fundamental laws of the States in question, and as obligations of international concern, were placed under the guarantee of the League of Nations.[12]

It is to be noted that these treaties and conventions imposed obligations only upon powers too weak to resist the pressure of the great powers and upon the onetime enemy powers. This was unfortunate, for it gave color to the objection that Poland in particular continued to press—that the minority treaties implied a stigma of inferiority upon the nations bound by their provisions. That this came to be felt by other nations is in the record of history. The fact is that the treaties did not embody a general principle but only a special device to ensure the good behavior of states that it was implied needed restraint. That the restraint was needed did not make the nations concerned willing to admit its necessity. "It was," as Professor Gilbert Murray puts it, "an error of principle in the Peace Treaties to impose the clauses for the due protection of minorities upon the new nations alone. The same obligation should have been accepted by the Great Powers, and made part of the common law of Europe."[13] Whether the nations are now prepared to recognize the principle as a part of the common law of Europe, or indeed of the world, remains to be seen. It is easier to state the Four Freedoms than it will be to secure their effective recognition.

[12]*The League of Nations and the Protection of Minorities* (Geneva: Information Section, League of Nations Secretariat, 1927), pp. 5–6.
[13]Gilbert Murray, Introduction to Mair, *Protection of Minorities*, p. vii.

It would take us too far afield to consider the weakness of administration and control that further prejudiced the prospects of the minority treaties. There were obvious inadequacies in the matter of supervision, difficulties of enforcement, and a reluctance to assume responsibilities on the part of the League Council. With the general collapse of the League system, the minority treaties lost whatever force they had. It is a mistake, however, to assume that the method of approach was wrong, or that the idea is not capable of more adequate expression and of more fruitful results.

The conclusion seems inescapable that there is no short cut to any possible reconciliation of the principles of democracy and of nationality. Certainly the bare principle of self-determination is too simple to be of much value in any attempted solution of so complex a problem. The important thing is to be clear as to what people really desire when the nationalist claim is made. After all, political independence is a means to certain ends that will be found to be fairly simple and that are generally desired, but independence may not be the necessary or the wisest and most effective means for the achievement of these ends. It is human for people to desire the freedoms that will enable them to live their own lives, cherish their own traditions, speak their own languages, worship in the manner they consider right and good, and develop their own particular culture. It is also an advantage to humanity as a whole that nations should be secure in the opportunity to do these things. The assumption that such security can be achieved only through political independence is the sad result of political incompetence and of undemocratic policies. Unfortunately, actual conditions under many governments have seemed to justify the assumption, but it must not continue to be justified.

Racial intolerance is a stubborn fact, agelong prejudices are hard to overcome, and political wisdom grows slowly. The growth of democracy and its spread depend upon the growth of tolerance, of understanding. As these grow, it may come to be realized that the existence of many nationalities within the boundaries of a particular state need not detract from its strength or endanger its stability. It may, indeed, enrich its life, secure conditions of material welfare that otherwise would be impossible, and give to it a strength that smaller unitary states cannot achieve. But all this depends on the ready acceptance of differences, the abandonment of privilege, evenhanded justice to all without distinction of race or creed, and the limitation of arbitrary authority—conditions that it will not be easy to realize or to maintain but that are not to be dismissed as utopian.

Meanwhile something may be done by international agreement. The acceptance of the Four Freedoms as basic principles of a new international order will help; the guarantee of minority rights faithfully observed and effectively administered would help still more. But they must not be "freedoms" imposed on unwilling peoples, who feel them as a discrimination because the powers that are prepared to impose them are not prepared to accept or to honor them. A new order is needed in Europe and in the world, but it must be one based on the fundamental principle of equality among nations and states as well as among individuals. And this is equivalent to saying that the new order, if it is to give any assurance of stability and permanence, must be democratic in this broader sense. It will probably mean in the present era the enlargement of states rather than the creation of new small states, but if progress rather than retrogression is to result, there must be an enlargement of liberty within the wider political boundaries. Then, if not until then, nationality will lose much of the political significance that has made it a disruptive force in the affairs of men and of nations. It will become more and more the interesting and beneficent condition that gives variety and color to the human scene and that enables each nation to make its different and characteristic contribution to the life of the whole.

A dream? Perhaps. But at least a dream upon the realization of which a democratic world order depends! It is certain that one of the most difficult problems of our generation will be that of resolving the apparent conflict between nationalistic claims on the one hand and the demands of economic stability and efficiency on the other. One condition of its solution would seem to be that frontiers should be made "invisible" at least in the economic sense, and less important in every other sense. The less they assume the character of barriers, of unscalable tariff walls, the better. This, however, leads us into the vast complex of international problems, and these demand separate treatment.

CHAPTER 14. Democracy and World Order

The discussion of democracy and nationality has brought us within sight of some of the broader implications of the democratic faith. The world of the twentieth century is too closely integrated to consider any political ideal merely in terms of a particular nation or state. If democracy as a principle is applicable to government at all, it must be applicable to the international structure that is slowly coming to birth in the titanic contests of our era.

Moreover, it is becoming clear now that democracy cannot remain static; it must spread or be continually on the defensive, threatened by forces that are antipathetic to it. The idea of "islands of democracy" in a totalitarian or hostile world is already discredited. In a sense the challenge of "we or they" is implicit in the world conditions of the twentieth century. This does not mean that it is necessary or even desirable to wage a crusade to secure the general adoption of democratic systems. It means, rather, that the conditions of our time impose upon us the necessity of greater world unity, economic and political, and this unity demands a principle as its basic condition. Democracy will not be safe anywhere if it is challenged by an armed doctrine, dynamic in character and violent in method.

Historically, the liberal tradition had definite implications for international policy. This is particularly apparent in the political history of nineteenth-century Britain. Here democracy had among its leading advocates writers and statesmen who developed their ideas in terms of an idealistic internationalism. The outstanding leaders of the Manchester school were the strenuous advocates of free trade not merely as a sound economic policy, but also as a means to, or as a condition of, world peace. Bright and Cobden were convinced that the principles they professed were essential to a stable and peaceful world order, and laissez faire meant for them not merely the limitation of governmental interference in internal commercial and industrial policies but also the removal of government restrictions upon the flow of international trade. This in turn might be expected to create a consciousness of common interest with international cooperation as its logical consequence.

In the world that would result, a world of almost universal free trade, it was to be expected that democracy would triumph, as it seemed to be doing in England. The antagonisms of nations would be appeased, and, with frontiers no longer impediments to trade and therefore no longer of such vital importance, the principle of nationality would be more readily recognized. Some of the most important economic consequences of political divisions between states would be eliminated. In such a world there would be no great difficulty in giving practical recognition to the aspirations of national groups, and there would be no serious consequences to the multiplication of states, even though some of them would certainly be too small for economic efficiency in a tariff-ridden world. Self-determination would not be an impossible ideal in such a world. Where trade was free, all the conditions of other freedoms might be expected to follow, if not speedily at least in due course.

It is indicative of the persistence of these ideas that World War I was represented by the Allied and Associated Powers as a crusade for democracy. It is easy to see now that the watchword of the period, "making the world safe for democracy," was an extreme oversimplification of the issues involved in that conflict, and possibly many of the governments and statesmen used this phrase for propaganda purposes. There is a danger, however, that the skeptical mood induced by a chastened retrospect may lead us to overlook the fact that for the liberals of that period the phrase was more than a slogan; it represented the logical expression of the liberal conviction that permanent peace could be assured only in a world established on democratic foundations. This, too, may have been a serious oversimplification, but the significant fact is that it represented a faith firmly held by many and accepted by the majority in the countries where democratic processes had become familiar. It may be said that Wilsonian idealism represented the flowering of Victorian liberalism. Its confident assertions and the assumption of its certain triumph were survivals, in a world to which it was inappropriate, of the optimistic temper of a century in which progress tended to be regarded as a part of the natural order. Nevertheless, the fact remains that democracy has always been regarded as an ideal for the world of nations as well as for particular nations.

Although the earlier optimism has passed, the ideal is still potent. A war, if it is to be endured at all by democratic peoples, must be a "people's war," and the peace, if it is to arouse enthusiasm and ardor, must be conceived as a "people's peace." If the disillusionments of the twenty years' armistice make men shy of the explicit idealist professions of an earlier day, this does not mean that the idealistic faith has been abandoned. It means, rather, that that faith is now more sober, more critical of its own implications, more conscious of the admixture of expediency that, in a world like ours, is found in all idealistic plans and purposes. World War II has not been represented generally as a war for democracy, but this does not alter the fact that it involves the future of democratic government. The Atlantic Charter and the growing demand for a people's peace are equally significant in their recognition of this fact. There is a growing appreciation of the vital bearing of the outcome of the war on the character and nature of the world of the future. The cause of the United Nations is related to, even if it cannot be identified with, the cause of democracy.

THE TOTALITARIAN NEW ORDERS

The decisive difference between the totalitarian conception of the future organization of the world and that of the United Nations is obvious. Whatever may be said of the new order conceived by the Axis for Europe, by Japan for the Far East, and by both for the world, it is clear that these new orders presupposed a political organization and a way of life that is not only the antithesis of democracy, but that would also constitute a challenge to the democratic ideal wherever it is professed. For Europe the essential features of the new system were stated in the literature of fascism. The system was to be based upon the principle of hierarchy, and the fundamental differences of race would determine the graduated stations and the various degrees of authority and power of the constituent parts. The "master race" would assume supreme power and would occupy a position comparable to that of the fuehrer in the political order of the Nazi state. The idea of equality as between nations and states would disappear and instead a regulated order of inequality and a systematic differentiation of function would be established in accordance with the necessities of the master race. To each of the various national or racial groups incorporated in the new order would be allotted its proper place and its proper tasks.

In Europe direction and control were to be exercised from the center, presumably Berlin, and the vital issues of policy, both political and economic, would be decided there. The economic activities of the smaller nations would be arranged so that they might blend harmoniously with the master plan. In some areas industrialization would be encouraged; elsewhere it would be forbidden. An agrarian economy would be imposed in one country and changed in another. The guiding principle in determining details of the plan would be, not the welfare of peoples, not the welfare of individuals, but the strength and power of the whole—and in particular, of course, the strength and power of the master race. The corporate state must expand into a corporate new order for Europe. The ruling group would be reminiscent of Plato's guardians, with the all-important difference that in the case of the Nazis the rulers were to be self-appointed and would need no training except in the fascist ideology. They would plan and execute measures of vital importance, would be responsible for defense and security, and would dominate the social arrangements of the whole. They would need no myth to justify this new order, for the racial doctrine of the Nazi creed implied that such is the order ordained by the gods. This was the armed doctrine that confronted the democratic faith.

It was unwise to dismiss all this as mere fantasy, for this new order promised an end to the destructive wars that have marked Europe's history. It promised a solution of Europe's major problem, the problem of disunity, and of the fierce antagonisms and economic inefficiency for which this disunity has been so tragically responsible. It was, in this respect, the realization of a dream cherished, in vastly different forms indeed, by men as far removed from one another in time and character as Dante and Napoleon. From this point of view it was another in a long succession of plans, from the "grand design" of Henry IV to that of the Holy Alliance, for the creation of a United Europe. It was based, however, on domination, racial superiority, and coercion, for these are the necessary assumptions and instruments of hierarchy. It declared that thus and thus only could Europe find surcease from its tragic conflicts and its peoples find peace and happiness.

The ideological bases of the new order for the Far East were not as clearly discernible as were those for Europe. It was an ancient dogma, modified to some extent by a somewhat transparent imitation of fascist concepts, that determined Japanese policy. There was in Japan no necessity to abandon or to repudiate democratic ideas, for these ideas had never been accepted. There was no need to elaborate the doctrine of a master race, for the doctrine was already an article of religious faith. The racial concept was not absent, for the new order was to mean Asia for the Asiatics, and this conveniently served the purposes of propaganda and of such self-justification as was felt to be necessary. It was not necessary for the Japanese to formulate their policy in a new philosophy. Despite all this, the new order in the Far East was not to be different in substance from the fascist order for Europe. The ascendancy of Japan, the dependence of tributary states upon its authority, the determination of the economic life of the component parts in the light of Japanese necessities and policy—these were as definitely the objectives of Japan in Asia as they were of Germany in Europe. And there was also the same assertion that this would bring stability and peace. China's resistance, according to this view, was due to lack of insight and to blindness to its own real interests.

It is not necessary to criticize the ideas implied in all this. What is important is to realize that the system issuing logically from these concepts of a new order is the antithesis of what we mean by democracy. It denies that self-government is a good to be cherished by nations, that it is desirable that all peoples be permitted to organize their lives as seems best to them. It challenges, too, the basic ethical assumptions of democracy. The good liberal asserts that it is impossible for any order based on coercion, as these new orders would be, to be permanent, that no people will be content to remain in a condition of tutelage and dependence forever. Peace secured thus would be short-lived. Fires of resentment would be kindled, which sooner or later would break forth in the flames of rebellion or of revolution. Even if this order were successfully imposed now, it would be doomed to failure and catastrophe in the long run. This would be so because human nature is what it is.

THE DEMOCRATIC ALTERNATIVE

What is the democratic alternative to these new orders? A democratic world order must surely mean something more positive, something better than a return to the chaotic prewar world. A return to conditions that prevailed before 1939 is not an inspiring prospect, for the world would then contain as little assurance of permanence as does the new order of the totalitarians. This old world crashed because of inherent weaknesses and imperfections. Restored with only some modifications and changes, it might crash again. The totalitarian challenge, therefore, must be met not only by force of arms, but by the creation of a world order in which such a challenge will not arise again, a world order that will not give to the fascist appeal enough power to entice and seduce whole peoples and nations, as it did in Germany, Italy, and elsewhere. It is from this point of view that the war has come to be regarded, and rightly, as a revolutionary war. It will not have been won unless it makes possible the establishment of a democratic new order, which must be conceived in opposition to the new orders the democratic nations have repudiated and to which they must be forever opposed.

Here we are not concerned with the detailed characteristics of this world of the future; certainly we are in no position to provide blueprints for its construction. What is relevant to our purpose is to consider whether the democratic faith involves principles that will serve as foundations for a new order and provide direction for its building. The tasks of reconstruction will be innumerable and difficult, and technical skills and specialized aptitudes will be necessary for their performance. These, however, will be of little avail if first principles are not clearly apprehended, and of still less avail if these principles are neither dependable nor true. The ideal of democracy, to change the figure, can provide no map or detailed chart of the course the world must follow in the years to come, but it must be capable of pointing clearly to the goal and of indicating the direction toward it; it must provide principles that will safeguard the world against the errors which have led the democratic nations into catastrophe and to the brink of irretrievable disaster.

We may begin our consideration with a frank recognition of the importance of one of the declared objectives of the totalitarian states. That a greater measure of unity among the states of the world is desirable and indeed necessary, is a conclusion to which the events of our time have forced men everywhere. From the point of view both of security and of economic efficiency, the existence of sovereign states sharply divided one from another, differing greatly in actual strength and in resources, and showing little regard for either the susceptibilities or the interests of one another, is a glaring anomaly. Occasional conferences in our time have not been adequate to overcome the serious disabilities that this condition of affairs involves. The League of Nations, beneficent in purpose, and its many organizations beneficent in action, did not provide adequately for the achievement of the necessary unity. The economic conferences of 1927 and 1933 sponsored by the League proved ineffective. They produced an abundance of information but no measures that could effectively remedy the world's economic ills. They ended in words, not in achievement. The disarmament conferences too split hopelessly on the rock of irreconcilable differences of needs and of points of view.

It is not possible to single out any one factor as *the* cause of these failures. Underlying them all, however, was the condition created by a fatal misinterpretation of the doctrine of sovereignty. Insistence upon sovereign rights became so dogmatic that any proposal for international cooperation was prejudiced in advance. Each strong state sought its own security, believing that this could be found by a rigid limitation of commitments that might involve responsibility. Each pursued the economic policy that seemed to serve its own particular interest, with little regard for the fact that no nation can possibly achieve economic stability and prosperity in isolation. In the integrated world of the twentieth century the interest of one nation cannot be separated from the interests of others. It is at least arguable that if the nations that still professed the democratic faith had been willing to cooperate politically and economically during the ten years that preceded the war, the tide of aggression might have been turned and the catastrophe of 1939 averted. Each nation, conscious of impending world catastrophe, hoped that it might not be involved in that catastrophe, if only it was scrupulous in its neutrality and jealous of its independence. The fate that befell the nations, independent and sovereign indeed but disunited, is history's verdict, written in letters of blood, upon this policy. The nations involved became the United Nations only when necessity forced them into unity in the desperate resistance of war. They achieved their unity in time to survive catastrophe but too late to avert it.

They did achieve unity, however, in the common experience of a fateful destiny. The question is whether the unity achieved in war can be maintained and developed in times of peace. The problem is not and can never be as simple for the democracies as it is for the totalitarians. Coercion is a short cut to unity, but a short cut the democracies can never take, for it is an article of faith with them that unity achieved by coercion is not real unity at all. The crucial problem, therefore, is whether there is a real democratic alternative to the kind of new order that was promised by Germany and Japan, whether it is possible to achieve, on the bases of consent and cooperation, the unity that modern conditions make necessary for survival.

Superficially the unity possible under democratic conditions will always seem less complete than that which totalitarianism promised; it will seem more fragile and above all more difficult to achieve. Nevertheless, democratic unity may prove to be stronger than that achieved by domination, and for precisely the reasons already adduced in discussing the relative weaknesses and merits of democracy and dictatorship. In any case, unity by consent is the only kind conceivable in terms of democracy. The only question is whether in a world of democratic states the difficulties of establishing essential unity are insurmountable.

The outlook is less gloomy perhaps than is generally supposed. There is surely some ground for believing that the kind of independence enjoyed and cherished before 1939 will hardly seem a boon worth the blood and tears that were paid for it by Norway, Belgium, Holland, and the other nations that were overrun by hostile armies—the nations whose peoples have been subjected to ruthless oppression and whose cities have been laid waste by fire and sword. *Sovereignty* may be a blessed word, but it connotes little that is real for the small weak state that must live under the shadow of a strong and powerful neighbor unrestrained by considerations of humanity. Its maintenance then will depend on the practical and material advantage that it affords, not to the small nation whose pride it is, but to the strong neighbor who tolerates it but who may cease to tolerate it when conditions change and the balance of advantage shifts. To be independent and sovereign but at the same time isolated and weak, is not a boon to be coveted in a world of power politics. However passionate nationalism is now, or may become hereafter, the harsh logic of events may convince the smaller nations that cooperation among themselves and some kind of unity with others is better than the unreal independence and the precarious neutrality to which they have been accustomed in the past. To depend on alliances or to live as satellites of a strong neighbor has not proved satisfactory in the past, nor will it give security in the future. The small nations will have every reason to welcome an alternative.

As the argument of the preceding chapter suggests, this need not mean the end of small nations. It means, rather, that the coordination and integration of small nations into stronger and more powerful economic and political combinations is desirable. More important, such integration could secure for small nations with inadequate resources not only greater security but also the benefits of balanced economies and of sounder social arrangements. This need not involve any restriction of real freedom or any frustration of sound and essential nationality. The condition of the peoples concerned could be vastly improved. Nationality may become more vital than ever in a world that has ceased to think of it primarily in terms of isolation and sovereignty, and in which it has ceased to be responsible for misery and want.

That there is a growing realization of this truth is indicated by some agreements made during the war.[1] It is true that these have not been implemented and the course of events since they were made makes it very unlikely that they will now be put into effect in their original form. Such agreements, which fell short of federation even in the restricted areas that were covered by them, have been outstripped by the march of events. It is reasonable to suppose, however, that agreements of this kind, and probably some of a more ambitious character, will be attempted in the period of general reconstruction. The discussion of a Danubian confederation, active and animated before and during World War II, was suspended as a result of the sweeping changes war wrought in that area, and it would be hazardous to venture any prediction of the shape of things to come in southeastern Europe. Nevertheless, it may be assumed that in the world of the future there will be a greater readiness on the part of most nations to enter into regional understandings both economic and political; confederations impossible before the war may be within the range of practical politics in the future. Fervid nationalism, intensified by the experiences of the war, will not prove so strong in the long run as to resist the forces set in motion by economic necessity.

Russia's entrance into the war complicated the situation in central and southeastern Europe for a time and altered the pattern that seemed to be in process of formation. Its opposition to a Danubian confederation, for example, seemed to dispel whatever hopes may have existed for the realization of that plan. And yet the U.S.S.R. is itself an outstanding illustration of the possibilities inherent in our present condition. Within the Soviet Union there has been achieved an economic unity, even a political unity, that has proved consistent with a respect for, and an encouragement of, nationalist aspirations. By what Owen Lattimore has called "the politics of attraction," the Soviet Union has won to cooperation and loyalty peoples and races of the most diverse characters and the most varied cultures. Nationalisms have not proved inconsistent with the unity that was demonstrated so powerfully in the fiery experiences of war. This, indeed, may be

[1] For texts of agreements between Poland and Czechoslovakia and between Greece and Yugoslavia see the Foreign Policy Association Report, March 15, 1942. See also the Joint Declaration of the Central European and Balkan Delegations in the same report.

Russia's greatest achievement, and it is not without significance for the other great powers of the world.

Economic regionalism may have greater significance and will probably have much less danger than political regionalism. It is important that both should be harmonized with, and integrated in, an effective world order. The smaller and weaker nations will not for long be blind to the advantages that may accrue to them through such developments. The changed policies of the Latin American nations in our time, their sudden reversal of traditional attitudes, is evidence of the possibilities that lie ahead.

THE LEADERSHIP OF THE GREAT POWERS

The chief difficulties that may arise in the movement toward a rational world order are hardly likely to come from the smaller nations. They will probably come from the great powers, for whom, under the conditions that have hitherto prevailed, independence *has* seemed real and isolation and relative self-sufficiency have seemed feasible. They may not be prepared to pay the price of a cooperative and integrated world order. This price, it may be argued, will consist in part of the abandonment of agelong prejudices and the renunciation of worn-out traditions, but it will involve the sacrifice of little or nothing of real value. Tradition is extraordinarily persistent, however. For the great powers sovereignty has meant the right and power to determine and shape their own policies without permission from, or consultation with, any other power or powers. They have been able to go their own way, masters in their own house, and with freedom of action in the world beyond!

Actually the world has never been as simple as this, nor has any nation's freedom been as unqualified as is suggested here. But these are the assertive claims that minister to national pride; they have been the distinctive marks of a great power; the demonstration of them has been the measure of its prestige. These are the implications of sovereignty in recent interpretations and this, in essence, is the condition so jealously guarded by independent sovereign powers in the past.

The principles of democracy have never been consistent with the complete irresponsibility of this attitude. "Community" for the world of nations, as for the world of individuals, must rest on a moral foundation, and in discussing the ethical bases of democracy the point has been made that freedom from the moral law is, from the democratic point of view, not real freedom but the negation of it. Moreover, the concept of international law assumes the existence of a society of nations with mutual rights and obligations that limit the irresponsible exercise of power and that contradict these extreme assertions of absolute sovereignty. If we assume that there is a society of nations at all, if once we abandon the atomistic and anarchic concept of entirely separate and irresponsible states, then it is necessary to recognize a measure of interdependence and to admit a mutuality of obligation. No state lives unto itself. So much was admitted in the custom and practice of nineteenth-century Europe. The characteristic assertions and policies of *Realpolitik* were developed in defiance of this tradition and were never assimilated into the main body of democratic doctrine.

Still, the tradition of irresponsible power, the jealousy of possible interference from others, the almost superstitious belief in sovereignty is deep-rooted. It has been, and may be again, the greatest obstacle to the organization of a community of civilized states. But it is now clear that it must be overcome, and the responsibility for leadership in the task will devolve on those states that emerge from the conflicts of our age with a relative preponderance of strength, military and economic. There has developed a remarkable consensus of popular opinion that accepts the proposition that sovereignty as interpreted in the past has outlived its usefulness and needs drastic modification. And there is a consensus of opinion, too, that this must be accomplished by democratic processes, that it must be achieved by the free consent of free peoples. When the demand is put in concrete and specific terms, however, public opinion is likely to prove less dependable than this consensus would seem to indicate. Agreement in principle is not always followed by agreement in practice, as the history of our time has demonstrated.

In two areas of cooperation, a recognition of corporate obligation and a readiness to adopt common policies are vitally important. In the realm of economic life the alternatives are either a cooperative international system or a world of states each striving for self-sufficiency and committed to autarchy, with all the devices of exchange control, barter, and unscrupulous competition with which the world was only too familiar in the years preceding the war. But an international system will involve organization, continuous negotiation, and a spirit of give and take between the parties to it. It will also involve a general recognition that the fiscal and commercial policies of each state are a matter of concern to every other state and to the whole world community. These policies should therefore be the subject of discussion, consultation, and agreement, and such consultation if it is to be effective must not be spasmodic or haphazard. Machinery must be devised for regular and periodic surveys and for negotiation in some kind of international economic council. How much power may be granted to such an organization will depend on the will of the member states. At first its powers will probably be limited, for there will be powerful interests that will fear the consequences of its activities, and public opinion, still influenced by a different tradition, will be reluctant to attempt drastic change.

Something will have been gained, however, by the explicit recognition of a principle. If a great power like Great Britain, for example, is prepared to accept the position that agreements such as the Ottawa agreements concern others besides members of the British Commonwealth, or if the United States is willing to submit to international consultation and debate before adopting, let us say, another Smoot-Hawley Tariff Act, a very important step will have been taken toward a better and a more democratic world. What is vitally necessary is the growth of a common sense of responsibility in relation to issues that have hitherto been regarded as matters entirely of internal politics. "Nations must agree to give up their unqualified right to change their economic legislation without regard for the effect on other nations. At the very least, they must agree to consult with the other parties affected."[2]

The functions of an international economic organization will go much farther than this and will be capable of wide extension in the course of time, as actual experience demonstrates increasing opportunities and increasing necessities. Some of these functions may already be anticipated. Fiscal controls, for instance, may be utilized to achieve economic stability, rather than as a means of economic warfare. The business cycle with its recurring booms and depressions is not ordained by any law of nature; it is capable of modification and control, but this demands international action, and this in turn will demand new international institutions. International investment, too, will take on a new importance in a world devastated by war and desperately needing reconstruction. There will be vast opportunities for developing the resources of countries

[2]Eugene Staley, "The Economic Organization of Peace," *International Conciliation*, April 1941, pp. 396, 407. For a fuller discussion of this subject see the whole article, pp. 394–423. See also P. E. Corbett, *Post-War Worlds* (Farrar and Rinehart, 1942), Chapter 11.

lacking the necessary capital and technique, as in the case of China. New projects for improving economic conditions and raising the standard of living in backward countries will demand a degree of enterprise and imagination far greater than have ever been displayed in the past.

These are conditions that will demand something very different from the scramble for concessions and the competitive bidding for opportunities to grant loans that were characteristic of the frenzied period of the twenties. Then credits were granted without regard to the purposes for which they were to be used, and without much regard for the interests of the peoples either of the borrowing or of the lending countries. Private enterprise will be utterly inadequate to meet the needs of the postwar world in this field, and no nation alone can be safely entrusted with the tremendous tasks involved. Stability and reconstruction must go together.

It is a good augury that the beginnings of a new approach in this field are already discernible. Beginning with the Food Conference held in May and June of 1943, increasing public attention has been directed to the problems of a cooperative international order. During the summer of 1943 not only were arrangements made for a conference of the United Nations to deal with the problems of relief and rehabilitation, but a new international organization (UNRRA) was actually formed, which held its first council meeting in November and December of 1943. It is now a functioning organization entrusted with the task of directing postwar economic reorganization in Europe and Asia. Even more significant are the plans formulated at the Bretton Woods Conference in July 1944 for a stabilization fund and an international bank for reconstruction and development.

It is true that the effectiveness of these and similar projects will depend on the approval and the dynamic support of governments and peoples, but they are significant of trends toward a more realistic approach to the problems of world organization. In particular they are evidence of a growing realization that a democratic world order must be based on effective and democratic economic foundations. The League of Nations was a more grandiose project, and the United Nations' plan formulated at the San Francisco Conference has naturally attracted more attention but it is doubtful whether any world organization of that character will ever function satisfactorily unless it is built on such foundations as are provided by UNRRA, the Bretton Woods agreements, and similar functional projects. In spite of appearances it may be that the implementation of plans for international stabilization and international credit such as were formulated at Bretton Woods is as important as was adherence to the Covenant of the League in 1920 or as the ratification of the San Francisco Charter in our own time. Sound economic foundations will condition the effectiveness of any political structure. A democratic world order cannot be created by a fiat; it must be constructed laboriously and strenuously by mastering concrete problems and achieving cooperation in their solution.

INTERNATIONAL ECONOMIC CONTROLS

The task that confronts the United Nations involves not only the creation of new institutions but also the removal or transformation of undemocratic institutions that already exist. There are certain areas of international life where controls have been established that have proved not only inadequate in operation but undemocratic in character.

The production of certain commodities may become a monopoly or a quasi monopoly owing to the conditions of production and the restricted areas in which these commodities are produced. Many of these commodities are of vital importance for purposes of both peace and war. Outstanding examples are tin and rubber, for which the world has, in the main, been dependent upon Malaya and the Dutch East Indies. The production and distribution of both these products have been subject to international control, but the policies of the agencies of control have been determined in the main by considerations of profit for particular groups and in the light of particular national interests, those of the Dutch and British in particular. Consumer interest has necessarily been a secondary consideration. If the public interest has been served at all, as no doubt it has in a measure, it is the indirect result of such coincidence of interest as may happen to exist between producer and consumer. The coincidence is not always clear and it is not assured.

Even if the coincidence were more assured than it is, it would still remain true that the nature of the controls exercised over the production and distribution of these natural monopolies is an anachronism in a democratic world order. There is no representation in the controlling organization for the vast majority of those whose welfare and lives are dependent upon the policies adopted. Authority is exercised by small but powerful interests, which are only indirectly responsible to public opinion in any form. Not only is the consumer interest unrepresented, but in comparison to its magnitude and importance its opportunity for effective criticism or for constructive influence is infinitesimal. Even government pressure and influence can be exercised only indirectly, and of course effective pressure can be brought to bear only by, or through, the governments in possession of the territories in which the producing areas happen to be situated.

With the growth of large-scale industry with international ramifications, the cases of tin and rubber are not likely to be exceptional in the postwar world. Trusts and cartels will undoubtedly extend their operations and the trend toward industrial integration, which has shown little regard for national frontiers and will certainly show less in the future, will be greatly accelerated. Conditions of quasi monopoly will tend to appear in the production and distribution of many of the products vital to modern industry. Steel, chemicals, and oil, to mention only three of these vital products, were before the war joining tin and rubber as commodities subject to undemocratic international control by cartels and vast combinations of capital. Somehow these controls must be made responsible to international authority if the demands of democracy are to be satisfactorily met. They must also be made as representative in character as possible.

The war has made clear the necessity for other controls not hitherto envisaged. The development of air transportation has been enormously stimulated and there can now be no doubt as to its vast importance and its global character. An international air code with an international authority to administer it is the only possible safeguard against the evils and abuses of unrestricted competition. A democratic economic order must be harmonized with the need for new international agencies to meet the complex problems that arise.

These suggestions, of course, fall far short of an adequate discussion of the problems that will confront the United Nations in their task of reconstructing the economic world on a democratic pattern. They indicate the direction in which democratic principles point, not the method of their application. They may also indicate the mental and moral readjustments that must be effected in the thought of peoples habituated to, and conditioned by, a different tradition.

The fundamental necessity of our time is a full recognition of the concept of world community and a readiness to make it practically effective. This will not mean the immediate creation of utopia. The more ambitious schemes of world federation or of hemispheric or European federation will probably have to wait. These are long-range objectives that may not be practicable for our generation, but they provide an ideal and a goal. The important thing is that policies adopted now shall be steps in the right path and that peoples shall determine to pursue them. The pace is less important than the direction. The changes wrought must be in line with democratic concepts. And of these concepts few can be clearer than that which recognizes the world of nations as a community, with community interests and community rights and duties. The acceptance of this concept in world economy will be one of the acid tests of the sincerity of the nations who profess their faith in democracy.

POLITICAL PRINCIPLES OF A WORLD ORDER

The economic conditions of a democratic world order have been given precedence in our discussion, but this does not mean that political conditions have been overlooked or are regarded as secondary. It does imply that an underestimate of the importance of economic factors was one of the errors of the peace settlement that followed World War I. No political order, democratic or other, can endure if economic conditions create misery and want or leave millions with no opportunity and little hope of employment. These are conditions that invite the appearance of the demagogue and predispose peoples to become victims of his appeal. It is not an accident that the March on Rome took place in 1922 in the first postwar depression and that Hitler achieved the chancellorship of Germany in the second. The failure of the League of Nations may be attributed largely to the fact that it was never able to come to grips effectively with the problems of economic maladjustment. It could appoint commissions and sponsor conferences, but it could not secure action, and therefore the basic economic causes of world unrest were beyond its control. No international political organization of which this can be said will endure.

Nevertheless, it is also true that political institutions and organizations are necessary for the maintenance of peace and the creation of effective security. "Let it be said clearly that the first requisite for any successful government, whether local, or supranational, is ability to make resorts to violence or breach of the law rare. Unless 'law and order' are reasonably well assured, extensive international economic co-operation is impossible except among allies preparing for war."[3]

There must be willingness to cooperate in preventing or suppressing aggression, and instrumentalities for that purpose must be created as a part of a political world order. In practice there has been little difficulty in our time in recognizing aggression when threatened, and still less when it has occurred. The League condemned aggression in Manchuria and in Ethiopia, but it was not able to prevent or suppress it in either of these cases. It lacked the ability and the will to deal with aggression in a decisive manner.

The League failed to do this because of the reluctance of its member states to assume responsibility and to take the risks of peace. Decisive action in those cases where aggression was clear involved the possibility of war, and there was no clear consciousness anywhere that to risk war may, under certain circumstances, be the only means of averting it. The sense of community among those nations that desired peace was not strong enough to guarantee united action, when only united action could possibly avail. The results were divided counsels, the evasion of responsibility, and ultimately the collapse of all resistance to aggression. No international organization will ever be able to go far beyond the general will of its members, and it will never prove effective if this will is divided. History has underlined this lesson so that it has been partially, and let us hope sufficiently, learned.

Admitting the need of an international organization to prevent aggression and to restrain violence, we still must deal with the problem of its creation. Here also, to attempt a solution lies beyond our present purpose, but certain principles seem to be dictated by any adequate conception of democracy.

Democracy involves the concept of a progressive world, and a world organization must secure opportunities for change. The world is dynamic, and any system that ignores this fact or assumes a static order will necessarily be doomed sooner or later. Any union of states, therefore, that aims merely at perpetuating the existing order at any given point in history will break under the strain created by the emergence of new forces. In a world society there must be room for growth for the constituent parts, for new alignments between its members, for adjustments to the changing needs of nations as they pass through the varying phases of their development. The balance of authority and of

[3] Staley in *International Conciliation*, April 1941, pp. 417–18, footnote.

influence within the association may be expected to change with the passing of the years, and flexibility will be necessary to prevent change from becoming disruptive. The equitable arrangement of today may be the reverse of equitable tomorrow. No distribution of power, no differentiation of function, no assignment of territory can be regarded as just or necessary *for all time*. Change is inherent in the nature of things, and to curb or to repress it is to invite catastrophe.

A revision, therefore, of things as they are in the community of nations must be regarded as a normal and continuous function of a satisfactory political order. As in the life of a state so in the life of the association of states, the primary objective of democracy will be not to prevent the tides of change but to harness them. Progress, as Plato puts it, "is the movement from force to persuasion," and this is the distinctive mark of the democratic method. It "counts heads instead of breaking them" within states, and it must follow the same principle in international affairs. Its concern, therefore, will be to develop and perfect the instruments of peaceful change, recognizing change not as a disturbing and distressing fact to which we will yield only when we must, but as the normal and beneficent condition of progress.

Since changes do not take place simultaneously in all parts of the world, controversy between the forces of stability and tradition on the one hand and those of revision and change on the other is inevitable. A world order that tried to prevent such controversy would have to prevent freedom of invention and experimentation by individuals, groups, and nations, and would, if successful, prevent progress, though it might also prevent retrogression. Its efforts, however, would in the long run be unsuccessful, and the thwarted forces of change would eventually break forth in violence.[4]

The one article of the Covenant of the League which passed into oblivion almost as soon as the Covenant was signed was the particular article providing for the revision of treaties. Revision might have redeemed the weaknesses of the Treaty of Versailles if it had been attempted, not as a series of spasmodic responses to pressure, but as a normal function of the League of Nations. The Covenant came to be represented, not without some justification, as an attempt to guarantee the *status quo*. The fundamental error of the nineteenth century in the Holy Alliance was repeated in the twentieth.

[4] Quincy Wright, "Peace and Political Organization," *International Conciliation*, April 1941, p. 455.

A more difficult question arises when we consider the basic political principle of a new international order. If it is asserted that this must be democratic, what exactly will this mean in practice? Will only democratic states be admitted to membership in the association of nations?

It has been admitted that the professed democracies at best achieve only an approximation to real democracy. In one sense there are no democratic states except by virtue of aspiration or commitment, and the degree of achievement varies greatly among nations called democracies. There are very few nations, perhaps none, that are not conscious in certain phases of their life of limitations and even of denials of the democratic faith. Racial conditions in the United States and the existence of class distinctions in Great Britain are instances that leap to mind even where the committal to democratic principles is most explicit and probably as sincere as anywhere in the world. In what sense is China a democracy, and what are the prospects there of a political order that is democratic according to our Western pattern? In many countries conditions will obtain for years to come that may make it difficult, if not impossible, to establish systems of democratic government in the American or European interpretation of that term. That there will be wide diversities of political conditions and marked differences of democratic achievement among nations in the future seems inevitable.

The attempt will be made to secure that new governments set up and recognized shall be really and truly representative. This is the clear implication of the third point in the Atlantic Charter. There ought to be, and probably there will be, a careful regard for the wishes of the peoples concerned, but it may be difficult to determine what those wishes are. In the disturbed conditions of a world distracted and torn by years of war, it will not be easy to provide the supervision and control that assure free and genuine elections. There will be danger of pressure and violence by interested parties possessing a power that has little relation to their numbers or to their representative character. The principle, however, remains. New governments set up or governments restored should be acceptable to the peoples whose governance is to be entrusted to them. To guarantee that their representative character shall be preserved will be beyond the competence of any international authority. Who can be sure even that governments democratically constituted will remain democratic?

The demand, therefore, that the new order shall be democratic in the sense that membership in its organizations shall be open only to democratic states needs critical consideration. No existing state can be sure enough of its own thoroughly democratic nature to justify too rigid an insistence on this point. The formulation by the American president of the Four Freedoms—freedom of speech, freedom to worship, freedom from want, and freedom from fear— as basic conditions of a new world order, brings out the difficulty. Even freedom of speech, the simplest of the four, is not entirely unlimited in any organized state, whether democratic or other. The last two of the Four Freedoms are clearly in the nature of ideals toward which all nations may aspire, but which none have yet come within measurable distance of achieving. Obviously, to insist upon them as marks of democratic character and as conditions of membership in a democratic association of nations is impossible in practice.

In any case, to impose democratic constitutions upon peoples even by indirect pressure is not only futile but is itself undemocratic. Such constitutions would remain "paper" and would probably be repudiated when pressure was removed. By ranging national sentiment in opposition to them the very existence of these imposed constitutions would give to antidemocratic forces an instrument of effective propaganda and thus defeat whatever purpose they may have been intended to fulfill. The history of the Weimar Republic is the significant illustration in this connection. There are no short cuts to a democratic world order!

This does not mean, however, that principle need or can be entirely ignored in laying foundations. It has been suggested that an international bill of rights may be drawn up to guarantee the individual against injustice and oppression and to give assurance of certain primary liberties.[5] This, it is urged, is not only a democratic necessity, but also a condition of an effective international order. "Effective international organization," declares Professor Quincy Wright, "is not possible unless it protects basic human rights against encroachments by national States."[6]

A democratic world order, according to this argument, implies and demands a world public opinion, and this cannot develop unless certain conditions are fulfilled. A rigid censorship of opinion, for example, in one state or in a few would be a bar to the formation of an international public opinion in general. And an association of states cannot be regarded as democratic if it does

---

[5] For an interesting discussion of this see *The World's Destiny and the United States* (Chicago: World Citizens Association, 1941), Chapter 3.
[6] *Ibid.*, pp. 102–3.

not secure and evoke the interest and loyalty of the peoples who are governed. Moreover, it is necessary to give to individuals a direct responsibility for, and interest in, the actual functions of the world organization. It is not easy to see how the necessary loyalty can be developed if the organization does not rest on basic principles. "A person cannot be a good world citizen unless he enjoys some rights from, as well as owes some duties to, the world organization directly."[7]

The difficulties this proposal must meet are great. Agreement on the essential rights to be included in such a declaration would be hard to secure. Any statement of rights will seem either too limited to be adequate or too extensive to be legally recognized and enforced. There would certainly be grave reluctance in most nations to entrust an international court with the onerous responsibility of interpreting a bill of rights and of making authoritative decisions with regard to its observance or its violation. An international bill of rights is a desirable objective, but it is not likely to be immediately practicable.

Perhaps it is not necessary that it should be. A declaration of rights may achieve a very useful purpose, even though it is not enforceable at law. It may serve as a standard of judgment exercising a salutary influence upon the conduct of nations and upon the formation of world opinion. A creed may have value even though no ecclesiastical courts are entrusted with the task of authoritative interpretation or of enforcement. For this purpose, the statement of the Four Freedoms may serve as well as any alternative that has been or can be suggested. The acceptance in principle of this declaration, leaving room for considerable latitude of interpretation and for varied methods of practical application, constitutes in itself a definite forward step.

Acceptance of the Four Freedoms in principle is not an unreasonable condition of membership in a world organization, and this would constitute at least a principle of unity. These freedoms have not been achieved by any nation, and there are differences of opinion with regard to their relative importance. Russia, for example, emphasizes its belief that freedom from want is primary, a condition of the achievement of the other three freedoms. The United States and Great Britain have a different approach. It may be a serious mistake to insist upon interpretations of democracy with which Western nations are familiar. The Four Freedoms are not easily reduced to specific rules.

[7] *Ibid.*, p. 104.

After all, perhaps ideological professions, like creedal subscription, may be less important than actual practice. Actual cooperation in democratic purposes may come before, and be the condition of, achieving unity in democratic faith. In the task of creating a democratic world the meaning of democratic ideas may reveal itself. And the measure of success achieved in that task, rather than lip service to doctrinal statements, will vindicate or condemn democracy. The important fact is that nations differing in political method and in economic system are now united in a common conviction that the world cannot endure half slave and half free, are united too in a common struggle to ensure that it shall be wholly free rather than wholly enslaved. It is in such struggles, and in the tragic experiences of suffering and exaltation they bring, that the consciousness that creates community is born, and it is out of such struggles that the sense of community emerges with a new clarity and a greater depth. Men achieve a common faith more often by working together, by suffering together, by enduring together, than they do by argument.

CONVERSION FROM WAR TO PEACE

It would seem, therefore, that to maintain and develop the unity already achieved, to provide it with opportunities of expression in constructive and beneficent purposes for the healing of the nations, will be the primary condition of a better, as well as a more democratic, world. There will naturally be differences of emphasis in different nations on the many phases of the democratic ideal; there will be differences in the possibilities that exist for giving full application to its principles; there will be variety in the political methods and systems with which experiment may be made for its achievement. These will not matter, or may be desirable, provided cooperation in constructive tasks is maintained, and so long as the determination to maintain peace and to restrain aggression is at once a common interest and a common purpose.

Unity is for the time being an accomplished fact; it has been achieved by a common realization of the threat to such liberty as had been achieved in this world. This threat is being met in the united conviction that it must be destroyed if liberty, as men have known it, is to survive. This gives no assurance that the unity will persist when the danger is past, but it is at least clear evidence that these nations had one interest in common that seemed precious enough to justify the utmost sacrifices and the ultimate risks. This interest will persist, and therefore the basic condition of unity will persist; whether or not that common interest preserves the unity it has created may be more decisive in the future of the world than any other single factor.

The task of creating a new order, therefore, is already being partially achieved, for the felt need of unity already exists; the nucleuses of the necessary international organizations are already present in the machinery set up for the united direction of the war effort. The unification of policy and of purpose that the exigencies of war forced upon the United Nations may be and ought to be regarded as one of the primary conditions of a stable peace. Unified direction and control, not only in matters of military strategy and operation, but also in political and economic planning, was achieved, and the resources of many nations were directed and allocated in accordance with a plan that took account of world conditions and needs. Economic activities in the various countries have been coordinated for the achievement of a common purpose, and political issues have been and are being discussed in continuous consultation between governments. A global war has taught us that unity must be translated into practical terms on every front and must extend into the multifarious concerns and activities of the nations involved. International bureaus and boards of all kinds have, therefore, had to be improvised to coordinate and regulate not only the vast operations of war, but also the economic policies, which are now as decisive in effect as campaigns and battles.

The vast international machinery and organization created for war purposes will not be adapted overnight to the purposes of a world at peace. Even in the conversion of national war economies to peace economies many difficulties will have to be overcome and vast readjustment will be necessary. No one doubts, however, that this will be done, and few suppose that it will mean merely the abandonment of those organs of industrial cooperation that have been formed in the crisis. The conversion of industry from a wartime basis will not be simply a return to the conditions and methods of the prewar period in any country.

Similarly in the international order the transition from a war to a peace economy will present vast and perplexing problems, but it will be neither desirable nor possible to return to the unregulated and haphazard methods of the world that collapsed in 1939. The tasks of feeding hungry millions and of reconstructing devastated continents are as onerous as that of waging total war, and they need as high a degree of integration and of international supervision. Issues depending on the successful accomplishment of these tasks are as grave as those depending on military operations. Much of the machinery of unified effort now in existence, or still to be created, will therefore be vitally necessary for the constructive tasks of the postwar world. There can be no wholesale scrapping of the complicated organization that the necessities of war brought into being. The allocation of commodities and shipping space and the apportionment by international agencies of raw materials and industrial products will have to be continued. International cooperation in such matters will not be a matter of choice; it will be dictated by inexorable circumstance.

It is in this task of converting an international war system to the purposes of peace that the vital importance of long-range objectives needs to be recognized and kept steadily in view. A definitive peace settlement after the pattern of Versailles will not be attempted. A transition period of some years must elapse before the major tasks of political and economic reorganization can be carried far. This period will be crucially important, for it is then that the lines of reconstruction must be drawn and the foundations of a democratic order laid. Not only industry but the vast machinery of war, political and social as well as military, will have to be converted from its wartime purposes to the tasks of recovery and peace. The task of orderly and systematic demobilization, with due regard to political necessities and the capacity of economic systems to absorb the men and women withdrawn from war services, will in itself be herculean. It will need more care, for it will be fraught with greater dangers, than the mobilization of armies. Only if these tasks are approached in a spirit of cooperation and understanding will it be possible to lay the bases for a well-organized world. But there is a decided advantage in the fact that in and during the waging of the war the task has been begun. All the machinery of war will not have to be scrapped.

Beyond the transition years major issues will await decision. The task of political world organization is a continuous one, of which the end cannot be foreseen. A world charter is, at best, only the inception of such a task, and even the most admirable constitution is, in a sense, a promise rather than an accomplished achievement. The charter opens up possibilities; it cannot guarantee their realization. To forge an instrument for world peace, as was done at San Francisco, is vastly important, but only if the nations are determined to use it. Humanity will be able to do so if it sees clearly just what has been done and what still remains to be done. It must have courage in action and wisdom in direction. The United Nations' Charter is an opportunity, not a magic formula. The lessons of the League's failure and of its weaknesses must be learned and safeguards devised against the pitfalls, which are obvious now as they were not in 1919 and in the years that followed. There will be neither necessity nor excuse for a repetition of the errors and the weakness of will that proved so disastrous in the past.

Preponderant power will rest with the victors at the end of the war and it will be maintained for a considerable period—how long no one can now tell. Whether the United Nations wish it or not, power will be theirs, to use or to abuse. However much they may wish to evade its responsibilities, that course will not be open to them. Only if they remember that power always threatens to corrupt those who possess it will its exercise be salutary.

Since no future peace can be maintained if land, sea, or air armaments continue to be employed by nations which threaten, or may threaten, aggression outside of their frontiers, they [the signatories of the Atlantic Charter] believe, pending the establishment of a wider and permanent system of general security, that the disarmament of such nations is essential.

A frank recognition of the imperative obligations that this article of the Atlantic Charter imposes upon those who are parties to it will help. Preponderance of power and of armed force must not be maintained by some powers to the exclusion of others permanently or beyond the point where it is necessary to guarantee the peace and stability of the world. Power must be exercised by the victors, but as soon as possible it must be converted into power exercised by all for the security and good of all. Consent and agreement must gradually replace force and power, for it is the democratic faith that in the last resort consent and agreement are the only permanent foundations of a just and peaceful world. How long the achievement of this task will take is less important than the sincerity of the United Nations in recognizing it and in their determination to achieve it however long it takes.

At the present stage of human development it will not be possible to abandon the use of coercive power in international affairs. The United Nations at San Francisco in recognizing and expressing that fact were registering the judgment of the vast majority of mankind. The primary task of our age is to make sure that the exercise of power shall become more and more responsible. The fundamental evil of war is not that it is a destructive and violent exercise of force but that it is an *irresponsible* use of force. Such use is anarchic because it is divorced from, and independent of, any rational arbiter. For many ages to come international government, we may suppose, will involve the use of coercive power, as does civil government now. But coercive power can be subjected to restraints, as it has been in democratic countries; it can be made responsible. The conversion of the preponderant power of the United Nations into the responsible power of an authoritative and organized world of nations—this is the supreme task that confronts the democratic governments of the world. It is not an easy task, nor is it likely to be speedily accomplished. Nevertheless, it is an imperative implied in the basic concepts of democracy. Democracies must be prepared to use decisive power while recognizing that a world of *irresponsible* armed powers is a contradiction of the faith they profess. This is the paradox that only time and incessant effort can resolve.

The extension of democratic government in the democratic states of today has been a long and laborious process. Democracy has triumphed, to the extent and in the measure of its achievement, by virtue of the refusal of the human spirit to be discouraged by difficulties or to be defeated by what may seem to be insuperable obstacles. In the wider sphere of international life, the difficulties may be greater and the costs may be higher. There is no reason to believe, however, that the human spirit is incapable of paying the price of success. In the last resort, it is the democratic faith in human nature that is being put to the test in our time.

CHAPTER 15. Democracy and International Relations

W E   C O M E now to certain international problems that in a specific sense are a test of democratic principles. The most important are those that have customarily been grouped as the problem of backward peoples, or of dependent areas. It is very doubtful whether there would be universal agreement as to the criteria for determining "backwardness," for the scheme of values generally implied in the activities of states is too uncertain to be regarded as unquestionably valid. For any particular group of nations to claim superiority as "advanced" nations in the present state of the world is presumptuous. Here, therefore, if use is made of the term *backward peoples*, it implies no moral or cultural judgment. The relation of recognized states to one another, however, is specifically different from that of states to peoples who have not achieved statehood, or to peoples once independent who for one reason or another are no longer so. Generally, in speaking of backward peoples, we have in mind lack of political status on the one hand and a primitive economic condition on the other. What does the democratic faith imply for the relations of states to peoples who are still in a condition of dependence?

RISE AND DECLINE OF IMPERIALISM

Generally, dependent political status and primitive economic condition, the marks of backwardness, go together, although this is not necessarily the case. Often the peoples concerned will have had no experience of ordered political life, while a general condition of illiteracy may make it improbable that capacity for government will be developed for a long time. In the extreme cases, conditions of life are primitive, there is no law save that which is implied in tribal custom, and no definite political consciousness exists. There are numerous gradations, from that of the savage tribe to that of peoples whose competence for self-government is asserted and who demand it.

The broad distinctions adopted in the mandate system of the League of Nations serve as a convenient and, for practical purposes, a sufficient basis of classification. Peoples "not yet able to stand by themselves under the strenuous conditions of the modern world" are divided into the three categories: (1) those who "have reached a stage of development where their existence as independent nations can be provisionally recognized subject to administrative advice and assistance," (2) those who "are at such a state that the Mandatory must be responsible for the administration of the territory under conditions" that will guarantee certain rights and prohibit certain abuses; and (3) "territories . . . which, owing to the sparseness of their population, or their small size, or their remoteness from the centers of civilization, or their geographical contiguity to the territory of the Mandatory, and other circumstances, can be best administered under the laws of the Mandatory as integral portions of its territory." These distinctions imply that peoples in the first category may be expected to achieve the status of self-government in a comparatively short period of time, those in the second in a considerably longer time, and those in the third in a time so long that the condition of tutelage may be regarded as indeterminate.

Generally, as we have already stated, backwardness in this political sense is associated with a very rudimentary development of economic life. The peoples, undeveloped politically, also occupy undeveloped territories. Industrialization has either not even begun or is in its very earliest stages; natural resources may exist which the inhabitants cannot develop. Strangers to the techniques of modern production, they are ignorant of their potential riches, and perhaps would be indifferent to them even if they knew of their existence; the idea of capital accumulation has not yet entered their minds. Where economic backwardness is not present in such extreme form, peoples may still lack capacity to develop industry or to exploit the resources in their possession. The basic conditions of economic effectiveness—roads, railways, means of communication—either do not exist or are exceedingly primitive. Implements and machinery necessary for the exploitation of natural resources or for building industries fitted to their needs and necessary for their material advancement must be supplied by others.

Wide differences of economic and political development have long existed. They achieved a new significance when peoples at different levels of development established contacts during the age of adventure and exploration. The history of what occurred when these contacts were made is more romantic than pleasant. The conquistadors of the West and the trading companies of the East carved out paths that were frequently stained with blood, and their activities were marked by deeds of ruthless cruelty.

Even in these early years, consciences were made uneasy—for instance, among the Spanish Jesuits in relation to the Western world and among the British in relation to India—by the startling accounts of the behavior of those who were supposed to represent Christian civilization. The world was being opened up while principles governing conduct in new relationships were still lacking.

With the rapid growth of trade and commerce and the coming of the Industrial Revolution in the eighteenth century, the development of intercommunication was greatly accelerated. Trading companies established their posts in the most distant reaches of the world, and in many areas company control developed into what was in practice a government of the territory within which the company operated. In the course of time the flag followed trade; governments took over the administrative and political functions of the trading companies. Where doors were closed to trade, governments battered them open. Later, in Africa particularly, came the second phase of imperialist expansion, where trader and soldier cooperated in opening up "the dark continent." This was accomplished with little concern for the social systems that happened to exist and with little regard for the peoples whose territory was annexed.

The process of expansion and penetration was effected by ruthless methods of force. Sometimes formal agreements were negotiated with chiefs who signed treaties they could not read. The customary fate of backward peoples was that of subjection. Where subjection was not avowed, the device of "protection" served, for except in the refinements of international law the differences between a protectorate and a possession was not of much practical significance. Where subjection, veiled or avowed, was not practicable or politic, concessions and privileges were extorted from reluctant governments too weak to resist, as in China, for instance. When necessary, violence would reinforce pressure, and always behind the demands of the "advanced" powers was the threat of war. The relationships created were relationships between the strong and the weak, the powerful and the helpless; the idea of consent on the part of the governed received hardly the tribute of lip service. The path of empire was carved by the sword and cleared by the mighty arms of power.

In the latter half of the nineteenth century conscience began to awaken among the democratic peoples regarding these developments. Sometimes this resulted in an attempt at a poetic, if not a mystic, justification of imperialism in terms that soothed the feelings of those who were not too profoundly disturbed and who were disinclined to look with too critical an eye upon the stark realities of empire. But the reassurance was neither profound nor permanent. "The white man's burden" was a dubious term when applied to tasks which most states were ready to assume with alacrity and at considerable cost. The attempt, characteristic of the late Victorian era, to idealize the imperialist urge never succeeded in convincing any except those who wished to be convinced. Romantic imperialism died in the first years of the twentieth century and was never really resurrected. The attempt to interpret the urge of expansion, economic and territorial, in terms of romantic national self-denial gave way before the realistic temper of a new age.

Evidence of this awakening of conscience is to be found in a new concern for primitive peoples and in a critical reaction against conditions of dependence and subjection. Knowledge of what happened in distant lands seeped out from regions that hitherto had been unknown. Occasionally a particular scene was highlighted by shocking stories of cruelty and oppression, as happened in the case of the African Congo and the Putumayo; dramatic accounts of the conditions of natives of India in South Africa and of natives on the plantations of the South Seas, or of indentured Chinese in mines, factories, or plantations in many places, sometimes became headline news. As knowledge of conditions spread a consciousness of responsibility grew.

Light was filtering into dark regions where hitherto imperialism had been subject to little restraint. Societies for the protection of natives in many lands came into existence; subject populations, incapable of agitation or of effective protest themselves, found defenders among humanitarians who lacked neither vigor nor facts. Their cause was championed in the parliaments of the world and particularly in the parliaments of the colonial powers. As a result, there was a marked improvement in the personnel of colonial administration and a keener sense of responsibility on the part of ministers in charge of colonial affairs.

In the democratic countries there developed also a new consciousness of responsibility toward peoples less backward and less entirely dependent. Even if democracy did not mean the immediate possibility of self-government for India, at least it meant a conscious and definite obligation to prepare the way for it. Groups like that of the Friends of India became active—and not only in relation to India. With the turn of the century the tide of liberal thought was running strongly in opposition to imperialist policy. China was far away, but not so far as to obscure completely the significance of unequal treaties, extraterritoriality, and enforced concessions. The onetime representation of the "heathen Chinee" was outmoded and soon became ridiculous. With the revolution of 1911 and the inauguration of the republic, China ceased to be a strange land, or at least an unknown land. The public opinion of the world was shocked into a new awareness of the possible meaning of democracy in new situations. No people suffering from avowed and patent inequalities of status was without its influential advocates in the assemblies of the democratic nations. Before World War I had come to an end, a realization of the gulf that existed between the democratic profession of Western powers and their actual practice in these and other countries was deep and general.

Moreover, a new consciousness had developed also among the subject peoples themselves. In many instances they were no longer in suppliant mood; they were now formulating demands, not asking for favors. This spirit had been fostered by the declared aims of the Allied Powers in the war; it was not possible to renounce those aims in the moment of victory. Repudiation of the principle of self-determination was not politically expedient. A war fought to make the world safe for democracy had not only aroused subject peoples but had greatly strengthened liberal sentiment. How democratic was the world?

Seen in these wider perspectives, the actual sway of democracy was not too impressive. The countries of Europe, the homes of democracy, were small areas on the periphery of the great world. There were vast regions and great multitudes that had not experienced its benefits or had the opportunity to practice it. In vast areas also, the conditions established by nations professing the democratic creed seemed a denial of that creed, not its fulfillment. The heritage of the ages of expansion, of colonization, and of imperialism was examined anew. It was an exercise more salutary than pleasant!

Perhaps in some quarters the reaction went too far. It was foolish to overlook what the old imperialism had accomplished in many areas. In India, in Egypt, and indeed in most of her colonies, Great Britain had much to her credit. Dams were built, vast areas of land were reclaimed and made fertile, education was provided, disease was combated with heroism and often with great success, and many other benefits were conferred upon her many dependencies. All this is true, of course, of the United States in the Philippines and of other colonial powers in North Africa, in the South Seas, and elsewhere. The beneficence of much that was accomplished by empire builders and empire administration need not be depreciated. The material well-being of the majority of mankind had been enhanced and misery and helplessness had been redeemed through the colonial policies of the great powers. In any case, the development of the modern empires, following upon the explorations of the age of discovery and later upon the growth of commerce and industry, lay in the logic of history. It was the phase through which the world had to pass on its way to the achievement of a world consciousness and of world unity. Not all that accompanied this was necessary, certainly not the cruelty, the oppression, and the inhumanity. But ruthless as imperialism was, it yet prepared the way for a measure of human progress that might otherwise have been impossible. This is not to excuse the sins of imperialism; it is merely to recognize that there was in this process an inherent historical necessity. Barriers had to be broken down; the world's resources had to be made available for the world's needs. These things were done no doubt with unnecessary violence, but they were done.

MUTUAL RESPONSIBILITY AS AN ALTERNATIVE

Imperialist expansion, described here only in rough outline, created both the opportunities and the problems with which we are now confronted. In the twentieth century the fruits of imperialism came to seem less pleasant than of old, but they could not be suddenly abandoned. The consequences of centuries of history could not be canceled at will, even though it seemed that the age of expansion was approaching its end. The problem confronting many nations was no longer that of acquiring new territories, but of disposing of at least some that had been secured in earlier times. Liquidating the gains of expansion and the assets of empire was almost as serious a problem as expansion had been in earlier times.

In certain cases the problem was simplified by virtue of the community of interest, of culture, and of political tradition that existed between the colonies and the imperial power. In these, dependence could be and was converted into partnership, as in the case of some of the colonies of Great Britain. The dominions were granted self-government without too much difficulty, and with a wisdom that overcame what difficulties there were. The

British Commonwealth of Nations is the best example of the application of democratic principle to the problem of empire. A vast political transformation was effected so successfully that the nature and significance of what had been achieved was hardly realized. The unity of empire was converted into the unity of commonwealth without serious or dangerous crisis, and onetime dependencies became dominions, with all save the formal marks of sovereignty—and this without the loss of a life or even a loss of temper!

Unfortunately, the problem of liquidating an empire is much more difficult in cases where basic unities of culture and tradition do not exist and where the ties of sentiment cannot be relied upon to maintain a consciousness of unity. India, naturally, is a much more perplexing problem than Canada ever was. How to dispose of it while still safeguarding vital British interests and also, let it be said, the welfare of the Indian peoples, is a problem that may be on the way to solution but is not yet solved. Can dominion status in this case mean just what it means in the case of Canada or of Australia, or even of South Africa? And if the effective independence that has been granted to these and the other dominions is accorded to India, will it have the same consequences? Similar questions arise in relation to Egypt and Iraq, where formal independence has been granted, but with limitations which indicate clearly that it is not possible or politic to rely entirely on the ties of sentiment and good will that are sufficient in the case of the dominions.

What to do with colonial possessions in the face of their growing demands for independence, which the democratic spirit cannot logically reject, is a problem that cannot be evaded by Great Britain or by the other imperial nations. What form will independence take and in what form will it be desired by the Philippines when the time comes to implement the treaty that promises it? The right policy in sundering ties may demand less power but more wisdom than was needed in forming them. Who would care to predict the future most desirable from the democratic point of view for Syria or for Morocco?

The primary necessities that inspired the movement of expansion and colonization will remain. The exploration of new lands and the opening up of new continents may have reached its limit, but the development of the world's resources and the utilization of nature's products is as necessary as ever. With the growth of industrialization, the need for freer access to, and a fuller use of, essential materials, mineral and other, will increase rather than diminish. The world will need more rubber and tin, more oil, more iron, magnesium, and aluminum—more of all the materials that make or feed its machines. It is clear that where the sources of supply lie in territories whose peoples are unable to develop or utilize them, political difficulties will not prevent their exploitation in some way or other. The East Indies and Malaya, the unexplored riches of the South American continent, the mineral deposits of China, cannot be permitted to remain undeveloped.

Who is to be responsible for this development, and under what conditions will it be carried out? Letting peoples that occupy areas of economic importance alone, letting them do as they will, is too simple a solution to be practical. These peoples may have neither the will nor the capacity nor the resources to do what is necessary. There is no coincidence between the possession of natural wealth and the ability to use it. The old imperialism at least recognized this fact, and, recognizing it, was able to increase greatly the material riches of the world and thus to make possible the enhancement of human welfare. Imperialism, in spite of its abuses, fulfilled a necessary function, and colonization made possible the great advances in technique and in economic effectiveness that the last two centuries have witnessed. The utilization of world resources cannot be left to the haphazard chance of geography. The occupation of rich territory by backward races cannot be permitted to bar access to commodities necessary to the progress of the world.

In democratic theory there is no recognition of the rights of irresponsible ownership. Possession has to be justified in terms of social purpose, just as the right to private property must be established by showing that it is socially expedient or beneficial. The assumption that possession involves responsibility is integral in the ethical tradition of Western civilization.[1] The fact that this doctrine has frequently been put to uses that savored of insincerity or even of hypocrisy does not affect its validity.

The application of this principle of responsibility or trusteeship to an established state, or to colonial territories occupied by peoples not yet organized as states, is obviously not without difficulty. The confused discussion of trusteeship at San Francisco was evidence of this. Nevertheless, it would seem that the concept of responsibility applies in the case of nations and peoples as in that

[1] See Ritchie, *Natural Rights,* Chapter 13; and also *Property, Its Duties and Rights* (New York: Macmillan, 1922), *passim.*

of individuals. The resources of a particular territory do not belong in any absolute sense to the people who happen to occupy it. If it is said that they own the land and its resources, it must be added that they own it, not to do with as they please, but in trust for humanity and the world. Here, of course, the argument moves in the realm of morals, not of law. International law recognizes the "right of the occupier," but we are not now concerned with legalistic distinctions. The concept of a community of nations carries with it the principle of all community: the action of one or of a few shall not frustrate and effectively hinder the purposes of the many, and the interest of the whole shall override the particular interests of each. Certain things should no more be done in the community of nations than in other communities, and certain things should be proscribed by the morality of nations.

It may, for example, be the will of a government to keep itself aloof from the rest of the world, guarding its doors to prevent the intrusion of strangers and building its walls to prevent access for the commerce of the nations to its markets. This is the policy it was impossible to maintain in the nineteenth century, as China and Japan discovered, and it is a policy that will never be possible again. Such isolation is incompatible with even the measure of community that has already been achieved among the nations of the world. If a people has within its territory the source of supply of some commodity of vital importance to the rest of the world, it will not be justified in withholding the commodity, nor will it, in the long run, be permitted to do so. If the conditions of producing the commodity or of its geographical distribution are such as to constitute a natural monopoly, the people will not be justified in exploiting that monopoly to its own advantage without regard to the interests of others. These are considerations chosen at random to illustrate the thesis that the world's wealth is the world's concern, that the control of particular portions of that wealth, dependent upon the occupation of a particular part of the earth's surface, is not and cannot be absolute or unlimited. The territory of a state or of a people is in the nature of a trust held for the world, to be administered for the good of the world.

This is a conception, as we have seen in another connection (Chapter 14), that cuts across the customary habit of thought of the governments of sovereign states. Peoples have been habituated to think of themselves as "masters in their own house," to be proud of the fact that they can do what they please with their own, and so on. Nevertheless, the recognition that such habits of thought mean the perpetuation of international anarchy is growing. The fact that the conception of national responsibility is strange does not prove that it is not true, and the fact that strong powers have shown little readiness to acknowledge it in practice does not make it any the less valid. It must be admitted that the great powers have generally disclaimed responsibility, resented outside "interference," and repudiated any attempt to establish international restraints on what they have called their "internal policies." This is the main reason why the case for colonization, even when it was most reasonably presented, smacked of hypocrisy; it assumed a principle which the great powers did not observe in practice.

The responsibilities of backward nations can only be urged by nations that are themselves prepared to acknowledge similar responsibilities. The responsibility is real in both instances and its recognition is a necessary condition of a better international order. The vast resources of a continent cannot be left unavailable and undeveloped simply because the peoples of that continent are neither willing nor capable of making them available. This was the real justification, certainly not for the methods used, but for the actual opening up of vast regions for exploitation and development. The obligation to open them existed, but the fact that it was done with self-seeking motives and with little if any sense of obligation toward the inhabitants of those regions must be admitted and deplored. The morality of nations had not developed sufficiently to meet the needs of the new age of industrial expansion!

During the last fifty years this has produced serious consequences. The clash of colonial ambitions and the rapacity of unscrupulous interests have been among the primary causes of international discord and have contributed to the making of the wars of our era. The arguments of the "have-not" nations in the thirties had some show of reason, but only because the practices of great powers gave them plausibility. There was a suggestion of unreality in assertions concerning the burdens of empire while those who bore the burdens steadfastly refused to be eased of them. Whether colonies were profitable or not was a question that merited discussion, but the fact was that, whatever conclusion the economists reached, the powers that had colonies were stubbornly clinging to them. In a world where war was more than a possibility, where tariff discrimination was practiced, and where government restrictions blocked the channels of trade, the possession of dependencies *was* an advantage; it was a safeguard against the fear of which other nations were conscious, that supplies could be cut in times of war and trade restricted in times of peace. In a peaceful world where trade was free the advantages might not be worth what the empire cost. But the world was not peaceful and trade was not free!

The Axis powers sought to remedy the situation in the worst possible way: not by striving for political stability and economic freedom, but by wresting from those who held it the power against which they complained. Even if they had succeeded, the basic problem would have remained. The way they chose meant war.

EMPIRE AND THE WAR

There is a certain irony in the fact that this Axis attack should have come just when the old imperialism was showing signs of decay. The imperialist method of "opening up the world" and of developing its resources had helped to produce the most alarming economic crisis in history. It had opened the closed doors in many areas of the world only to obstruct access to them by all sorts of restrictive policies. It had secured access to raw materials only to permit them in many cases to accumulate wastefully in storehouses because they could not be sold profitably. Competitive industrialism was closing the avenues through which the riches of the world might flow to satisfy human needs. Whatever justification there may have been for the old imperialism, it was not advancing general welfare, and even many of the sectional advantages it produced proved illusory when the depression came.

In another way and in more dramatic fashion the advantages of imperialism were proved to be doubtful. On crucial occasions far-flung possessions turned out to be liabilities rather than assets, even for the purposes of security, for they proved singularly vulnerable to attack. Such economic advantages as they possessed for war purposes depended on naval or air supremacy, and their defense was not greatly aided by native peoples. This should not have been surprising. It was not logical to expect subject peoples to display heroism in defense of a freedom they did not possess. The millions of Burmese did not mean manpower for the defense of Burma, because those millions did not feel that they were fighting for their own homeland. Egypt remained neutral even with its land invaded, and its neutrality was not too benevolent. Five decades of British rule and administration had undoubtedly conferred enormous material benefits upon the Egyptian people, but freedom had come late, and, when achieved, it was a restricted freedom. Subject peoples do not put up the sturdy defense of peoples consciously free. There was evidence of something that went deeper than military ineptitude in the loss of Malaya and the fall of Singapore. France could not rally the people of Indo-China to fight for their country, because the people had not been encouraged to think that they had a country. Were these people essentially different from the neighboring peoples of China, whose resistance won the amazed admiration of the world? And if they were, what was it that made them different?

No doubt the old imperialism with all its faults was preferable to the more ruthless imperialism that Axis domination would have imposed. But people have never been very ready to fight to the death either for or against a mere change of masters. The story of the Philippines was in many ways a striking contrast to the general pattern in the Straits Settlements, in the East Indies, and elsewhere. Was it different because the Filipinos are different in character from the other Pacific peoples? Or did the definite pledge of independence, precise and dated, have something to do with the difference? The Filipinos fought bravely because they were consciously fighting for freedom and independence. Where rule had been kindly and by traditional standards beneficent, as for instance in the East Indies, it made some difference, but not enough. It did not, and could not, make alien rule equivalent to self-government or paternal protection equivalent to independence. Even a kindly but imposed government is not a satisfactory substitute for the hope of self-government.

It would seem, therefore, that continued subjection is in many ways not good policy. If peoples are permitted to remain backward, their backwardness will involve dangers and penalties for those who acquiesce in it or who do too little to overcome it. If subject peoples remain ignorant, illiterate, and miserable in condition, they may make satisfactory laborers for the mines or the plantations, but they certainly cannot be effective material for the defense of their homeland. Self-reliance does not grow in conditions of servitude, however pleasant that servitude may be.

This is not an indictment of any particular colonial system, certainly not of the British or the Dutch, for these have been among the best, not the worst, of the world's colonial systems. Yet the fact remains that in a great crisis even these systems have been a source of weakness rather than of strength. A loyal Burmese people, moderately efficient, reliable and intelligent, and with a real prospect of independence, might have been of greater value to Britain than Singapore. If we must have empire, we must have different and better "bastions of empire," and they must be founded in the heart and spirit of peoples. The age of empires, as empire has been understood in the past, is drawing to its close. If this is a revolutionary war, then the decay of empire may be not the least significant aspect of that revolution.

Not only has the war demonstrated the fatal weaknesses of subjection as the cement of empire; it has raised questions concerning the morale of armies fighting for the defense of empire. The British soldier no doubt will fight bravely under any conditions, but will British armies be as effective when they feel, rightly or wrongly, that they are fighting to retain control of the tea of Penang as when they are fighting for the homes of England? The same British character that withstood the terrors of the blitz in England had to endure the rigors of sand and heat and the attacks of tanks and dive bombers in Libya. In both conditions it displayed a capacity for heroism and tenacity. But what if there had been no blitz? Was the morale of British troops in Malaya as high as at Dunkirk?

The idea of imperial glory has lost its potency. The youth of England has no interest in "painting the map red" or in keeping it as red as the old imperialism painted it. They will fight if they are sure of what they are fighting for and if they feel that what they are fighting for is worth the sacrifices entailed. They will not fight as their forebears fought, merely for empire. These are the signs of the end of an epoch.

And yet it must be repeated that for a good many years there will still be peoples who have neither capacity nor experience for self-government; there will be peoples whose condition will necessitate a measure of tutelage and control. And there will also be primitive peoples with little knowledge of the meaning of government and no ability to manage their own affairs. There will be regions wealthy in resources badly needed for reconstruction but inhabited by peoples who have no notion of their potentialities and no will and capacity to realize them. In short, the problem that the old imperialism solved, or failed to solve in its ruthless way, will remain. The world needs an alternative, one better than the old imperialism and certainly one better than was promised by the new imperialism of the Axis nations. A new order can be worse than the old!

To provide this alternative or to indicate its nature is a problem for democracy. Is it possible on the basis of democratic principle to provide a system that will be at once equitable and efficient, fulfilling the necessary functions of imperialism and yet avoiding its abuses and its cruelties? To what extent may we hope to find in consent and cooperation a foundation that will be firmer and better than that of rule and subjection? The capacity of the United Nations to meet the challenge of these questions will in large measure decide whether or not democracy is a faith for the modern world and a suitable method of government for the world of the future.

A GENERAL PRINCIPLE

Universal self-government is no solution of the problem, since it is neither practical nor expedient. It has been sufficiently stressed that even among the independent nations, many will necessarily fall far short of democratic government for a long time to come. There can be no magic transformation of subject countries into self-governing democratic states. Nor is there any fixed pattern into which peoples just emerging into a definite political consciousness can be fitted. Political experience comes slowly and its lessons must be learned over long periods and with difficulty.

There are some cases, however, where the demand for independence has become vocal and clear, and where there is at least a presumption that the demand is not unreasonable. Here there is no simple formula that can be applied without regard to the circumstances and conditions that obtain in each case. Nor is it possible to define the stages or to outline in advance the method by which ties are to be severed or the relation of dependence transformed into that of partnership. The method adopted by the United States in the case of the Philippines or by Great Britain in the case of Iraq and Egypt may not be suitable or expedient in the case of India. The complex of economic interests and political relations must be taken into consideration in each particular case. The vital importance of the Suez Canal, for example, may have justified some limitation of Egyptian sovereignty when independence was granted, for obviously Egypt was in no position to provide for the adequate and effective defense of the canal.

Nevertheless, a general principle may be logically deduced from democratic principle. The paramount power in the relation of empire and dependency must justify the control it exercises by furthering the conditions and encouraging the qualities that will lead in time to its own elimination. The aim of colonial government is to render that government unnecessary. The sincerity of a democratic state may be judged by the effort it makes to achieve this end and by the spirit of urgency with which it pursues it. It will seek opportunities, and perhaps create them, for transferring responsibility to the peoples whose government it has undertaken. If risks must be taken in this progressive transfer, it will risk going too fast rather than too slow. There is less danger in a certain measure of inefficiency than in a sense of frustration and grievance. A wise democratic state will never regard the relationship of rule and dependence as normal or permanent, for it is committed to the belief that alien government, however efficient, is no satisfactory substitute for self-government. It must regard its task as a trust. The crowning achievement of its rule will be the elimination of the necessity that was its justification.

There will be a strong temptation for a democratic state to forget this principle. In the dependency interests will be created through much sacrifice on the part of the nationals of the ruling state, interests that have grown through a long period of time. The government will naturally be concerned to safeguard these, and it will be conscious of the risks to them that a change of political status may involve. An ideal disinterestedness is too much to expect under such circumstances. What may be expected, however, is a recognition of the democratic assumption that the preservation and defense of such interests in the long run will depend on good will and understanding, not on the exercise of power. There are more satisfactory defenses even of material interests than those an alien authority can provide! The friendship of a partner is a more certain guarantee of security even in material concerns than the subservience of an inferior.

The just tempo of change in transferring responsibility and authority in any given case will depend on circumstances. In most cases it will be desirable that change should be gradual and progressive rather than sudden. One need not believe in the inevitability of gradualness in order to recognize that a sharp and sudden change of status might have disastrous economic and political consequences. A steady devolution of authority, increasing participation in government of the people, progressive transfer of administrative functions—these will normally constitute the safest path to independence. These steps a democratic state will take willingly and as rapidly as conditions permit. They are the necessary conditions for developing capacity and providing experience. Competence in government is not to be expected overnight; the important thing is that people should be on their way!

A MANDATE SYSTEM?

Beyond the issues raised in any particular case, however, lies the difficult problem of liquidating or transforming a colonial system deeply imbedded in the structure of the modern world. There is a consensus of opinion that its solution demands international action. After World War I, President Wilson gave definite expression in speech to this opinion, and first steps toward a solution of the problem were taken at the Peace Conference in setting up the mandate system of the League of Nations. The idea that system embodied was almost universally approved, and if the more realistic or cynical among the political leaders who gathered at Paris had reservations, doubts, and misgivings, as a rule they refrained from expressing them. Of all the departures from traditional usage that the Covenant of the League embodied, none seemed to have greater promise than that which provided for the establishment of mandates. Here at least was a new approach to a problem that had hitherto seemed almost insoluble.

Unfortunately, the mandate system proved to be much less fruitful in operation than it had been promising in conception. It was an advance toward a rational world order, but it was exceedingly tentative and uncertain, as first steps are apt to be. That it improved conditions to some extent in certain areas and prevented abuses in others must be reckoned to its credit. Nevertheless, the fact remains that it did not fulfill the high expectations of its sponsors. It did not involve a sufficiently sharp and decisive break with the imperialist tradition. The history of the various mandates has been told elsewhere, and there is no need to repeat it here. At best it is the history of modest, if not meager, achievement.

The mandate system, like the minority treaties, was unfortunate in the circumstances of its birth. From the outset its prestige was prejudiced by the fact that the system was applied only to the territories taken from the defeated powers. It had, therefore, the appearance of being punitive in character. No member of the victorious Allies, although some had records of colonial administration that were far from unblemished, felt called upon to surrender its control of even the smallest of its colonial possessions or to place any of its territories under the mild supervision for which the mandate system provided. This fact gave color and plausibility to the suspicion that mandates were a polite, but not too effective, disguise for what was actually the appropriation of new territories by those who possessed power. The suspicion seemed to be confirmed by the attitude of the governments entrusted with mandates toward the mandate commission of the League when its constitution and powers were under discussion. Too great a readiness to evade its supervision and to whittle down its authority was evident.

The manner in which the mandates were assigned and in which their terms were drawn up was not reassuring. The distribution of them was entrusted, not to the Assembly of the League, where at least there would have been a chance for discussion, but to the Supreme Council, where British and French influence was decisive. Its decisions were believed to be dictated by consideration for British and French interests, not by considerations of equity. Little attempt was made to discover the wishes of the peoples involved, or where they were fairly well known, as in Syria, no attempt was made to meet them.[2] The Supreme Council decided, as might have been expected, that Germany should not retain any of her colonies, even under mandate. France, Great Britain, and Japan, together with certain British dominions, were naturally chosen for the onerous task of administering the mandates! It was a choice that could hardly be made to look disinterested.

The mandatory powers were also entrusted with the task of drawing up the text embodying the terms of their own mandates. They were instructed to do so "in the spirit of Article 22 of the Covenant." The mandates were then submitted to the Council of the League, their terms were examined by the legal and mandates sections, and finally, on their report, were approved and adopted by the Council. The precise status of a mandate in international law was left in doubt—a doubt that has never been resolved. This clearly was not a good beginning for what had promised to be a democratic development of great significance. It prejudiced the prospects of the mandate system from the outset by creating doubt as to the sincerity of its chief sponsors. Was "new mandate" merely "old colony," written not large perhaps, but all too clearly nevertheless? The mandate system got off to a bad start.

Its history has been one of moderate success and of qualified achievements. Its machinery was imperfect and the authority of

[2] A commission was sent by President Wilson to ascertain the wishes of the peoples of former Turkish territories. The King-Crane report was so embarrassing that it was not published for ten years after its presentation! Its findings were completely ignored.

its directing organization, the mandates commission, was inadequate from the outset. Cooperation of the mandatories with the commission was either almost completely absent, as in the case of Japan, or reluctant and suspicious, as in the case of France and of Great Britain. The procedure for supervising the mandates was cumbersome and ineffective, making delay and evasion far too easy. The machinery established to secure the information necessary to make the commission's supervision real was unsatisfactory. The peoples of the mandated territories had no representatives on the commission, and the commission had no independent representatives in the mandated territories.

No official visits to these territories were ever made by members or officers of the League for the purpose of investigating complaints or reporting on conditions. Petitions to the League had to be presented first to the responsible government of the mandate, which forwarded them to the commission after adding such observations as it saw fit. No oral testimony by the petitioners was permitted and of course examination and cross-examination were impossible. In many of the territories, moreover, the method of petition was entirely inappropriate for peoples who were illiterate and primitive and had no capacity to formulate or present complaints in this form.

Some of these weaknesses were inevitable in a new and untried system, and perhaps some reluctance on the part of the mandatories to rely on international supervision was excusable. But the limited achievement of the mandate system was due fundamentally to the underlying factors that were also responsible for the failure of the League. Chief among these were distrust of international government, the reluctance of sovereign states to relinquish authority and power, and the refusal of these states to provide means for implementing the policies that the League or its organizations might adopt or approve. The mandate commission, like the League itself, had in general no difficulty in making decisions, but it had no means for giving effect to them. Often admirable intentions expressed in suitable resolutions were the only results achieved, resolutions followed so often by complete inaction. The system was undermined by waning confidence in its effectiveness.

Nevertheless, it must be recognized that in spite of the weaknesses of the mandate system, the idea of mandates or of trusteeship is sound and its principle valid. It was its application and its practical operation that was defective. What is needed, therefore, is not the abandonment of the system, but its drastic reform and its wider extension within the new international organization. Some of the changes most urgently needed are implied in the criticisms stated above. An effective system must give decisive authority to those responsible for its operation, authority to investigate, to report, and above all to give effect to their decisions. It must develop organs of effective supervision. This may be secured in a system of international representatives or officials acting as advisers, not in the particular city that happens to be the seat of the international organization, but in the mandated areas; officials who will therefore be familiar with conditions and in close touch with events. It must also secure for the peoples concerned, by means suited to their abilities, easy and convenient access to the responsible international agency, to the mandates commission or whatever may be established in its place. These changes are not revolutionary and can be effected if there is a will to do so. They are primary necessities, revealed and suggested by the history of the mandate system during the last twenty years.

Beyond these changes of constitution and administration lies the necessity for an extension of the mandate principle to other regions and territories. Will colonial powers in the future be prepared to accept a wider application of the principle, and not merely to the territories of defeated nations? Surely it is applicable to the government and administration of all territories "inhabited by peoples not yet able to stand by themselves." It cannot be applied universally at once, but experiments in its extended application are possible and desirable. The important thing is to take seriously and to interpret sincerely the conception of trust rather than possession, of responsibility rather than domination, in relation to territories needing control and to peoples needing guidance. Colonial rivalries will pass only when colonies are no longer regarded as areas of special privilege and exclusive advantage, as they were in the age of imperialism. They must be regarded as areas of special responsibility both to the peoples concerned and to the community of nations. The concepts of empire must give way to the concepts of commonwealth. The frank acceptance of this principle would mark the beginning of a new era.

The liquidation of empire and the replacement of the colonial system by an international one cannot be accomplished by great cataclysmic changes. Again it is not the tempo but the direction of change that is of supreme importance, although the tempo is important too. It should be as rapid as existing conditions permit.

In the case of certain colonies occupied by Axis powers during the war, conditions will be fluid, as they have not been in the past. There will be possibilities of change, in the South Pacific and in the Carribean for example, that would have been entirely impracticable before the war. These possibilities should be explored. Where opportunities for international administration exist they should be seized and developed. Councils for consultation and the formulation of policy, with representation for the powers that have special interests in these areas, might be a great advance over what has existed in the past.

The United Nations did not engage in war for the restoration of empire or to enable colonial powers merely to win back their lost possessions. Countries occupied during the course of the conflict had to be freed from their conquerors, of course, but the fate of Burma, Syria, or Java, for example, is no longer a question merely of restoring lost property but of establishing conditions that will facilitate and further human progress. How best to do this in particular cases must be decided in view of all the facts, but it ought to be clear that liberation does not necessarily mean merely the restoration of conditions that existed before the war. The interests of the imperial powers must be taken into account, as they no doubt will be. But these ought not to be given precedence over the interests of the peoples of liberated areas. These areas must be held in trust, their future determined by the principles of a new and democratic world order. Self-government may not be immediately possible in any of these territories, certainly not in many of them. But what democratic principle demands is that the wishes of the people should be recognized as far as possible and that their interests should be given equal consideration with those of the imperial powers. The old order that collapsed so tragically in these countries ought not to be revived. What measure of autonomy is consistent with prudent policy, how the best interests of the community of nations may be served, what new international organs are desirable—these are questions that in the future should not be left entirely to the decision of imperial governments.

The conclusion to which this discussion points may be stated simply. They were not in error who saw in the mandate system the first faint promise of an international colonial administration, even though this is yet some distance from fulfillment. They were too generous in their appraisal of what had actually been accomplished and too optimistic in their expectations of speedy change.

The imperfections of the system were fairly obvious and the lack of enthusiasm, perhaps even of sincerity, on the part of the powers chiefly interested gave little promise that the imperfections would be remedied in practical operation. The San Francisco discussions of the trustee issue leave little room for illusions now, and sober realism may be safer than facile optimism. To such dependencies and possessions as they have, the great powers will probably cling tenaciously, and they will be able to point to the undoubted hazards of hasty change.

Nevertheless, new beginnings may be hoped for and must be attempted. It would be a great advance if, within a reasonable period, Britain and France were willing to entrust some, if not all, of the mandates they already hold to an international administration directly responsible to an international authority; if some of the Japanese islands in the Pacific were administered, not as American or British or Chinese possessions, but as international bases. The establishment of an international commission—which in such cases would have the power of appointment, direct responsibility for supervision and control, and specialized knowledge— would prepare the way for still further advance as experience is gained. There might emerge a trained international civil service, free from the suspicions that are not unnatural in the case of colonial administration at present. The pressure of selfish national interest would be removed in some areas and weakened in others. The possibilities of even faint beginnings such as these would be great.

Is it possible that some of the colonies at present in the possession of great powers should be converted into mandates within a new and reformed system? This would not only be a gesture indicating the sincerity of democratic professions made in the stress of war; it would also serve as a precedent for the progressive transformation of the imperialist order into a democratic order. Such a change might involve no real sacrifice for the nation that made it, or if it was felt to be a sacrifice, the gain of a more stable and peaceful world would be more than adequate compensation. Nothing would more surely enhance the credit of a mandate or trustee system than the voluntary transfer to it by a great power of one or more of its colonies. It would immediately improve the prospects of democracy in the world of the future.

Finally, one principle that was implied in the mandate system should be preserved for whatever new order may be formed. In Section 5 of Article 22 in the Covenant it is explicitly stated that in the mandated territory the mandatory shall provide conditions that will "secure equal opportunities for the trade and commerce of the other members of the League." Is there any reason why this obligation should not be made universal? It seems to be the clear implication of Article 4 of the Atlantic Charter: "They will endeavor, with due respect for their existing obligations, to further the enjoyment by all States, great or small, victor or vanquished, of access, on equal terms, to the trade and to the raw materials of the world which are needed for their economic prosperity." A sincere application of this principle would remove grievances and abate those irritations and jealousies from which the world has suffered so much.

Certain advantages in trade and commerce will inevitably accrue to colonial powers and even to mandatories by virtue of the political connection that exists. These are fair compensation for the costs of administration and of other necessary services. Discrimination that creates exclusive privilege and restrictions that limit opportunities of fair trade for others are the factors that arouse envy and antagonism. They are also the conditions that may again give plausibility and even some substance to the complaints of "have-not" nations. On the other hand, with the frank acceptance of this principle of equal economic opportunity and nondiscrimination some of the supposed advantages of the old imperialism would vanish and some of the incentives of expansion would disappear. Empire would lose some of its attraction if it was no longer a condition of unfair privilege. It would not destroy the lure of colonies but it would remove one of the potent causes of the spirit that breeds war.

The conversion of an anarchic world, where dominion went to the strong and subjection to the weak, into a world order based on democratic principles is no easy task, and it will not be accomplished in a day. It is something, however, and it may be much, that there are opportunities for new beginnings. Some of the traditions of the world that is passing will have to be renounced, some of its practices abandoned, much of its achievement conserved. It is important that we should perceive clearly the first stages of the path that may lead us to our goal of an ordered democratic world. It is even more important that we should willingly and steadfastly set out upon this path.

Conclusion

It has been the underlying thesis of this book that a redefinition of democracy is a primary necessity of our time, and that this redefinition must be attempted in terms of the concrete political and economic order of the twentieth century. Vast industrial developments, technological advances, and the deepening of social consciousness have created new conditions and new problems. They have also brought into play new forces. Many of the presuppositions of the classical economists have been abandoned while the assumptions of nineteenth-century liberalism have been profoundly modified. Democracy therefore must develop a new dynamic quality; it must demonstrate its ability to control and direct the forces of this new age.

The crisis of democracy in our generation cannot be resolved in terms of nineteenth-century ideas. Nor, on the other hand, can it be resolved without a just understanding and appreciation of those ideas. If this age and the conflicts in which we are engaged are revolutionary, it means, not that the changes our situation demands involve a violent break with the past, but that they must be far-reaching and must go deep. With wisdom the "crisis of democracy" can be resolved without violence, for the democratic faith contains a principle of life and has therefore the capacity to adapt itself to new conditions. Democracy will survive if it demonstrates this vitality. It is not mere wishful thinking to believe that it can and will.

It was of England in particular that Harold Nicholson was thinking when he wrote, "I believe that when the dust of war has settled upon the ruins of past catch-words we shall find that our political genius will again assert itself, and that we shall show the world that we can achieve an economic revolution without tyranny even as in the past we achieved a political revolution without chaos."[1] This is a belief that we may well cherish for America and for all nations. We may believe also that a revolution in the attitudes and policies of states can be achieved without either tyranny or chaos. We may learn even how such changes, in the future, can be achieved without war. Progress, like victory, may demand blood and tears as its price, but humanity in other crises has proved its readiness to pay this price and to endure the sacrifices demanded. To believe that it can and will do so again

[1] *The Spectator*, July 31, 1942, p. 105.

is not unreasonable. It must do so if democracy is to triumph. But it will do so only if democracy is seen and felt by those who believe in it, not as a shibboleth or a form, but as a dynamic faith. For only a dynamic faith, imbued with vision and intelligence, is capable of providing the urge and the inspiration that will set peoples and nations on their way toward a democratic new order.

Index

Ability, 12; special, 133-36, 196-99; natural, 199
Absolute government, 26, 59, 85, 89, 142; in Western world, 67, 88; contrary to natural law, 77, 80-81; in Stuart England, 88
Absolute rights, *see* Natural rights
Abyssinia, *see* Ethiopia
Acton, Lord, 210, 221, 224
Africa, colonization of, 261-62, 264
Air, freedom of, 114; international control of, 247
Alexander the Great, 124
American Declaration of Independence, 78, 103, 120, 129, 143-45
American Revolution, 68, 75, 81, 143, 148, 218
Americans in the Philippines, 264
Aquinas, Thomas, 68
Aristotle, 14-15, 23, 60, 69, 94, 100, 122-24; on education, 20; on representative government, 23; "good life" of, 82, 94; attitude toward slavery, 92, 123, 126
Arkwright, Sir Richard, 153
Art, subject to rules, 114-15
Associations, foster democracy, 162-63
Athens, democracy in, 1, 7-8, 10, 14, 28, 80, 94, 116
Atlantic Charter, *1941*, 235, 280
Augustine, Saint, 73
Austria-Hungary, nationality, 226
Autocracy, *see* Absolute government

Backward and dependent peoples, 240, 259-80
Balkan Peninsula, wars, 211; nationality, 225-26
Barker, Ernest, quoted, 86
Becker, C. L., quoted, 3, 171, 206
Belgium, fascism in, 5; in World War II, 35, 240
Bentham, Jeremy, criticized by Sir Henry Maine, 28-29; attack on natural rights, 144-45; conception of rights, 150
Bismarck, Otto von, 16, 18, 48
Bradley, A. C., quoted, 30, 60
Bretton Woods agreements, *1944*, 245
Brierly, J. L., quoted, 81
Bright, John, 233
British, in Africa, 261; in India, 261-62, 265; in Egypt, 265
British Commonwealth of Nations, 265
Brotherhood of man, *see* Fraternity
Browning, Robert, quoted, 94
Bryce, James, quoted, 3-4, 9, 63-64, 215
Bureaucracy, 25-26
Burke, Edmund, doctrine of rights, 145; on natural rights, 146-47; quoted, 153; on group loyalty, 164, 220; on Rousseau, 165
Burma, in World War II, 269-70
Burns, Delisle, quoted, 10-12, 131
Burns, Robert, quoted, 140, 165

Capacity to govern, 19-25, 27-30, 37, 148. *See also* Citizenship; Will to govern
Capek, Karel, quoted, 117
Carlyle, R. W. and A. J., quoted, 68, 70-72, 122-23
Carritt, E. F., quoted, 56, 69
Cartels, 200, 247
Cavour, Camillo di, 211
Censorship, 52, 106, 118
China, foreign interventions, 261-63; revolution, *1911-1912*, 263
Christianity, natural law congenial to, 76-78, 81; and equality, 120-21, 127
Church, The, 67, 212; teachings of, 68, 71, 73, 78, 85, 141; and state, 74, 213
Church unity, 163, 212
Cicero, 70, 76, 122; on natural law, 77
Citizenship, in a democracy, 22, 24-25, 30, 85, 104, 111, 131, 164
Civilization, Teutonic, democrac in, 72-73, 80; Western, democracy in, 76, 78, 80-82, 94, 130, 266
Class interests, 31, 62
Cobban, Alfred, 69
Cobden, Richard, 233
Colonial government, 260-74. *See also* Mandates
Communism, 43, 202-5, 208
Compromise, true spirit of, 85, 135
Conference, on international organization, *1945*, 245-46, 256-57, 266; on limitation of armaments, *1921-1922*, 239
Conscience, liberty of, *see* Freedom of thought
Constitutions and democratic government, 12-18
Consumer, 199-200, 246-47
Cooperation, 130-31, 160-65, 204-6; international, 165, 232-82; necessary to nationality, 220, 228
Corinthians I, quoted, 131
Croats, in Yugoslavia, 226
Crompton, Samuel, 153
Culture, factor in nationality, 215-19
Czechoslovakia, democracy in, 4; in World War II, 107-9; nationality, 225, 227

Daladier, Edouard, 49
Dante, belief in world empire, 165, 212, 236

283

284 TOWARD A DEMOCRATIC NEW ORDER

Danubian confederation, 241
Declaration of Independence, *see* American Declaration of Independence
Democratic government, 1–5; definitions of, 8–10, 54; weaknesses of, 33–40; compared with totalitarianism, 35, 53, 59–60, 89, 96–97, 167, 207; ethical bases of, 82–97, 242; and industry, 166–86
Democracy, defined, 1, 8–12; social, 8–12, 117–18, 149–85, 188–209; and education, 19–22, 194–95; economic, 59, 86–96, 113, 131, 162, 166–86; primary characteristics of, 98–165; and rights of man, 141–58; ideal, 159, 234; industrial, 166–87; and nationality, 210–32; and world unity, 233–58; and international organization, 233–80; and international relations, 259–80; political, *see* Democratic government
Denmark, fascism in, 5
Dependent nations, *see* Backward and dependent peoples
De Roussy de Sales, Richard, quoted, 49
Dewey, John, quoted, 113
Dictatorship, 41–43, 49–53, 81; contrary to natural law, 81
Disarmament conferences, *1921–1922*, 239
Divine right of kings, 67, 71, 73–75, 82
Dunkirk, 271
Dutch East Indies, natural resources, 246

East Indies, 266
Economic conferences of *1927* and *1933*, 238
Education, function of, 19–22; and democracy, 19–22, 27–29, 34, 118, 194–95; and social conditions, 21–22, 118; in Great Britain, 194–95; in the United States, 194–95
Egypt, colonization of, 265; in World War II, 269; independence, 270, 272
Emerson, R. W., 218
Emotion and reason, 37–40, 90–92, 141
English Revolution, *1688*, 75, 143
Equality, 120–65; in a democracy, 12, 98, 120, 160, 171, 188; Sabine on, 76; in Greek and Roman philosophy, 121–23; not acknowledged by Greek culture, 123–24; and natural law, 129; defined, 130–32; of opportunity, 133, 189–201; of sovereign states, 235
Espionage, *see* Secret service
Ethics, political, 29, 79, 82–97
Ethiopia, Italian occupation of, *1936*, 249
Experience, 25, 30, 90, 92, 216

Family, 56; as pattern of ideal social democracy, 159–65
Fascism, 89; Italian, 4, 89, 209; in Western world, 5; Mussolini on, 89
Feudalism, 127, 168, 213

Finer, Herman, quoted, 41–42
Food Conference, *1943*, 245
Force, use of, 17, 110–11; in German Republic, 17; and natural law, 77, 81; government not based on, 82; in totalitarianism, 109
Four Freedoms, 232, 252–53
Fowler, Warde, quoted, 13–14
France, fascism in, 5; democracy in, 49, 128; constitution of *1848*, 120
Franchise, 23, 148, 167, 170, 193
Frankfort parliament, *1848–1849*, 16
Fraternity, 85, 98, 159–65, 201; in Roman Empire, 125; ideal of democracy, 159; cooperation essential to, 161–62, international, 163
Free enterprise, 112, 170, 177, 180, 194–95, 202; and freedom, 161, 233
Free trade, 233–34, 268–69, 280
Freedom, 23, 92–94, 98–119, 171, 188, 234; of discussion, 23, 34, 58, 105; of thought, 23, 105; of worship, 23, 105, 195; of speech, 23, 105–6, 149, 195; defined, 99; negative, 99–111, 243; of spirit, 108; positive, 111–19, 195; from want, 155, 194, 231, 252–53; essential to fraternity, 160; from fear, 195; limitations of, 197–201. See also Four Freedoms; Natural rights; Rights of man
French Declaration of the Rights of Man, 103, 120, 144–45
French Revolution, 68, 75, 81, 98, 102, 141, 209, 211, 214
Friends of India, 262
Fulton, J. S., quoted, 194

Garden of Eden, 78
General will, 14, 45, 54–59, 143, 152; Rousseau on, 54–55.
German Republic, democracy in, 15–18; constitution, 15–17; threatened by national socialism, 110
Germany, in World War I, 15–16, 47–48; in World War II, 47–48
Germans, in the Balkans, 35; in Latin America, 36; in Wisconsin, 222; in Czechoslovakia, 225; in the Tyrol, 229
Gettysburg, 217
Gierke, Otto von, quoted, 73, 79–80, 88
Gladstone, W. E., leadership, 45
Göring, Hermann, quoted by Gooch, 51
"Good life" of Aristotle, 82, 94
Gooch, G. P., quoted, 50–52, 68
Government, by experts, 25–33, 53; functions of, 116, 141; relation to general will, 143. See also Democratic government
Great Britain, democracy in, 2, 128, 233–34; nationality, 216, 221
Greece, ancient, democracy in, 7, 60, 68, 123–24, 141, 220; natural law in, 76, 141;

INDEX

modern, war of independence, *1821–1829*, 211; nationality, 229
Gregory the Great, 73, 165

Haldane, R. B., on education, 20
Hattersley, A. F., quoted, 127
Hawthorne, Nathaniel, 218
Hebrew prophets, 120
Hedonism, 94
Hegel, conception of general will, 55; ethics, 83
Henlein, Konrad, 107
Henry IV of France, "grand design" of, 236
Hindenburg, Paul von, 18
Hitler, Adolf, 4, 154, 203n, 235, 248
Hobbs, Thomas, view of natural rights, 54, 75, 100, 103, 128–29, 142–45; on public welfare, 95; on equality, 128–29
Hobhouse, L. T., 87n
Holland, *see* Netherlands
Holy Alliance, 236, 250
Human nature, 2, 28–29, 40, 76, 78, 80, 92–93, 122–23, 161, 165; democratic view of, 90–94, 208
Human welfare, *see* Social welfare
Hypocrisy, in government, 82–83, 268

Idealism, 94
Imperialism, 259–74, 280; British, 83–84, 261–65; idealized, 262; American, 262–63; beneficence of, 263–64, 266; and World War II, 267–72; Dutch, 270
India, self-government, 262, 272
Individual, and the state, 87–89, 95, 104, 195
Individualism, 84, 87–89, 95–96, 101, 112–13, 127, 130–31, 170, 193–94, 202
Indo-China, in World War II, 270
Industrial Revolution, 101, 116–17, 168, 261
Industry, self-government in, 167, 171; and political power, 167, 189–93; and democracy, 167–88, 247–69; organization and control, 168–87; management and labor in, 169–76; and state, 170–86; growth of labor unions in, 175; and social democracy, 188–209
Inequality, in totalitarianism, 41–44, 96–97, 235; and social democracy, 188–209; and democratic government, 189–209; economic, 189–209; of opportunity, 193–201
International cooperation, *see* World unity
International good will, *see* World unity
International law, 243, 267; status of mandate in, 275–76
International organization, 233–58; economic, 236, 246, 279–80; political, 248
International relations, 83–84, 239–80. See also World unity

Iraq, independence, 265, 272
Isolationism, 239, 241, 267
Israel, nationality, 219
Italy, democracy in, 4; fascism in, 4, 89, 209; in Ethiopia, 82; revolution of *1848*, 211

Japan, foreign policy, 35; in Manchuria, 83; plans for world order, 235–37
Jarrow, England, steel industry in, 156
Jefferson, Thomas, 78, 218
Jesuits, as colonizers, 261
Joad, C. E. M., quoted, 32–33, 95
John of Paris, 214

Kellet, E. E., quoted, 53
King-Crane report, 275n

Labor unions, 176–79, 203; leadership in, 177–78; power in politics, 178
Laissez faire, *see* Free enterprise
Laski, H. J., quoted, 104, 158, 169
Latin America, government in, 4, 242; Germans in, 36
Lattimore, Owen, quoted, 241
Law, guarantee of freedom, 103, 111; of gravity, 114; natural, *see* Natural law
Leadership, 39, 42–45, 177; in a democracy, 42–45, 177–78; in totalitarian states, 43–44, 154, 177; positive, 154–55; in labor unions, 177–78; training for, 178; of strong nations, 242–43
League of Nations, 229–31, 238, 245–50, 259; and mandates, 259–60, 274–76
Lecky, William, quoted, 2–3
Leisure, use of, 116–18
"Levellers," 121
Liberalism, 23, 89–93, 102, 112–13, 118, 167, 170–71, 189, 198, 210–80; German, 16; function in history, 89; and nationalism, 212
Liberty, *see* Freedom
Lincoln, Abraham, leadership, 40; quoted, 90
Lindsay, A. D., quoted, 38, 47, 187, 197
Lippincott, B. E., quoted, 2–3
Locke, John, 54, 75, 80, 90, 100–3, 109, 129–30, 142–45, 157
Longfellow, H. W., 218
Loyalty, 163–64

MacCunn, John, quoted, 151
Machiavelli, Niccolo, 29, 83
Mackenzie, J. S., quoted, 55–56
Maine, Sir Henry, quoted, 1–2, 9–10, 28–29
Majority government, *see* Democratic government
Malaya, natural resources, 246, 266; in World War II, 270

Manchester school, 233
Manchuria, 249
Mandates, 259–80; and League of Nations, 259–60, 275–76; in international law, 275
March on Rome, *1922*, 4, 248
Marsilius, Hippolytus de, 68
Marx, Karl, 147, 202, 204
Masterman, J. H. B., quoted, 45–46, 82
Mazzini, Giuseppe, 211
Middle Ages, democracy in, 68, 72–73, 212; natural law in, 76–79, 141; equality in, 127
Middle classes, political influence of, 168–69
Mill, J. S., quoted, 24–26, 31, 90, 106, 210, 215, 221
Milton, John, *Areopagitica*, 106
Minorities, 13, 29–31, 54, 58–66, 105, 168, 210–32; rights and duties of, 61–66
Monopoly, 189, 197, 199–200, 246
Morley, John, quoted, 30
Morris, William, on equality, 121
Motion pictures, and public opinion, 190–91
Munich agreement, *1938*, 35, 227
Murray, Gilbert, quoted, 230
Mussolini, Benito, 4, 41, 154; quoted, 89, 91, 96, 98; repudiates liberty, 98
Myth, use by Plato, 11, 38; in propaganda, 90–91; in totalitarianism, 91, 236

Napoleon I, 236
National characteristics, 57; factor in nationality, 219
National socialism, 43, 108–9; and proposed organization of Europe, 236
National socialist movement, *see* National socialism
Nationality, 57, 163, 210–14, 242; and democracy, 210–34; meaning of, 214–19; in the United States, 216–18, 251; in Great Britain, 221–22; and smaller states, 240
Natural law, 76–81, 100–3, 114–15, 141–58; and equality, 129. *See also* Natural rights; Sovereignty of the people
Natural resources, not possessions but trusts, 244–58, 265–71
Natural rights, 103, 141–52; Paine's defence of, 141; from theory of natural law, 141; in Middle Ages, 142; in a civil society, 142–52; in 18th-century philosophy, 143–45; Burke's attack on, 145–47
Nature, law of, *see* Natural law
Nepotism, 163–64
Netherlands, in World War II, 35, 240
Nettleship, R. L., quoted, 46
Neutrality, 228
Newspapers, and public opinion, 190–91
Niebuhr, Reinhold, 85n; quoted, 168

Norway, fascism in, 5; in World War II, 240
Noske, Gustav, 17
Nourse, E. G., quoted, 174, 177, 182

Occam, William, *see* William of Occam
Opportunity, 11, 133, 193–97, 201
Opposition, function of, 60–61. *See also* Minorities
Ottawa agreements, 244

Paine, Thomas, 155; *Rights of Man*, 141; quoted, 150
Panic of *1929*, 180, 269
Paris, Peace Conference, *1919*, 225–27, 274
Parties, political, 42–43
Paul, Apostle, on natural law, 77; on equality, 126–27; on fraternity, 160
Pearl Harbor, 35
People, sovereignty of, *see* Sovereignty, of the people
Pericles, 7–11, 124; pride in Athens, 7–8; contrasted with Plato, 11; on slavery, 123
Perry, Ralph B., quoted, 5
Philippines, American intervention, 264, 272; independence, 265, 270; in World War II, 270
Plato, 10–12, 122; contrasted with Pericles, 10; condemnation of democracy, 10–11, 21, 69; use of mythology, 11, 38; *Republic*, 11, 141; "guardian class," 11, 236; quoted, 21, 123; on progress, 250
Poland, in World War II, 82, 224; nationality, 216
Polybius, 13–14, 70
Popular government, *see* Democratic government
Popular sovereignty, *see* Sovereignty, of the people
Portugal, government in, 4
Poverty, 31, 117–18, 171, 195, 227
Prerogative, royal, 70–72. *See also* Divine right of kings
Primo de Rivera, Miguel, 50
"Principles of 89," 103, 120, 144–45
Propaganda, 34–39, 90–91, 109–10, 190–91, 224; democratic, 34–35, 38–40, 90–91, 110, 189; totalitarian, 38–40, 91, 109, 237; revolutionary, 109; use in World War I, 234
Property, right of, 143, 145, 157
Public opinion, 23, 34, 55–56, 58–59, 63, 65–66, 119, 189–92, 243; in totalitarianism, 52
Public spirit, necessary to democracy, 1, 21, 34, 49, 55, 92, 112, 178, 201, 206–7
Public welfare, *see* Welfare, public
Puritan Revolution, *1642–1660*, 88, 102, 121

Puritanism, English, 81, 88

Race, factor in nationality, 215–16, 218–24; foundation of totalitarianism, 235–36; in Europe, 235–36; in Asia, 236–37
Radio, and public opinion, 190–91
Raditch, Stephen, 228
Rationalism, 39–40, 76; in democracy, 40, 90, 100, 122; in Roman law, 76, 122
Realism, in government, 91
Reason, 76–81, 122, 141; and emotion, 37–40, 90–92, 141
Reconstruction, World War I, 34, 210, 229; World War II, 51, 238, 245
Reformation, 67, 74, 127, 213
Regionalism, and world organization, 242
Religion, factor in nationality, 215
Renaissance, 212–13; rise of nation states in, 67; beginnings of democratic tendency in, 74
Representative government, 23–24, 28, 42, 74
Revolution, 51, 109–10, 141–44, 155, 201–9, 227, 238
Rights of man, 88, 141–58; Paine on, 141, 150; revolutionary implications of, 142–44, 155; American and French declarations of, 144–45; civil, 144–58; Burke's doctrine of, 145–50; ideal, 149–51; social, 146–58; and private interests, 156–57; in a democracy, 157–58; recognition of, 157–58; natural, *see* Natural rights
Ritchie, D. G., quoted, 65, 128, 145
Roman Catholic church, 127
Romans, Epistle to, quoted, 77
Rome, ancient, democracy in, 13–14, 68–70, 122; natural law in, 76–78, 141; colonies, 125; cosmopolitan quality of, 125; slavery in, 125; equality in, 125–27
Roosevelt, F. D., 252
Roosevelt, Theodore, antitrust campaign, 200
Rousseau, J. J., 23, 43, 130; quoted, 9; theory of general will, 54, 57, 61, 75, 100, 103, 142–47; criticized by Burke, 165
Rowntree, B. S., on democratic government, 180; plan for industrial democracy, 180–81
Russell, Bertrand, quoted, 95
Russell, G. W. (A. E.), quoted, 174
Russia, Constitution of *1936*, 12; in World War II, 35, 48, 241–42; leadership in, 43; equality in, 134; nationality, 241–42
Russo-German treaty, *1939*, 35

Sabine, G. H., quoted, 70, 76, 126
Salter, Arthur, quoted, 154
Sandburg, Carl, 218

San Francisco Charter, *see* United Nations, Charter
San Francisco Conference, *see* United Nations, conference on international organization
Scandinavians, in Minnesota, 222
Schneider, H. W., quoted, 89
Scotland, home rule, 221
Secret service, in totalitarian states, 52
Self-determination, 210, 221, 234, 263
Self-government, *see* Democratic government
Self-preservation, right of, 143
Shaw, G. B., 196, 225
Sherman Antitrust Act, *1890*, 200
Singapore, in World War II, 270
Slavery, 85, 92, 123; and natural law, 77; in Greece, 125; in Roman Empire, 126; and Christianity, 127
Smith, Adam, 156, 161–62, 167; on cooperation, 162
Smoot-Hawley Tariff Act, 244
Social contract theory, 54, 75, 82, 141, 143, 146; Rousseau on, 54
Social democratic party, Germany, 17–18
Social security, 112
Social welfare, purpose of democracy, 82, 94–97
Socialism, 2
Socrates, 1, 27–28, 86
Sophists, 141
South Seas, colonization of, 264
Sovereignty, 79, 213; of the people, 23, 69–75, 239, 265, 267; of the king, 77–79, 82, 142, 213
Spain, democracy in, 4; civil war, *1936–1939*, 50, 93
Spoils system, foreign to democratic government, 65
State, 55, 60, 74; and church, 74; subject to natural law, 79; and individual, 87–94; and public welfare, 95
Steel industry, England, 156
Stoicism, 76, 78, 80, 122, 125–27, 129; and state of nature, 141
Stuart, House of, parliamentary struggle against, 68, 75
Sudeten movement, 107–10, 227
Suez canal, 272
Suffrage, universal, 2, 170, 193; for women, 24
Sweden, fascism in, 5

Tawney, R. H., 188, 197
Taxation, right of, 148
Technology, 117, 196, 200, 281
Teutonic civilization, *see* Civilization, Teutonic
Thomas Aquinas, 68
Tolerance, 105–11, 223; racial, 231

Totalitarianism, 35–36, 94, 166, 202; in Europe, 4; in Latin America, 4; compared with democracy, 35–53, 59–60, 89, 96–97, 109, 167, 207, 236–37, 240, 269, 271; contrary to natural law, 81; proposed international organization, 233, 235, 239
Trade unions, *see* Labor unions
Trading companies, 260–61
Tradition, 16, 57, 208, 217, 242; factor in nationality, 219
Trafalgar, 217
Transylvania, nationality, 225
Turkey, nationality, 229

Unemployment, 152–56, 171, 195
United Nations, 239, 247; and international organization, 235, 248, 255–58, 272, 278; relief and rehabilitation administration (UNRRA), 241, 245; Charter, 245–46, 256–57; conference on international organization, San Francisco, *1945*, 245–46, 256–57, 266
United States, nationality, 216–18, 251
Unity in government, democratic and totalitarian compared, 46–49; in diversity, 59–61; social, 201–9

Valley Forge, 48, 217
Vernon, A. W., quoted, 36
Versailles, Treaty of, 250
Vocation, choice of, 197–99

Wales, home rule, 221

War psychology, 206–7, 234, 241
Washington, George, 218
Watt, James, 153
Weimar Republic, *see* German Republic
Welfare, public, 94–97
Western world, democracy in, 1–5, 30, 75–76, 80, 87–88, 121, 211–12, 263
White Mountain, Battle of, 217
Whitman, Walt, 218
Will of the people, *see* General will
Will to govern, 14, 18–19, 43, 92
William of Occam, 68
Wilson, Woodrow, 17; Fourteen Points, 210; idealism, 234; on mandates, 274
Wordsworth, William, quoted, 132, 217
Work, right to, 152–54, 195, 199
Workers educational association, England, 178
World of states, 243
World unity, 159, 165, 202, 210–82; and democracy, 233–82; advanced by mandate system, 274
World War I, 15; minority treaties, 230–31; crusade for democracy, 234, 263
World War II, and world unity, 235, 239; revolutionary nature, 238; and imperialism, 269–72
Wright, Quincy, on political organization, 250
Wycliffe, John, doctrine of lordship, 128

Yugoslavia, nationality, 225–26, 228

Zimmern, A. E., quoted, 216

DATE DUE

DEC 5
JAN 1